Gringo Injustice is a path-breaking collection, destined to be the definitive resource on Latinos/as in the criminal justice system. Combining a range of sociological and legal frameworks with "insider" experiences, the book casts new light on the dual system of justice that produces some of the most pressing challenges facing Latinos today.
Maxine Baca Zinn, Michigan State University

Alfredo Mirandé and the book's contributors have produced an audacious volume of theoretically grounded and empirically driven work treating each with lucidity and grace.
Rodolfo D. Torres, University of California, Irvine, and coauthor of *Capitalism and Critique: Unruly Democracy and Solidarity Economics*

Books on the criminal "justice" system have typically focused on African Americans. Alfredo Mirandé's *Gringo Injustice* is a wonderful correction to this trend. The chapters are powerfully written by scholars, activists, lawyers, and historians and address various justice issues affecting Latinos (e.g., police shootings of unarmed Latinos, projects to attempt to curb police violence against Latinos, inter-ethnic conflict in prisons, racialized anti-gang policies, and surveillance). I highly recommend this book and will use it myself in my classes.
Eduardo Bonilla-Silva, Duke University, and author of *Racism without Racists*

Gringo Injustice

The recent mass shooting of 22 innocent people in El Paso by a lone White gunman looking to "Kill Mexicans" is not new. It is part of a long, bloody history of anti-Latina/o violence in the United States. *Gringo Injustice* brings this history to life, shedding critical light on the complex relationship between Latinas/os and the United States' legal and judicial system.

Contributors with first-hand knowledge and experience, including former law enforcement officers, ex-gang members, attorneys, and community activists, share insider perspectives on the issues facing Latinas/os and initiate a critical dialogue on this neglected topic. Essays examine the unauthorized use of deadly force by police and patterned incidents of lynching, hate crimes, gang violence, and racial profiling. The book also highlights the hyper-criminalization of barrio youth and considers wide-ranging implications from the disproportionate imprisonment of Latinas/os. *Gringo Injustice* provides a comprehensive and powerful look into the Latina/o community's fraught history with law enforcement and the American judicial system. It is an essential reference for students and scholars interested in intersections between crime and communities of Color.

Alfredo Mirandé, a native of Mexico City and the father of three children, is Distinguished Professor of Sociology and Ethnic Studies at the University of California, Riverside. He is a practicing attorney who previously taught at the Texas Tech University School of Law. Mirandé received a BS in social science from Illinois State University, MA and PhD degrees in sociology from the University of Nebraska, and a JD from Stanford University. Mirandé's teaching and research interests are in Chicano sociology; masculinity; constitutional law; civil rights; and the relationship among law, race, class, and gender. He has also published numerous journal articles on sociology, law, and ethnic studies and is the author of *The Age of Crisis; La Chicana: The Mexican American Woman* (co-authored with Evangelina Enríquez); *The Chicano Experience: An Alternative Perspective; Gringo Justice; Hombres y Machos: Masculinity and Latino Culture; The Stanford Law Chronicles: 'Doin' Time on the Farm; Jalos USA: Transnational Community and Identity*; and *Behind the Mask: Gender Hybridity in a Zapotec Community*.

Gringo Injustice

Insider Perspectives on Police, Gangs, and Law

Edited by Alfredo Mirandé

Routledge
Taylor & Francis Group

NEW YORK AND LONDON

First published 2020
by Routledge
52 Vanderbilt Avenue, New York, NY 10017

and by Routledge
2 Park Square, Milton Park, Abingdon, Oxon OX14 4RN

Routledge is an imprint of the Taylor & Francis Group, an informa business

© 2020 Taylor & Francis

The right of Alfredo Mirandé to be identified as the author of the editorial material, and of the authors for their individual chapters, has been asserted in accordance with sections 77 and 78 of the Copyright, Designs and Patents Act 1988.

Library of Congress Cataloging-in-Publication Data
A catalog record for this title has been requested

ISBN: 978-0-367-27605-8 (hbk)
ISBN: 978-0-367-27606-5 (pbk)
ISBN: 978-0-429-29685-7 (ebk)

Typeset in Bembo
by Taylor & Francis Books

In Memoriam

This book is dedicated to Francisco Arias and José Chamales, two young Californios hanged in Santa Cruz, California on May 2, 1877* by an angry lynch mob, and to the memory of the countless other victims of American injustice.

*Figure 1.1 (p. 27) "Hanged at the Water Street Bridge." 1877.

Contents

Figures

Contributors

Richard A. Alvarado, the author of *10–33 on the West Yard* (Infinity, 2015), has more than 32 years of experience in the criminal justice system and retired in December 2011 as the Chief Deputy Warden at the California Institution for Men in Chino, California. Alvarado received a Bachelor of Science degree in Chicano Studies and History from the University of California, Riverside, and a master's degree in Public Administration from the University of La Verne. He serves on the Advisory Board for the Presley Center for Crime and Justice Studies and is co-author of a forthcoming fictional story, "Chile Town" about Latino youth experiences.

Robert J. Durán has a PhD in Sociology from the University of Colorado and is Associate Professor of Sociology at Texas A&M University. A former gang member, he later served as a youth probation officer before becoming a scholar activist, focusing on gangs and police use of deadly force. He has published numerous articles in academic journals on crime, gangs, and officer-involved shooting, and two books, *Gang Life in Two Cities: An Insider's Journey* and *The Gang Paradox: Inequalities and Miracles on the U.S.-Mexico Border,* both with Columbia University Press."

Katherine L. Maldonado, PhD student in the Department of Sociology at the University of California, Riverside, American Sociological Association Minority Fellow, and Ford Foundation Pre-Doctoral Fellow, was formerly a gang-affiliated teen mother from South Central Los Angeles. Her areas of specialization include race and class inequality and critical criminology, focusing on gangs, gender, teen motherhood, and how stigma and violence impact barrio youth survival strategies. Her research unpacks the way that race, class, and gender inequalities play a role in institutional and systemic racism, embedded in the criminal justice and child welfare system toward women and children of Color.

Alfredo Mirandé, a native of Mexico City, Distinguished Professor of Sociology and Ethnic Studies at the University of California, Riverside, and a practicing attorney, received a PhD in Sociology from the University of Nebraska and a Juris Doctorate from Stanford University. Mirandé previously taught at the Texas Tech University School of Law; he has published numerous articles and ten books focusing on law, gender, and Chicano Sociology.

Maritza Pérez, Esq. is a policy analyst for criminal justice reform at a think tank in Washington, DC. She evaluates and advises federal legislation to minimize the harmful impacts of the criminal justice system in the lives of individuals. Maritza began her advocacy career as a Soros Justice Fellow at MALDEF where she advanced policies to end mass incarceration. She earned her J.D. at the University of California, Berkeley, School of Law, receiving the highest distinction for her pro bono work in the areas of criminal justice reform, immigrant rights, and education access for disadvantaged students. Before attending law school, Maritza joined Teach For America and was a fourth grade teacher in New Orleans. She received her B.A. in Journalism and Spanish from the University of Nevada, Reno with academic honors. The proud daughter of Mexican immigrants, Maritza is the first in her family to receive a higher education and earn a professional degree. She is originally from Elko, Nevada.

José S. Plascencia-Castillo, Chancellor's Doctoral Incentive Program (CDIP) Fellow from California State University and recipient of the prestigious Eugene Cota Robles Fellowship, is a PhD student in the Department of Sociology at the University of California, Riverside, specializing in race and class inequality and critical criminology. with a focus on gangs and adolescent subcultures. His work interrogates the individualistic logic of the criminal justice system that pathologizes and criminalizes youth of Color. His current research focuses on panoptic surveillance and control in a Southern California barrio.

Roberto Rivera is a doctoral student in Sociology at the University of California, Riverside, and a Fulbright Fellow, retired after a twenty-year career in law enforcement. A practitioner in the Restorative Justice Movement, as an officer he developed and implemented the Move Forward Project, an innovative community police model initiative that sought to promote a more holistic positive engagement of mutual trust and respect between the police and the Latina/o community. He has presented at numerous conferences and workshops on community policing and restorative justice, has several articles in progress on policing in minority communities, and was a contributor to the book, *Lawyers as Change Makers: The Global Integrative Law Movement*, published by the American Bar Association. He is currently working on his first book, on holistic policing, which should be released in 2021.

Ernesto Vigil is a community activist and former member of the Crusade
for Justice in Denver, Colorado, from 1968–1981, who worked closely
with its founder Chicano Civil Rights leader, Rodolfo "Corky" Gonzáles. He was previously a research associate at the Center for the Study
of Ethnicity and Race in America at the University of Colorado at
Boulder, and is the author of *The Crusade for Justice* (University of Wisconsin Press), the definitive account of the Chicano movement in the
1960s.

Preface

The legal and extra-judicial killing of Mexicans along the border and beyond has been an endemic feature of American life since the signing of the Treaty of Guadalupe Hidalgo, which ended the Mexican-American War in 1848 and resulted in the acquisition of more than half of Mexico's territory, or approximately one-fourth of the United States. Historically Chicanos and Chicanas have been subjected to a double standard of justice that applied one standard to Anglo-Americans and another one to Mexicans (Mirandé 1987). Irrespective of citizenship or immigration status, they were characterized as "greasers," bandits, criminals, and members of an inferior indolent race.

In preparing the Introduction to this volume, I consulted my book, *Gringo Justice*, published more than 30 years ago and was surprised to discover that the issues it raised are as relevant today as ever. In pointing to the importance of providing a historical context for the contemporary situation, I sought to justify the laconic title noting that:

> Titles such as *Law, Justice, and the Chicano* and *Chicanos and the Legal and Judicial System* were considered and discarded because they implied that the American legal and judicial system had been just and equitable in its treatment of Chicanos. The title *Gringo Justice* seemed to more accurately capture the reality of the Chicano experience before the American Tribunals.
> (ibid., ix)

This book presents a fresh look at *Gringo Justice*, or more accurately *Injustice*, nearly two hundred years after the end of the Mexican-American War and the signing of the Treaty of Guadalupe Hidalgo. It presents a unique in-depth insider look at the relationship of Mexicans and Latinos in the United States to the legal and judicial system in the twenty-first century. I begin by reviewing the Treaty of Guadalupe Hidalgo, which provided special protections of property and legal rights of former Mexican citizens incorporated into the United States, and addresses the contemporary system of "Gringo Injustice."

This book places the Chicano/a experience in historical perspective and presents an insider view of Gringo Injustice which rejects the traditional objective, neutral, value-free stance of academic scholarship, and is grounded in the belief that it is neither possible nor desirable to be indifferent or neutral toward racism or the prevailing unequal system of justice in the United States. There is currently increasing public debate about crime, police violence in minority communities, racial profiling, the victimization of people of Color, and a powerful "Black Lives Matter" movement which was sparked by the Rodney King beating and acquittal of the officers involved, but came directly in response to the Trayvon Martin killing and subsequent acquittal of George Zimmerman, Ferguson, and other recent incidents of excessive use of police force, which has evolved into a global network.

While Latinos continue to be overrepresented in the prison population, and as victims of racial profiling and police use of deadly force, the topic remains relatively neglected. A recent report by the Office of Inspector General of traffic stops by a sheriff's department team concluded that "Latinos were both stopped and searched at much greater rates than other racial or ethnic groups" but that "there was a very low rate of success in finding contraband" (Lin and Poston 2019). According to the California Department of Justice, for example, approximately 43 percent of the victims of police shootings in California over the past ten years were Latino (Reese 2016). There is considerable scholarship focusing on Latino youth gangs and crime, some written by former gang members, but there is a compelling need for a comprehensive look at Latinos and the legal and judicial system, particularly a work written from the perspective of those who are in the trenches with first-hand, personal experience and understanding of the topic. The contributors to this volume are experts who have not only solid academic credentials but also direct personal experience, inside knowledge of the law, and are eminently qualified to write on the topic. Three of the contributors (Rivera, Durán, and Alvarado) have worked as police officers; two are retired law enforcement officers (Rivera and Alvarado), and another worked in juvenile probation early in his career (Durán). There are also three previously gang-affiliated youth (Durán, Plascencia-Castillo, and Maldonado), two attorneys (Pérez and Mirandé), and a community activist (Vigil).

This work is also distinguished by incorporating both sociological and criminological theories of crime as well as providing a close examination of the legal and constitutional frameworks on the topic. The chapters in this volume explore neglected issues on Latinos and the law in the twenty-first century and are geared toward experts in Sociology, Latino and Chicano Studies, Crime, Delinquency, and Law. It will appeal to students, faculty, practitioners, and lay readers interested in México and Latino América, crime, delinquency, law, criminal justice, and ethnic studies.

The structure of the book

Among the contributors, Roberto Rivera is a doctoral student in sociology and Fulbright scholar who was a police officer for twenty years and has emerged as a leading figure in the holistic policing movement (Wright 2016, 348–350). Richard Alvarado was Chief Deputy Warden at the California Institution for Men, Chino, retiring in 2011 after 32 years in law enforcement. Alvarado was the Deputy in Charge during the major, bloody Chino prison riot on August 8, 2009, involving Black and Chicano inmates, a riot apparently orchestrated by the Mexican Mafia, and wrote a book about the incident. In Chapter 3 and Chapter 6, Rivera and Alvarado take a critical retrospective gaze at policing and the relationship between law enforcement and Latino communities from the inside out, with Alvarado providing a law enforcement perspective on prison gangs and the Mexican Mafia, or La Eme, and Rivera critically examining three police shootings of Latinos in a city in California, and a program designed to improve the relationship between police and the Latino community.

Ernesto Vigil is a community activist and former member of the Crusade for Justice in Denver, Colorado, from 1968–1981, who worked closely with its founder, Chicano Civil Rights leader, Rodolfo "Corky" Gonzáles. He was previously a research associate at the Center for the Study of Ethnicity and Race in America at the University of Colorado at Boulder and is author of *The Crusade for Justice*, the definitive account of the Chicano movement in Denver in the 1960s (Vigil 1999). In Chapter 4, Vigil presents an insider perspective on the wrongful death of Ismael Mena, a Mexican immigrant who was killed by the Denver Police SWAT team after they raided Mena's apartment, mistakenly suspecting it of being a drug house.

José Stalin Plascencia-Castillo and Katherine Lucía Maldonado, an American Sociological Association Doctoral Fellow, are doctoral students in sociology who have lived the barrio lifestyle and have directly experienced the hyper-criminalization of barrio youth. In Chapter 7, Plascencia-Castillo uses a Foucauldian theoretical lens to understand the panopticon and mechanisms employed in controlling and criminalizing barrio youth. In Chapter 8, Maldonado offers an insider, intersectional perspective on gang-affiliated teen-mothers and their unique experience with both sexism and hyper-criminalization.

Robert Durán, sociologist and criminologist, is a transitional figure who has published extensively on gangs and police use of excessive force on Latinos. A professor and activist scholar, he was previously a gang member and subsequently became a member of law enforcement working in juvenile probation. He brings his knowledge of gangs and law enforcement to the table in Chapter 2.

Maritza Pérez is a policy analyst and attorney who has advocated for policies to end mass incarceration and the disproportionate representation of Latinos in the criminal legal system. In Chapter 1 and Chapter 5, Pérez and Mirandé, a sociologist and practicing attorney, bring a legal lens to examine the problems of mass incarceration, excessive use of force, extrajudicial killings, racial profiling, and the exclusion of Mexicans from grand and petit juries.

The idea for the book project came from years of teaching graduate and undergraduate students and writing about Gringo Injustice and the relationship of Chicanos to the legal and judicial system. One of the contributors, Richard Alvarado, was an undergraduate student in the early 1980s at the University of California, Riverside, who along with other students, joined me in teaching a Chicano Studies class to inmates at the California Rehabilitation Center in Norco, California. Once retired after a long career in law enforcement, we reconnected and began talking about common interests and the possibility of collaborating on a collective project that focused on Chicanos and the law. Several years ago, Roberto Rivera, a retired law enforcement officer, became a graduate student in sociology and I have served as his advisor and faculty mentor. I have also worked and mentored two other contributors, José Stalin Plascencia-Castillo and Katherine Lucía Maldonado, who enrolled in my Chicano Sociology graduate seminar last year and began sharing ideas about policing, surveillance of barrio youth, and contributing to a volume on the topic.

I had never met Robert Durán when he reached out to me several years ago and thanked me for writing *The Chicano Experience* and *Gringo Justice,* thereby blazing the trail for future generations of young Chicano/a scholars. Once I became familiar with his work on gangs and police shootings, I asked him to submit a chapter for this volume. I sat in on a presentation by Maritza Pérez at the LatCrit Conference in Orange County in 2015. I was very impressed with her presentation and research and invited her to submit a chapter on lynchings of Mexicans and contemporary hate crimes for the volume. I met Ernesto Vigil several years ago when he made a presentation at UC Riverside, "Holes in the Door," based on a 2009 documentary focusing on the unlawful killing of Ismael Mena by the Denver Police in 1999 and asked him to contribute to the volume.

I owe a special thanks to all the contributors to this volume who worked diligently to meet deadlines and make this project a reality. Evelyn Pruneda provided valuable editorial assistance and helped in editing and formatting an earlier draft of the book. Evangelina Enríquez read and edited the manuscript and provided ongoing and valuable input on the project. Although a number of persons have contributed to the successful completion of this work, I am ultimately responsible for any errors or omissions.

References

LinII, Rong-Gong and Ben Poston. 2019. "Sheriff's I-5 Unit Faulted in Report." *Los Angeles Times*, B-1. April 20.

Mirandé, Alfredo. 1987. *Gringo Justice*. Notre Dame, IN: Notre Dame University Press.

Reese, Philip. 2016. "The Facts About Police Shootings in California: Black, White and Latino." *Sacramento Bee*. July 12, 2016. Vigil, Ernesto V. 1999. *The Crusade for Justice: Chicano Militancy and the Government's War on Dissent*. Madison, WI: The University of Wisconsin Press.

Wright, J.Kim. 2016. *Lawyers as Changemakers: The Global Integrative Law Movement*. American Bar Association.

Introduction

Alfredo Mirandé

The Treaty of Guadalupe Hidalgo, 1848

ARTICLE VIII

Mexicans now established in territories previously belonging to Mexico, and which remain for the future within the limits of the United States, as defined by the present treaty, shall be free to continue where they now reside, or to remove at any time to the Mexican Republic, retaining the property which they possess in the said territories, or disposing thereof, and removing the proceeds wherever they please, without their being subjected, on this account, to any contribution, tax, or charge whatever ...

In the said territories, property of every kind, now belonging to Mexicans not established there, shall be inviolably respected. The present owners, the heirs of these, and all Mexicans who may hereafter acquire said property by contract, shall enjoy with respect to it guarantees equally ample as if the same belonged to citizens of the United States.

(Treaty of Guadalupe Hidalgo, 1848)

Signed on February 2, 1848, in Guadalupe Hidalgo, Querétaro, a city north of the Mexican capital where the government fled to avoid the advancing US forces, the Treaty of Guadalupe Hidalgo ended the Mexican-American War (1846–1848). With the defeat of its army in September 1847, the Mexican government had entered into negotiations to end the War. The peace talks were negotiated by Nicholas Trist of the United States and representatives of the Mexican Government, Don Bernardo Couto, Don Miguel Atristain, and Don Luis Gonzago Cuevas.

Per Article VIII of the Treaty, property of every kind belonging to Mexican citizens "shall be inviolably respected." Article IX of the Treaty, as amended by the US Senate, further guaranteed that,

The Mexicans who, in the territories aforesaid, shall not preserve the character of citizens of the Mexican Republic, conformably with what is stipulated in the preceding article, shall be incorporated into the Union of the United States and be admitted at the proper time (to be judged of by the Congress of the United States) to the enjoyment of all the rights of citizens of the United States,[1] according to the principles of the Constitution; and in the meantime, shall be maintained and protected in the free enjoyment of their liberty and property, and secured in the free exercise of their religion without restriction.

According to the terms of the Treaty, Mexico ceded Upper California and New Mexico to the United States. Known as the Mexican Cession, this also included the present-day states of Arizona and New Mexico and parts of Utah, Nevada, and Colorado (Article V) and in addition, Mexico relinquished all claims to Texas, recognizing the Rio Grande as the southern boundary with the United States (Article V).

Overall, Mexico ceded more than 525,000 square miles of territory, or 55 percent of its land base. The United States paid Mexico $15,000,000 "in consideration of the extension acquired by the boundaries of the United States" (Article XII of the Treaty) and agreed to pay American citizens' debts owed to them by the Mexican government (Article XV). In addition, the Treaty protected the property and civil rights of Mexican nationals living within the new boundaries of the United States (Articles VIII and IX), with the promise of the United States to police its boundaries (Article XI), and the compulsory arbitration of future disputes between the two countries (Article XXI).

Although successful in negotiating the terms of the Treaty, President Polk was furious with Trist and had initially ordered him to end the negotiations and return to the United States because he wanted more territory for less money (Mirandé 1987, 9). Polk was incensed with the Treaty but was anxious to end the war and reluctantly submitted it to Congress for ratification.[2]

It should be noted that the Senate significantly altered Article IX, and struck Article X, which protected land grants made to Mexican residents in the ceded territory:

> All grants of land made by the Mexican government or by the competent authorities, in territories previously appertaining to Mexico, and remaining for the future within the limits of the United States, shall be respected as valid, to the same extent that the same grant would be valid, if the said territories had remained with the limits of Mexico.
> (Treaty of Guadalupe Hidalgo, 1848, Article X, Deleted)

It more specifically declared as valid all land grants issued by the Mexican government or competent authorities prior to March 2, 1836, in Texas, and May 13, 1846, in all other territories.

Article IX was amended and a lengthy set of conditions were condensed into a single paragraph. The original phrase, "shall be incorporated into the United States and admitted into the Union of the United States, and admitted as soon as possible" was changed to read—"shall be incorporated at the proper time (to be judged by the Congress of the United States)." The rights of the Catholic Church and guarantees protecting Church property were also struck. The omission of Article X was especially significant because it virtually protected "all prior and pending titles to property of every description" (Perrigo 1971, 176).

While the Treaty of Guadalupe Hidalgo ended the Mexican-American War and hostilities between Mexico and the United States, it also marked the beginning of conflict between Anglo-Americans and Chicanos, formerly displaced Mexicans who now found themselves within the territorial boundaries of the United States (Mirandé 1987, 17). Despite its many protections of land, property, and the cultural rights of displaced Mexicans, the Treaty's important provisions were breached even prior to its ratification by both countries.

Once the Treaty was ratified by the United States on March 13, 1848, there was concern that Mexico would refuse to ratify it because of the deletions and amendments introduced by the Senate. Mexico's vigorous protests over the Senate's Amendments and the deletion of Article X resulted in the issuance of the Protocol of Quererato, signed by the United States Commissioners four months later on May 26, 1848. The Protocol affirmed that the American Government, first of all:

> by suppressing the IXth article of the Treaty of Guadalupe and substituting the III article of the Treaty of Louisiana did not intend to diminish in any way what was agreed upon by the aforesaid article IXth in favor of the inhabitants of the territories ceded by Mexico ... all the privileges and guarantees, civil, political and religious, which would have been possessed by the inhabitants of the ceded territories, if the IXth article of the Treaty had been retained, will be enjoyed by them without any difference under the article which has been substituted.

Then,

> by suppressing the Xth article of the Treaty of Guadalupe did not in any way intend to annul the grants of lands made by Mexico in the ceded territories. These grants, notwithstanding the suppression of the article of the Treaty, preserve the legal value which they may possess; and the grantees may cause their legitimate titles to be acknowledged before the American tribunals.
>
> Conformably to the law of the United States, legitimate titles to every description of property personal and real, existing in the ceded territories, are those which were legitimate titles under the Mexican law in California and New Mexico up to the 13th of May 1846, and in Texas up to the 2d March 1836.

and then,

> by suppressing the concluding paragraph of article XIIth of the Treaty, did not intend to deprive the Mexican Republic of the free and unrestrained faculty of ceding, conveying or transferring at any time (as it may judge best) the sum of the twelve [*sic*] millions of dollars which the same Government of the United States is to deliver in the places designated by the amended article.
>
> (Protocol of Querétaro)

For Mexico, the Protocol became a critical and binding part of the Treaty but the United States countered that the Protocol did not alter the original terms of the Treaty and was non-binding. There was so much confusion over the Protocol and the Treaty that it raised concern in Congress relative to whether the Protocol might have essentially abrogated the Treaty (Miller 1937, 383). Since the Protocol induced Mexico to ratify the Treaty, it can be argued that the Protocol is valid only if the Treaty is valid, and if they are both valid, the United States has failed to adhere to the terms of the Treaty (Rendón 1972, 77). On the other hand, if the Treaty and the Protocol are not valid, the hostilities between the United States and Mexico are ongoing, and as a result of its unlawful possession of seven Southwestern states, the United States is in violation of international law. Mexico eventually ratified the Treaty and ratifications were exchanged in Querétaro on May 30 with the Treaty of Guadalupe Hidalgo officially proclaimed by the President of the United States on July 4, 1848.

No document is more important for the Chicano people than the Treaty of Guadalupe Hidalgo. The Treaty meant that except for American Indians, Chicanos were the only other group who entered the United States as a result of war and conquest who had their legal, civil, and constitutional rights guaranteed by treaty (McWilliams 1990 [1968], 103). This is significant because United States Treaties, like the Constitution, are "the ultimate law of the land." Per Article VI, Clause Two of the Constitution which states:

> This Constitution, and the Laws of the United States which shall be made in Pursuance thereof; and all Treaties made, or which shall be made, under the Authority of the United States, shall be the supreme Law of the Land; and the Judges in every State shall be bound thereby, any Thing in the Constitution or Laws of any State to the Contrary notwithstanding.

Gringo Injustice

The Treaty had afforded special treaty rights to Chicanos that extended beyond constitutional protections. In addition to the rights and duties of American citizenship, Mexicans would have special privileges derived from their previous customs in language, law, and religion. But the Treaty differed from treaties with tribal nations in that it did not recognize the sovereignty rights of Chicanos as a people, or their collective right to occupy land. Although individual land titles were to be respected, the Protocol's wording implicitly called into question the validity of these titles. Per the Protocol, these grants "preserve the legal value which they may possess; and the grantees may cause their legitimate titles to be acknowledged before the American tribunals."

In retrospect, it is clear that the United States has failed to honor the terms of the Treaty of Guadalupe Hidalgo or to respect the land, cultural, or linguistic rights of Chicanos.[3] As I previously concluded:

> Chicanos did not fare very well before the American tribunals. Within two decades most were landless. Since the Mexican-American War, the treaty has been largely ignored and its provisions have not been adhered to by the United States. Chicanos have been exploited economically, politically, and culturally, and much violence has been perpetrated against them. At the same time that the legal and judicial system has worked to advance the interest of the dominant society and to maintain Chicanos in a subordinate position, Chicanos have been depicted as a lawless and violent people.
>
> (Mirandé 1987, 16)

Subsequent to the Mexican-American War, Chicanos and Chicanas were subjected to a double standard of justice, or more accurately, injustice that applied one system to Anglo-Americans and another one to Mexicans (ibid., ix). George Marvin, for example, reported that:

> The killing of Mexicans ... through the border in these last four months is almost incredible ... Some rangers have degenerated into common man-killers. There is no penalty for killing, for no jury along the border would ever convict a white man for shooting a Mexican ... Reading over the Secret Service records makes you feel almost as though there were an open game season on Mexicans along the border.
>
> (McWilliams 1990 [1968], 112)

While these observations were recorded on the eve of World War I, the legal and extra-judicial killing of Mexicans along the border and beyond has been an endemic feature of American life since the signing of the Treaty of Guadalupe Hidalgo.

The Treaty was significant in that it sought to protect the property and cultural rights of former Mexican citizens and recognized displaced Mexicans (Chicanos) as a unique national minority. Mexicans were given one year to declare their Mexican citizenship and return to Mexico. Article VIII further stated that "[T]hose who shall remain in the said territories after the expiration of that year, without having declared their intention to retain the character of Mexicans, shall be considered to have elected to become citizens of the United States" (Treaty of Guadalupe Hidalgo 1848, Article VIII). Mexicans were, thus, implicitly granted unconditional amnesty and US citizenship. The Treaty distinguished between displaced Mexicans who remained in the United States and Mexican nationals. Although there are important differences in the rights and experiences of Chicanos and *mexicanos* today, particularly "unauthorized" Mexican nationals, who enter the United States without inspection, there are also important commonalities between them. The Treaty's distinction between Mexicans living in the acquired territory and those residing in Mexico and along the newly established international border—a 1,945-mile-long strip stretching from San Ysidro, California, to the Gulf of Mexico—has been blurred by law enforcement.

The proximity of the US/Mexican border subjected Mexicans to a double standard of justice and to regulation not only by local police agencies and private police forces like the Texas Rangers but also to an international police force, the Border Patrol. In short, the proximity of the border and the legacy of conflict between the United States and Mexico have placed Mexicans on either side of the border in a disadvantaged position relative to the legal and judicial system. Persons who cross the border without authorization, for example, are often victims of crime and subjected to abuses and mistreatment not only by gangs and bandits, but by the police and Immigration and Customs Enforcement (ICE) agents, yet they are reluctant to complain or seek legal redress to their injuries in American tribunals.

Law enforcement, on the other hand, regularly engages in racial profiling, regardless of a person's place of birth or citizenship status. In fact, it is argued in Chapter 10 that there is a "Mexican Exception" to the Fourth Amendment, reinforced by the Supreme Court that has made Mexican appearance alone a legitimate factor in making an immigration stop, although it cannot be the only factor. A large number of Chicanos have consequently been subjected to unnecessary questioning and detention along the border, and some have even been deported.

Gringos and Greasers

Because racism knows no borders, Mexicans, irrespective of their citizenship or immigration status, have typically been characterized as "greasers," bandits, criminals, and members of an inferior, indolent race. Historian Carey McWilliams and other observers have noted that in the US borderlands Anglos have always been "gringos" to the Mexicans, whereas Mexicans have always been "greasers" to Anglos and the two terms accurately reflect the level of mutual hostility that each group had for the other (McWilliams 1990 [1968], 112). For

many years, the term Gringo was said to have been associated with a song—
"Green Grow the Rushes, O!"—that the Americans sang as they marched into
Mexico in 1846 (ibid., 112). Gringo in all Spanish dictionaries is a corruption
of the word, *griego* (the Spanish word for Greek). To talk in "gringo" was to
speak in gibberish. Prior to the Conquest, gringo referred to any foreigner who
spoke Spanish with a foreign accent but it was much less pejorative than its
counterpart, greaser (ibid., 112).

The origin of greaser is less clear. One explanation is that a Mexican
maintained a small shop at the crest of Raton Pass where ox-carts and
wagons on the Santa Fe Trail were greased before descending down to the
New Mexico plateau. According to this account, a Mexican was thus literally "a greaser" (ibid., 112). In California, the word can ostensibly be
traced to the days of the hide-and-tallow trade, when American sailors used
it to refer to Indians and Mexicans who loaded greasy hides on clipper ships
(ibid., 112). Regardless of the origin of these terms, they accurately reflect
the hostility and contempt between Mexicans and Anglos in the Southwest.
Greaser was clearly the more offensive and pejorative of the two terms.

According to historian Arnoldo De León, the contemptuous word greaser
which Anglos applied to Mexicans may also have been associated with
Indians, since the Indians' olive color was thought to have resulted from the
oils and greases they used to paint their faces (1983, 16). As John C. Reid
traveled through Texas in the 1850s, he attempted unsuccessfully to ascer-
tain why Mexican men were called "greasers" and the women "greaser
women" (ibid., 16).

In California, the Anti-Vagrancy Act of 1855 was also known as the
"Greaser Act" and was only renamed after it had been on the books for a
year (Gonzales-Day 2006, 24). Section §2 of the statute was aimed at "all
persons who are commonly known as 'Greasers' or the issue of Spanish or
Indian blood ... and who go armed and are not peaceable and quiet persons" (Heizer and Almquist 1977, 151). The Foreign Miners' Tax of 1851
was similarly aimed at Mexicans and other non-Anglos in the California
mines and required that all foreign-born miners pay a tax of $20 each
month and was intended to bolster the state's empty confers. While the
Act was ostensibly aimed at all foreign miners, in practice, it served to
drive thousands of Mexican and Latin American miners from their claims.
Despite the guarantees contained in the Treaty of Guadalupe Hidalgo,
they were required to pay for the tax regardless of their citizenship status
(Gonzales-Day 2006, 25).

Interestingly, dark Mexican skin tone was also associated with Blacks.
Justice of the Peace, Adolphus Sterne, who attended a wedding in Texas
between a Mexican *criollo*, a member of the upper class and descendant of
Spaniards, and a White woman, remarked about mestizo members of the
groom's party, observing that "they would be taken anywhere for Negroes"
(De León 1983, 16).

Contempt for the Mexican intensified after the Texas Revolt in the 1830s and Texas Independence. Anglo migrants to Texas were from the South and their antipathies toward Blacks were readily transferred to the swarthy, dark-skinned Mexicans (Mirandé 1987, 7). According to De León,

> From the Southern and frontier-oriented culture they had acquired a certain repulsion for dark-skinned people and a distaste for miscegenation ... By conditioning, they were predisposed to react intolerably to people they found different from themselves but similar to those they considered as enemies and as inferior.
>
> (1983, 6)

Oscar M. Addison similarly commented in a letter to his brother in the 1850s that Mexicans were of "a class, inferior to common nigers [sic]" (ibid., 17). A journalist from Chattanooga wrote, "Mexicans were a race of mongrels" and "dark to the point of blackness" (San Antonio Standard 1889, 1).

Anglo perceptions of Mexicans as primitive, inferior, and standing in the way of progress preceded the signing of the Treaty in 1848 and just a year later in a letter to his wife in 1849, Thomas B. Eastland described the people in the border city of El Paso as:

> A poor, miserable, dirty town, badly built, containing a population of some 5,000 Mexicans, and a few foreigners—the greater portion of the former are *Peons* or slaves, and as miserable a set of looking *greasers*, as you would see, nowhere else in the wild but in this land of "*God and Liberty.*"
>
> (1939, 125)

In another letter on March 26, 1864, George L. Robertson wrote to his sister about the greasers he encountered on the border:

> There is a report in camp that our company has been ordered to Corpus Christi which I hope is so. I am getting rather tired of the Rio Grande and the *greasers*, of all the contemptable [sic], despicable people on Earth the greasers in my estimation are the lowest, meaner even than the Cummanche. They are ugly, thieving, rascally in every way and to be educated only makes a greaser the grander rascal. I think the whole nation ought to be peoned rich and poor, they would make the best plantation hands in the world. They fear and respect authority and are a great deal more humble and less intelligent than our negroes.
>
> (De León 1983, 1)

Although Mexicans were subjected to a double standard of justice and were often the victims of denigrating attitudes and crime, ironically as men like Tiburcio Vasquez (Figure 0.1), one of the Chicano Social Bandits, responded

Bradley & Rulofson. } {Entered according to Act of Congress in the year 1874, by Bradley & Rulofson,} San Francisco.
in the office of the Librarian of Congress, at Washington }

Figure 0.1 Noted Bandit, Tiburcio Vasquez, circa 1874; Portraits Collection, PC-PT; California Historical Society; PC-PT_00161.

to their systematic displacement from their land and property and to abuses at the hands of the legal and judicial system, they were also labeled criminals and bloodthirsty outlaws (Boessenecker 2010). In fact, one of the most perduring images throughout the history of the Southwest is that of the greasy Mexican bandit, or "*bandito*."

Negative images of Mexicans even penetrated scholarly works. Distinguished Texas historian, Walter Prescott, for example, has this to say about Mexicans:

> Without disparagement, it may be said that there is a cruel streak in the Mexican nature, or so the history of Texas would lead one to believe. This cruelty may be a heritage from the Spanish and of the Inquisition; it may, and doubtless should be, attributed partly to the Indian blood
> …
>
> (Webb 1965 [1935], 14)

This image has evolved from the greasy *bandito* of the old West, to crazed Zoot-Suiters and *pachuco* killers in the 1940s, to contemporary *cholos*, gangsters, and gang members. Media portrayals in newspapers, film, and news are particularly pernicious in reinforcing the image of Mexicans as violent criminals (Martinez 1971; Trujillo 1974; De León 1983, 75).

In 1970, sociologist Thomas Martinez led an attack on the Frito Bandido and other advertisements that reinforced media images of Mexicans as treacherous bandidos. He argued, for example, that the Frito Bandido promoted racist thinking because "Mexicans were portrayed as sneaking and thieving. Mexican American children were paying the price in loss of self-esteem for the Frito-Lay Corporation's successful advertising" (Martinez 1971).

The greasy and treacherous Mexican bandit was portrayed in director John Huston's classic 1948 film, *The Treasure of the Sierra Madre*. A famous phrase, popularized in the film, occurs when three Americans who have secretly agreed to split the treasure are confronted by a group of Mexican bandits headed by their greasy and bearded leader played by famous Mexican actor, Alfonso Badolla. When the leader, "Gold Hat" tries to convince Fred C. Dobbs (Humphrey Bogart) that he and his men are *federales*, Dobbs demands that the bandit produce a badge to prove that they are police. Badolla defiantly responds, "We ain't got no badges! We don't need no badges. I don't need to show you any stinkin' badges!"

The original version of the quote, which appeared in B. Traven's 1927 racist novel, *The Treasure of the Sierra Madre*, edited and censored for the film, was even more indignant:

> "All right," Curtin shouted back. "If you are the police, where are your badges? Let's see them."

"Badges, to god-damned hell with badges! We have no badges. In fact, we don't need badges. I don't have to show you any stinking badges, you god-damned cabrón and chinga tu madre!"[4]

The Racial Binary: "White But Not Equal"

In the context of this book, it is important to point out that the US Constitution was drafted and written to protect the interests of the founding fathers who were propertied Anglo-Saxon White men and slaveholders. The Constitution was an openly pro-slavery document. Several sections specifically protected the institution of slavery. Article I, §9 prevented Congress from banning the importation of slaves until 1808, and Article V prohibited this provision from being altered. Article I, §2, known as the "Three Fifths" clause required apportionment to the House of Representatives be based on the "whole Number of free Persons" and "three fifths of all other persons." Finally, the Fugitive Slave Clause in Article IV, §2 further provided that

> No person held to Service or Labour in one State, under the Laws thereof, escaping into another, shall in Consequence of any Law or Regulation therein, be discharged from such Service or Labour, but shall be delivered up on claim of the Party to whom such Service or Labour may be due.

In short, prior to the adoption of the Thirteenth Amendment in 1865, slavery was constitutionally permitted in the United States and prior to the 1868 adoption of the Fourteenth Amendment, there was no constitutional protection against racial discrimination, or assurance of due process or equal protection of the law.[5]

One of the major themes of this work is that Mexicans and other racial/ethnic groups have occupied a unique and ambiguous position in the US legal and judicial system which is based on the Black/White racial binary. Because Mexicans do not fit the binary as either Black or White, they have occupied an ambiguous, intermediate status. Although often defined as legally White, Mexicans were not White enough to gain equal treatment. In short, they are what Critical Race theorists have termed racially indeterminate and have been defined as White only when it was politically expedient, or in order to pit them against Blacks. An example is when schools that were predominantly Black and Latino were rendered "integrated" because Mexicans students were magically defined as legally "White."

It was not until the 1954 landmark *Hernandez v. Texas* case that Mexicans were first recognized as a legally cognizable category, separate and apart from Blacks and Whites. However, in rejecting Hernandez's appeal of his murder conviction, the Texas Supreme Court reinforced the racial binary by holding that Hernandez had been convicted by a jury of his peers because he was "White," as were the all-White members of the jury which convicted him.

In his treatment of the *Hernandez* case, Ignacio García aptly describes the experiences of Chicanos as "White But Not Equal" because their "in-between" Black and Whites status permitted "rampant discrimination and exclusion of people of Mexican descent" (García 2009, 3). In other words,

> They were not seen as able to fulfill their role as full citizens—that is of being white—but at the same time did not merit inclusion in the Equal Protection clause of the U.S. Constitution because they were not black.
>
> (ibid., 3)

Long after the historic *Brown v. Board of Education* decision, which ironically came in the same term as *Hernandez* and outlawed racial segregation as unconstitutional and a violation of the Fourteenth Amendment Equal Protection clause, Mexican children continued to be segregated because they were deemed to have special language and other social needs. In the little known 1931 *Lemon Grove* case, twenty-five years before *Brown*, the San Diego Superior Court ruled that you could not legally segregate Mexican children because they were "Caucasian" (Alvarez 1986). Similarly, in the landmark *Westminster School District of Orange County v. Mendez, et al.* (1947), some seven years before *Brown*, the Ninth Circuit Court of Appeals overturned the segregation of Mexican children, but it did so for the wrong reason, holding that the practice violated the equal protection clause because Mexicans were Caucasian and the specific California statute at issue did not specifically permit the segregation of Mexican students (*Westminster School District of Orange County v. Mendez, et al.* 1947, 774).

Overview

The relationship of Mexicans and Chicanos to the legal and judicial system, from the Constitution, written by propertied White slaveholders who subscribed to a racial binary, to the Treaty of Guadalupe Hidalgo, which was not honored, to Anglo settlers, journalists, and authors, who saw them as greasy, primitive, and less than slaves, has subjected them to a dual standard of justice and denial of equal protection under the law. Many Chicanos came to see Anglo "justice" as meaning "just us."

In the 1970s, there was a wave of police shootings of Chicanos. At the height of the Chicano Movement in 1975, a crowd of over 2,000 Chicanas/os showed up at National City's City Hall demanding the firing of police officer Craig Short for the killing of Luis "Tato" Rivera (Figure 0.2), a 20-year-old Chicano shot in the back with a .357 Magnum for allegedly snatching a purse (La Prensa 2003). Incredibly San Diego District Attorney Ed

Figure 0.2 Luis "Tato" Rivera shooting and protest march. 1975.   Courtesy of Herman Baca Papers, Special Collections & Archives, UC San Diego.

Miller indicted Short for manslaughter. Not only was Short acquitted of any wrong-doing, the Chicano/Latino community was further insulted in 2003 when Short was appointed as Acting Chief of Police by the City Council and mayor of National City (ibid.).

In 1977, three Houston policemen received one-year prison sentences for the killing of Vietnam veteran, Jose Campos Torres (Mirandé 1987, 21). A US Border Patrol agent similarly shot a 13-year-old boy for allegedly throwing rocks across the border (San Francisco Chronicle 1985). Ricardo Falcón, a student at the University of Colorado and a leader of the United Latin American Students (UMAS), was murdered and has become a martyr of the Chicano Movement. Falcón was a popular leader not only at UC Boulder, but throughout the rural areas of northeastern Colorado. In late August 1972, Falcón and other Chicano leaders set out in several cars for a meeting of La Raza Unida Party in El Paso (*Latin American* Herald Tribune, October 29, 2017). When the radiator in Falcón's car began to overheat, the caravan pulled into a gas station in Orogrande, New Mexico. The gas station owner, Perry Brunson, a member of the segregationist American Independent Party, refused to give them water unless they paid for it. Falcón and Brunson got into an argument. Brunson fired four shots, two of them struck Falcón, and he died shortly afterwards (ibid.). Brunson was tried for manslaughter and acquitted by an all-White jury.

More recently in Los Angeles, a Mexican wrongly suspected of bike theft was shot near a CVS/pharmacy. Investigators say police received a call about a report of a theft of a bicycle near a CVS/pharmacy store nearby. Arriving officers say they saw two individuals matching the description with a bicycle. Officers stopped those individuals. That's when officers say a third person in his late thirties appeared and tried to intervene. "He started to walk towards the officers. At that point, officers believed that he was reaching for a weapon and an officer-involved shooting occurred. He was shot multiple times. He was pronounced dead here at the scene," said Lt. Eddie Hernandez of the Los Angeles County Sheriff's Department (*CBS News* 2013).

Videos of the shooting released only after a federal court order, showed the Gardena police shooting two unarmed men, one of them, Ricardo Diaz Zeferino, fatally (Mejia et al. 2015). The men had actually been victims of a bike theft and were falsely accused of stealing a bicycle at the pharmacy. The grainy video shows that two of the men remained motionless, while Diaz Zeferino, a Mexican national, appears to be confused by the officers' instructions. He drops and raises his arms, showing the police his hands so they can see he is unarmed and steps backward and forward for a few paces. After Diaz Zeferino removes a baseball cap from his head, he is seen being gunned down by a volley of gunfire from police (ibid.). Diaz Zeferino appears not to have understood the officers' instructions.

Although there is much concern today with police treatment of barrio youth and gangs, Mexican gangs were not identified as a major problem in Los Angeles until the 1940s when the *pachuco* mania that led to a public outcry over the 1942 Sleepy Lagoon Incident and the 1943 Zoot-Suit Riots. Young Mexican and Mexican American youth were often labeled not only as *pachucos* and Zoot-Suiters but also with other pejorative, descriptive terms such as hoodlums, gangsters, and crazed killers. One such term is *cholo*, a contemporary version of *pachuco* in the1940s (Mazón 1984, 2). In *The Decline of the Californios*, historian Leonard Pitt described the bands of *cholos* who migrated to California in the 1830s and 1840s (Pitt 1971, 309), which he translated as "scoundrel" (Mazón 1984, 2). Interestingly, the derisive term was used to refer not to Chicanos but to lower-class, uneducated persons who had recently arrived from Mexico.

The Sleepy Lagoon case preceded and set the stage for the 1943 Zoot-Suit Riots. The defendants, alleged members of the 38th Street Gang, were accused of murdering José Díaz on August 2, 1942, after a fight was said to have erupted when members of the gang crashed a party at the Williams Ranch. The ranch was near a reservoir and popular "lover's lane" known as the Sleepy Lagoon (Mirandé 2011, 32). The conviction was obtained despite the fact that the prosecution failed to prove that the boys had beaten or murdered Díaz.

One of the most outrageous aspects of the case is that the young defendants were jailed for three months without being allowed to get haircuts or clean clothing because "their style of haircut, the thick heavy heads of hair, the duck tail comb, the *pachuco* pants and things of that kind" were important "evidence" in proving their guilt (Endore 1944, 31). The girls associated with 38th Street, particularly Lorena Encinas, played a critical role in the criminal proceedings and were incarcerated. They were incarcerated at the infamous reform school, the Ventura School for Girls, after they refused to testify against the Sleepy Lagoon defendants (O'Bregón Pagán 2003, 75–77; Ramírez 2009, 1–23). The Sleepy Lagoon case and the Zoot-Suit Riots were thus important in signaling the beginning of the current hyper-criminalization of Chicana/o youth.

Police Killings of Latinos

There has been increased public debate not only about police violence in minority communities but also mass incarceration, racial profiling, and victimization of people of Color. A powerful "Black Lives Matter" movement came in response to the killing of Trevor Martin, Ferguson, and other incidents of excessive use of police force, which evolved into a global network. These include numerous examples, such as the recent police killing of Philando Castile in Minnesota and Alton Sterling in Baton Rouge, Louisiana. Sterling was selling CDs outside a convenience store, and was on the ground and on his back when he was alleged to have been "reaching for a gun" when shot by Baton Rouge police. The chapters in this volume focus on Latinos and Gringo Injustice and are written in solidarity with and in support of the Black Lives Movement.

Although Latinos in general, and Mexicans in particular, continue to be overrepresented in the prison population, and as victims of racial profiling and police use of deadly force, the topic remains relatively neglected and unexplored. According to the California Department of Justice, for example, over the past ten years California police have shot and killed approximately 1,300 persons, including 130 in 2015, or an average of one person every three days (Reese 2016). Despite public concern with the recent shooting of police in Dallas and Baton Rouge, approximately four police were killed in the line of duty each year over the same period of time.

The most common justification for officer-involved killings, especially subsequent to the *Garner* decision (*Tennessee v. Garner* 1985) was that the suspect was believed to have posed a threat to the police or was in the act of committing a felony. Prior to the 1985 Supreme Court decision in *Garner*, the common law and a number of state statues allowed a police officer to kill a suspected felon and be free from criminal and tort liability if killing the felon proved necessary to effect an arrest (Tighe 1985, 151). In *Garner*, the court held that the shooting of an unarmed burglary suspect by the police violated the Fourth Amendment right to be free from unreasonable searches and seizures because the officer could not have reasonably believed that the suspect posed a threat to the officer or to others (ibid., 152). In overturning the Tennessee statute, the Supreme Court concluded that deadly force "may not be used unless it is necessary to prevent the escape and the officer has probable cause to believe that the suspect poses a significant threat of death or serious physical injury to the officer or others" (*Tennessee v. Garner* 1985, 4). Unfortunately, police officers have often misinterpreted *Garner* to justify deadly shootings by simply asserting that they believed the suspect "had a weapon" or "posed a threat to the officer or others," even when such a belief was not reasonable or justifiable.

Significantly, Latinos made up almost half of all persons killed by California police. Approximately, 43 percent of the victims of police killings in the past decade in the State were Latino, 30 percent were White, 20 percent were Black, and the remaining 7 percent were members of another race (Reese 2016).

Although a number of women have been killed by police, the killings of women are less likely to be reported or widely publicized. The death of Jessica Hernandez, an unarmed 17-year-old, queer Colorado girl, who was fatally shot by police on January 26, 2017, was ruled a homicide by the medical examiner's report (*NBC News* 2017). Although the Denver Police Department claimed that she was shot after she drove a stolen vehicle toward them, the autopsy performed by the Denver Chief Medical Examiner shows that Hernandez was shot two times on the left side of her torso (ibid.). The autopsy report did not indicate that Hernandez was driving toward the officers, since the wounds entered the body from the left side and were not fired at close range (ibid.). More recently, community members in Salinas, California, protested the killing of a young Latina, Brenda Mendoza, in a standoff with police on March 1, 2019 (The Californian, 2019).

The killing of Latinos by the police is not confined to the Southwest but is an endemic problem that has not received the national public exposure and attention it deserves. Oklahoma City Police, for example, were on their way to a hit-and-run collision when they stopped Magdiel Sanchez for holding a pipe. The 35-year-old deaf man was shot and killed by police even after neighbors had yelled that he could not hear their commands (Hayes 2017). The officer who fired the shot, Chris Barnes, was placed on administrative leave.

According to *Newsweek*, there has been a lack of media attention of police shootings of Latinos (Perez 2017). Of the 715 people killed by police in 2016, 112 were Latino (*Washington Post* 2017). Many of these fatalities have not been reported nationally. Blacks and Latinos have interaction rates with police that are proportional to their numbers, but, according to the US Bureau of Justice Statistics, they are overrepresented when it comes to traffic searches and arrests. Latinos make up 17.8 percent of the US but 23 percent of all searches and almost 30 percent of all arrests (Eith and Durose 2011). According to the *Huffington Post*, police killing of Latinos has garnered less public attention (Planas 2016).

Given the national attention on police killings one would have expected the shooting of Sanchez and other Latinos to have received more national media attention beyond the local and state level (ibid.). A number of community activists and analysts have suggested that the widespread killing of Latinos deserves to be more closely examined in order to better understand the complex relationship between law enforcement and Latino communities (ibid.). Brady Henderson, the legal director of the American Civil Liberties Union, offers several reasons for why police shootings of Latinos receive less media attention, noting that media outlets tend to look for the major story of the day. Henderson observed that the recent high profile shootings of African-American men have been "the big story," "but that's not the whole story. There is a much larger issue at the forefront" (Perez 2017). Henderson added that the lack of trust between the police and the various communities has a major impact on how people perceive the police.

The most common justification for officer-involved killings, especially subsequent to the *Garner* decision (*Tennessee v. Garner* 1985) was that the suspect was believed to have posed a threat to the police or was in the act of committing a felony. Significantly, African Americans and Latinos were killed at disproportionate rates, as police shot and killed blacks at almost five times the rate of Whites and three times the rate of Latinos. Most victims of police killings are men.

The Structure of the Book

This book seeks to initiate a very important conversation about the relationship between Latinas/os and the legal and judicial system, the unauthorized use of deadly force by the police in our communities, and the racial profiling of Latinos, particularly those of Mexican origin. The volume highlights racial profiling and the excessive use of force, the hyper-criminalization of barrio youth, as well as asking why there is so little public concern about these issues. Finally, it offers important policy recommendations and alternative solutions to these problems.

The chapters in this volume deal with a broad range of topics surrounding Latinos and the legal and judicial system or what I characterize as "Gringo Injustice" (Mirandé 1987). Part I focuses on state-sanctioned violence. In Chapter 1, Maritza Pérez uses an historical context to examine lynchings of Latinos in the nineteenth and early twentieth centuries, hate crimes, and how current anti-Mexican political rhetoric correlates to the rising number of Latinos falling victim to hate crimes and state-sanctioned violence. She concludes by offering policy recommendations for addressing these issues.

Robert J. Durán's Chapter 2 addresses officer-involved shootings of Latinos/as in the Southwest. He presents an overview of reflections and conclusions derived from years of studying officer-involved shootings in four counties in the Southwestern states of Colorado, New Mexico, Texas, and Utah. The study involved archival and ethnographic research used to compile a revisionist history of officer-involved shootings of Latinos in these geographic locales along with observations and interviews on police community interactions. He also offers important policy suggestions and recommendations.

In Chapter 3, Roberto Rivera applies Derick Bell's Interest Convergence Theory to racially biased policing in Latina/o communities and discusses a police initiative aimed at quelling conflict between barrio residents and the police. He critically evaluates why the Move Forward Project, a community-policing program that emerged in response to three police shootings of Latinos in a California community in five days, was discontinued, despite its apparent success in reducing violent crime in the community.

The final chapter in Part I, Chapter 4, is a first-hand account by community activist, Ernesto Vigil, documenting the wrongful death of Mexican immigrant, Ismael Mena, at the hands of the Denver Police and the cover-up that ensued. Colorado officials launched a drug raid in September 1999, which resulted in the death of the 45-year-old father of nine, who was shot to death by masked SWAT officers who broke down his door in the middle of the night. The officers, who had obtained a fatally flawed, no-knock warrant based on a tip from an informant who claimed there were drug dealers in the house, later said they shot Mena after he pointed a gun at them and fired. No drugs or evidence of drug dealing were found in Mena's house, and an autopsy revealed no drugs in his body.

Part II focuses on the Youth Control Complex and looks at Gringo Injustice from the perspective of barrio youth. Chapter 5 by Alfredo Mirandé is a case study of Chicano twins and their cousin who were charged with attempted murder pursuant to California's Street Terrorism and Enforcement Act (STEP); a new chapter in the War on Gangs. Based on his own experience as the attorney representing one of the twins, Mirandé perceptively discusses the constitutional implications of the Act.

In Chapter 6, Richard Alvarado addresses prison gangs and the Mexican Mafia. His analysis of the Mexican Mafia or "La EME," traces its inception in the 1950s to a web of influence in urban communities and shows how it has infiltrated all levels of the prison and jail system in California. He also discusses the role of prisons in perpetuating prison gangs and gang violence and offers possible recommendations and solutions to address this problem.

Chapter 7 is based on ethnographic field research, participant observation, and in-depth personal interviews with youth in Barrio Pico, a working-class neighborhood in San Diego County. José Plascentia-Castillo insightfully describes "a dual system of justice," where low-income urban Chicanas and Chicanos are targeted and receive harsh punishment for things that are considered innocuous outside of stigmatized neighborhoods and the criminalized status of gang membership. In addition to formal controls, he talks about the effects that panoptic surveillance has on Chicana and Chicano youngsters in the barrio.

In Chapter 8, Katherine L. Maldonado addresses the important and neglected topic of teen gang-affiliated mothers. She argues that the forms of control experienced by young women in the barrio who are not only gang affiliated but also teenage mothers, have not been adequately explored. Employing a Chicana feminist, intersectional analytical frame, she seeks to go beyond the Youth Control Complex, arguing that for young women like herself, a teen-mother at 15, the complexity of hyper-criminalization is one that becomes not only intergenerational but also inextricably gendered and race-based (Díaz-Cotto 2006).

The final section of the book, Part III, "Race, Citizenship and the Law," centers specifically on two important constitutional issues: (1) the exclusion of Latinos from juries; and (2) illegal searches and seizures, or what I have labeled the Mexican exception to the Fourth Amendment. Chapter 9 by Alfredo Mirandé examines the systemic exclusion of Mexicans and Latinos from grand and petit juries in violation of the Sixth and Fourteenth Amendments, as applied to the states. It also looks at the social construction of Whiteness and how language has become a proxy for race in the exclusion of bilingual jurors.

Finally, in Chapter 10, Alfredo Mirandé returns to the racial binary and discusses not only the social construction of Whiteness but also how White privilege plays out in an immigration context. This chapter speaks to how race affects the selective enforcement of the Fourth Amendment prohibition against unreasonable searches and seizures by ICE and the Border Patrol, as well as the legal doctrine surrounding the constitutionality of border stops and searches.

Recent Supreme Court rulings, including the Arizona SB 1070 case (*Arizona v. U.S.* 2012), for example, have held that being "Mexican-looking" is so closely linked to immigration status that it can be used as a legitimate factor in making an immigration stop; race thus serves as a proxy for immigration status. I conclude that in an immigration context, there has been a gradual and systemic evisceration of Fourth Amendment protections for Mexicans and "Mexican-looking" people residing on both sides of the border.

Notes

1 This provision proved to be controversial. At the California Constitutional Convention of 1849, for example, an amendment was adopted to essentially "amend" the provisions of Article IX of the Treaty to insert the word "white" before "male citizens of Mexico" (Heizer and Almquist 1977, 98), so that only White Mexican citizens would be granted citizenship. Although the final vote was left to the legislature, there was also a great deal of opposition to granting citizenship to Indians and descendants of African slaves residing in the former Mexican territory (ibid., 118–119).
2 There was much opposition to the Treaty in the Senate from diverse political groups. Some like Secretary of State, Buchanan, and Secretary of the Treasury, Walker, opposed the Treaty because they wanted more territory, including parts of northern Mexico. Others feared that the Treaty would upset the balance of power between slave and abolitionist states. The opposition party, the Whigs, feared that it would annex too much territory and increase the power of the slaveholding states (Griswold del Castillo 1990, 44).
3 Ironically, when Treaty Provisions have been enforced, the primary beneficiaries have not been Chicanos but "Anglo American land corporations and the state and federal governments" (Griswold del Castillo 1990, 87).
4 *Cabrón* is roughly translated as "bastard" and "*chinga tu madre*" as "Son of a bitch."
5 The Fifteenth Amendment, ratified in 1870, provided that the "right of citizens of the United States to vote shall not be denied or abridged by the United States or by any state on account of race, color, or previous condition of servitude."

References

Alvarado, Richard A. 2015. *10–33 On the West Yard: A Crime Story about Politics, Policies, and Prison Gangs*. West Conshohocken, PA: Infinity.

Alvarez, Robert, Jr. 1986. "The Lemon Grove Incident: The Nation's First Successful Desegregation Court Case." *The Journal of San Diego History*, 32(2): 2.

Boessenecker, John. 2010. *Bandido: The Life and Times of Tiburcio Vasquez*. Norman, OK: The University of Oklahoma Press.

CBS News. 2013. "Man Killed in Officer-Involved Shooting in Gardena." June 2.

De León, Arnoldo. 1983. *They Called Them Greasers: Anglo Attitudes toward Mexicans in Texas, 1821–1900*. Austin, TX: University of Texas Press.

Díaz-Cotto, Juanita. 2006. *Chicana Lives and Criminal Justice*. Austin, TX: University of Texas Press.

Eastland, Thomas B. 1939. "To California Through Texas and Mexico: The Diary and Letters of Thomas B. Eastland and Joseph G. Eastland, His Son." *California Historical Society Quarterly*, 18 (June): 99–135.

Eith, Christine and Matthew R. Durose. 2011. "Contacts between Police and the Public, 2008." Special Report. Washington, DC: U.S. Department of Justice, Office of Justice Programs, Bureau of Justice Statistics. October.

Endore, Guy. 1944. *The Sleepy Lagoon Mystery*. Los Angeles, CA: Unidos Books and Periodicals.

García, Ignacio M. 2009. *White But Not Equal: Mexican Americans, Jury Discrimination, and the Supreme Court*. Tucson, AZ: University of Arizona Press.

Gonzales-Day, Ken. 2006. *Lynchings in the West: 1850–1935*. Durham, NC: Duke University Press.

Griswold del Castillo, Ricardo. 1990. *The Treaty of Guadalupe Hidalgo: A Legacy of Conflict*. Norman, OK: University of Oklahoma Press.

Hayes, Christal. 2017. "Police Shootings: Oklahoma Cop Kills Deaf Man in Latest Attack on Disabled." *Newsweek*, September 21.

Heizer, Robert F. and Alan J. Almquist. 1977. *The Other Californians: Prejudice and Discrimination under Spain, Mexico, and the United States to 1920*. Berkeley, CA: University of California Press.

La Prensa. 2003. "Chicano Community Insulted." July 18.

Latin American Herald Tribune. 2017. "Chicano Leader Ricardo Falcón Remembered 40 Years After Murder." October 29.

Martinez, Thomas M. 1971. "Advertising and Racism: The Case of the Mexican-American." *El Grito: A Journal of Contemporary Mexican American Thought*, 2 (Summer): 3–13.

Mazón, Mauricio. 1984. *The Zoot-Suit Riots: The Psychology of Symbolic Annihilation*. Austin, TX: University of Texas Press.

McWilliams, Carey. 1990 [1968]. *North from Mexico*. New York: Greenwood Press.

Mejia, Brittny, Richard Winton, and Joel Rubin. 2015. "This Is the Shooting Video Gardena Police Didn't Want You to See." *Los Angeles Times*, July 15.

Miller, Hunter. 1937. *Treaties and Other International Acts of the United States of America*. vol. 5, Doc. 129. Washington, DC: U.S. Government Printing Office.

Mirandé, Alfredo. 1987. *Gringo Justice*. Notre Dame, IN: Notre Dame University Press.

Mirandé, Alfredo. 2011. *Rascuache Lawyer: Toward a Theory of Ordinary Litigation*. Tucson, AZ: University of Arizona Press.

Mirandé, Alfredo. 2012. "Latinos and the Fourth Amendment Protection Against Unreasonable Searches and Seizures." In Martín Guevara Urbina (Ed.), *Hispanics in the U.S. Criminal Justice System*. Springfield, IL: Charles C. Thomas, pp. 145–161.

NBC News. 2017. "Death of Denver Teen Jessica Hernandez Killed by Police Ruled a Homicide." February 28.

O'Bregón Pagán, Eduardo. 2003. *Murder at the Sleepy Lagoon: Zoot Suits, Race, and Riot in Wartime L.A.* Chapel Hill, NC: University of North Carolina Press.

Perez, Maria. 2017. "Police Shootings Are Killing Latinos." *Newsweek*, September 23.

Perrigo, Lynn. 1971. *The American Southwest: Its Peoples and Cultures*. Albuquerque, NM: University of New Mexico Press.

Pitt, Leonard. 1971. *The Decline of the Californios*. Berkeley, CA: University of California Press.

Planas, Roque. 2016. "The Fatal Police Shootings You Aren't Hearing About." *Huffington Post*, August 28.

Ramírez, Katherine. 2009. *The Woman in the Zoot-Suit: Gender, Nationalism, and the Cultural Politics of Memory*. Durham, NC: Duke University Press.

Reese, Philip. 2016. "The Facts about Police Shootings in California: Black, White and Latino." *The Sacramento Bee*, July 12.

Rendón, Armando B. 1972. *Chicano Manifesto*. New York: Macmillan.

San Antonio Standard, 1889. September 21, 1.

San Francisco Chronicle. 1985. "13-Year-Old Mexican Shot by a U.S. Guard." April 20, 12.

The Californian. 2019. "PHOTOS: District Attorney Reveals New Details in Death of Salinas Woman by Police." April 2, 1. Available at: www.thecalifornian.com/p icture-gallery/news/2019/04/02/photos-new-details-emerge-police-shooting-sa linas-woman/3345381002/

Tighe III, Frank P. 1985. "*Tennessee v. Garner*: Fourth Amendment Limitations on a Peace Officer's Use of Deadly Force to Effect an Arrest." *Loyola University Chicago Law Journal*, 17(1): 151–170.

Trujillo, Larry D. 1974. "La evolución del 'bandido' al 'pachuco': A Critical Examination and Evaluation of Criminological Literature on Chicanos." *Issues in Criminology*, 9 (Fall): 43–67.

Washington Post. 2017. "Police Shootings 2017 Database." December 31.

Webb, Walter Prescott. 1965 [1935]. *The Texas Rangers*. Austin, TX: University of Texas Press.

Public Document

The Treaty of Guadalupe Hidalgo. National Archives. Available at: www.archives. gov/education/lessons/guadalupe-hidalgo

Cases Cited

Arizona v. United States 567 U.S. (2012).

Hernandez v. Texas 347 U.S. (1954).

Tennessee v. Garner 471 U.S. 1 (1985).

Westminster School District of Orange County v. Mendez, et al., 161 F.2d 774 (1947).

Part I

State-Sanctioned Violence

Chapter 1

A History of Anti-Latino State-Sanctioned Violence
Executions, Lynchings, and Hate Crimes

Maritza Pérez

Introduction

In June 1874, Jesus Romo was arrested in La Puente, California, on charges of robbery and other crimes. Subsequent to his detention, a group of masked men seized him from the arresting officers and hanged him. Local opinion celebrated the lynching of the "hardened and blood-stained desperado" (Delgado 2009). More recently, in 2010, Alberto Alvarez, a Latino from Palo Alto, California, was sentenced to death for a 2006 altercation with a White police officer in which the officer was killed. Local media described Alvarez as an "evil" man who had committed such a "savage" crime (Lee 2010). "Hardened," "blood-stained," "evil," "savage"—these are some of the many dehumanizing words used to describe Latinos who find themselves entrapped in the criminal legal system.

Today, violence against Latinos is evident in state-sanctioned institutions that are based on the criminal legal system, such as capital punishment. Indeed, nationwide, the number of Latinos receiving capital sentences has increased throughout the years, with half of all capital sentences for Latinos coming from California in 2007 and that state steadily contributing to the toll since then (Minsker 2010; Snell 2014). State-sanctioned violence against Latinos is also evident in police brutality, mass incarceration, and immigration enforcement. One also cannot ignore the surge of hate crimes against Latinos since the beginning of the 2016 presidential election (Southern Poverty Law Center 2017). Though hate crimes are usually offenses committed by civilians, they are influenced by the same forces that motivate state-sanctioned violence, and are often tacitly supported or tolerated by the state. What is more, the current administration has failed to address the rise in hate crimes and, in fact, contributes to racial tensions and racialized violence.

This chapter argues that state-sanctioned violence against Latinos is propelled by the pervasive, dehumanizing political rhetoric in discourse surrounding immigration reform and Latinos.[1] Further, it shows that state-sanctioned violence against Latinos is not unlike the rampant, extrajudicial lynching of Latinos that took place in California between

1850 and 1935; a time when Latinos represented 50 percent of all victims of extrajudicial lynching in the state, while constituting less than 10 percent of the population (Attanasio 2015). In support of this position, I provide a brief history of the prevalence of, and the motivations behind, Latino lynching in California between 1850 and 1935. I then highlight troubling examples of modern anti-immigrant rhetoric, and anti-immigration practices and policies across the country, and discuss how today's political climate breeds racial bias and violence, including institutionalized violence against Latinos in the criminal legal system.

Latino Lynching: A Brief History

From 1848, following the end of the Mexican-American War until 1928, mobs lynched thousands of Mexicans across the United States.[2] Lynching—or the practice in which mobs hang someone without judicial process for the victim or legal sanctions for the perpetrators—was an informal political practice driven by rampant racism, diplomatic tensions, and economic competition[3] (*People v. Jones*, 19 Cal. App. 3d 437, 443 1971). Latino lynching primarily occurred in the southwestern states bordering Mexico, such as Arizona, New Mexico, Texas, and California, which have historically maintained significant Mexican populations (Carrigan and Webb 2015). Lynch mobs were predominantly Anglo, but sometimes included other Mexicans from the upper echelons of society who had been in the United States for generations (Attanasio 2015). Very few, if any, of the Anglo perpetrators ever had to stand trial for lynching a Mexican, perhaps because many of the extrajudicial killings were organized or led by law enforcement officials (Delgado 2009, 302; Attanasio 2015). More so than with lynching of African Americans, "Latino lynching went on with the knowledge and, in some cases, active participation of Anglo law enforcement authorities" (Attanasio 2015). On occasion, these same state and local law enforcement authorities, under pressure from the federal government, were tasked with investigating a lynching, inevitably failing to identify the perpetrators (Carrigan and Webb 2003). Like the lynching of African Americans, the lynching of Latinos was often a public spectacle "marked by hilarity and an atmosphere of righteous celebration," with many of the victim's bodies mutilated after death (Delgado 2009, 300–301).

Gonzales-Day has compiled an extensive dataset on lynching in California between 1850 and 1935, and found that "Latinos were nearly five times more likely to be lynched than Chinese immigrants, three times more likely to be lynched than American Indians, and nearly sixteen times more likely more likely to be lynched than African Americans" (Gonzales-Day 2006, 27).

It should be noted, however that there were only 962 African Americans in California in 1850, compared to 92,597 Anglos, and that Latinos outnumbered all other groups as victims of lynchings, despite being less than 10 percent of the population (ibid., 27) (Figure 1.1).

Figure 1.1 "Hanged at the Water Street Bridge." 1877. Courtesy of Covello and Covello Photography, Santa Cruz, California.

The perpetrators of lynching tried to justify the killings as necessary to maintain order (Carrigan 2015). Latinos were, in fact, lynched for violating nonsensical vagrancy laws and for acting "uppity" to maintain the façade that lynching was necessary to "solidif[y] society and reinforce civic virtue" (Delgado 2009, 299–301). In reality, Anglos believed that Mexicans' closer connection to Native Americans simply proved they were "ungodly" and needed to be corrected (Attanasio 2015). Further, Anglos believed Mexicans "possessed a culture, political system, and religion at odds with American society" (Carrigan 2015). As a result, Mexicans were lynched on stereotypical grounds like making advances toward White women, cheating at cards, practicing witchcraft, or simply for being "cowards" (Delgado 2009, 299). Sometimes Mexicans were lynched for acting "too Mexican," speaking Spanish too loudly or reminding Anglos too defiantly of their Mexicanness (ibid.). While the national narrative painted African Americans as sexual predators, in the public imagination Mexicans were largely bandits, murderers, or thieves (Carrigan 2015).

Adding fuel to the fire, diplomatic tensions amplified racist sentiment toward Mexicans in the period before and after the Mexican-American War, which took place between 1846 and 1848. Although the Treaty of Guadalupe Hidalgo of 1848 formally established peace between the United States and Mexico, continued conflict along the southwest border heightened tensions (ibid., 422). The most severe mob violence against Mexicans occurred during the 1850s, 1870s, and 1910s when war drove ethnic divisions to their peak (ibid.). In fact, in the decade following the Mexican-American War, Anglos lynched at least 160 Mexicans in the borderlands of the Southwest. During the Mexican Revolution, from 1910–1920, Anglos lynched 124 Mexicans (ibid., 423). Anglos questioned the loyalty of Mexicans, fearing they were informants or spies for Mexico. Diplomatic relations continued to deteriorate as each country blamed the other for the outbreaks in violence, further propelling the bloodshed (ibid., 422).

Lynching was also a mechanism for Anglos to gain and keep control of property and resources in the mid-nineteenth and early twentieth centuries as more people migrated to the Southwest in search of wealth and opportunity. As population numbers in California swelled, competition over resources escalated tensions between Anglos and Mexicans. Lynching and physical intimidation became a popular form of control. For example, the California Gold Rush attracted as many as 25,000 Mexican migrants between 1848 and 1852. Mexicans not only arrived at the gold mines earlier than the Anglos, but they brought with them superior expertise and skills. Mexicans quickly prospered in this industry, arousing "the bitter animosity of those Anglos who believed in their own natural sovereignty over the mines" (ibid., 422). As a result, between 1848 and 1860, at least 163 Mexicans were lynched in California (ibid.).

Mexicans were similarly lynched because of job competition or the perception that they were "taking away jobs" from Anglos (Delgado 2009, 299). For instance, in California, economically powerful and industrious Mexicans were intimidated, assaulted, and murdered by state authorities in order to keep power within the Anglo community. Joaquin Murietta, for example, one of the most infamous figures of

Mexican resistance, began to defy Anglo rule in California after his experience as a successful merchant brought him unwanted attention from rivals. Noticing his business acumen, local authorities accused him of horse theft and whipped him. They also accused his half-brother of the same offense and hanged him (Carrigan 2015, 424).

Although researchers have officially confirmed 597 instances of mobs lynching Latinos nationwide, hundreds of similar cases have been uncovered without enough evidence to draw definite conclusions (Delgado 2009, 299).[4] In California alone, researchers have documented 352 instances of lynching between 1850 and 1935 (Berger 2012). While the victims included African Americans, Asian Americans, and Native Americans, Latinos comprised the majority of those lynched in the state, although they were less than 10 percent of the residents of the state (ibid.). In total, lynching people of Color in California outnumbered White-on-White vigilantism nearly two to one, revealing how race was likely a contributing factor in many of the cases. Nevertheless, rampant racism, diplomatic tensions, and economic competition are not relics of the past and are manifested today in heated debates over immigration and the Border.

Contemporary Backlash Against Immigrants in the Public Sphere

Opposition to liberal immigration policies is closely linked to racial animus toward Latinos in that those who support restrictive immigration laws are more likely to harbor anti-Latino attitudes and beliefs (DeFrancesco Soto 2012). While "immigrant" and "Latino" are not synonymous, in the public imagination, they are often viewed as one and the same. Immigration reform has become an increasingly contentious topic over the last decade. Some of the reasons behind this increasingly charged and divisive topic include:

- Anglo resentment over the real and/or perceived ever-expanding Latino population in the United States;
- economic insecurity;
- the fact that significant immigration laws have been centerstage on the national platform.[5]

The media and politicians have probably had the most influence in building the combative narrative surrounding immigration reform, with the repercussions of this rhetoric manifesting themselves in the many anti-immigrant laws that have been crafted across the country. In 2005, for example, the House of Representatives presented the Border Protection, Anti-terrorism, and Illegal Immigration Control Act. This bill (also known as the Sensenbrenner Bill) would have done the following:

- made it a felony for undocumented persons to be in the United States;
- imposed new penalties on employers who hired undocumented people;
- required churches to check the immigration status of parishioners before aiding them;
- erected a fence along one-third of the United States-Mexico border (*Associated Press*, 2006).

Thousands upon thousands of Latinos took to the streets in the spring of 2006 to protest the bill (Engler and Engler 2016). Although the bill was never passed, the United States had to come to grips with the fact that the Latino population was growing and becoming increasingly politically relevant. In fact, for at least the last decade, the Latino population has been the largest minority group in the United States—even boasting one of the largest overall group growth rates—with its most significant populations in the Southwest (Passel, Cohn, and Lopez 2011). Yet, when communities undergo demographic shifts, growing tensions and anxieties increase the propensity to dehumanize the "Other."

Public perception of the Latino community has undoubtedly been negatively shaped by media coverage. Studies have shown that the news media rarely tells individual stories about Latinos, but instead will talk about this group in the context of an event-driven news report, such as when reporting on the Mexican drug wars or immigration reform (Pew Research Center 2009). In fact, although the Latino population continues to multiply, representation in the media has not kept up (Negron-Muntaner 2014). Media stories about Latinos compromise only 1 percent of all news coverage and the majority of these stories feature Latinos as lawbreakers (Planas 2015). Commercial, conservative media, often masked as "news media," erases the experiences of Latinos on a whole other scale. While immigration is one of the most popular topics of discussion on shows hosted by conservative pundits like Glenn Beck and Rush Limbaugh, a full 89 percent of all guests on these programs—who overwhelmingly express anti-immigrant sentiment—are White; only 4 percent are Latino (Noriega and Iribarren 2012). Undoubtedly, the program hosts themselves contribute to the problematic dialogue, too. For instance, Glenn Beck has suggested, on at least one occasion, that the United States create an alternative energy source out of the bodies of undocumented immigrants (Alexovich 2008).

Popular media does not fare better than the news media. In popular media, stereotypical portrayals reign supreme and overwhelmingly depict Latinos as criminals, disposable immigrant laborers, or hypersexualized personalities. The result of xenophobic media coverage is that Latinos are dehumanized and reduced to stereotypical characterizations. Consequently, "[v]iolence or discrimination against Latinos does not tend to resonate among most Americans because Latinos are generally not perceived as Americans" or even human (Planas 2015). Instead, Americans perceive

Latinos as recent immigrants and foreigners with no deep roots and histories in this country, "[s]o, abuses of power or injustices toward Latinos remain out of sight and out of mind" (ibid.).

Many politicians reinforce these limited views of Latinos, which in turn make their way back to the media. The 2008 presidential election offered many examples of this phenomenon. While Republican candidates mostly spewed typical anti-immigrant talk, such as Republican candidate Mitt Romney accusing immigration reformists of "letting illegal immigrants take jobs from American workers" (Navarrete, Jr 2012) some candidates were more sinister in their delivery of anti-immigrant sentiment.

Tom Tancredo of Colorado, for example, jump-started his political career as a Congressman by espousing nativist views. For instance, in 2004, Tancredo cautioned that undocumented immigrants are "coming here to kill you and to kill me and our families" (Israel 2013). He ran his unsuccessful 2008 presidential campaign on the single issue of immigration (ibid.). In one of his most infamous campaign advertisements, he showed bloody images of terrorist attacks and warned that open borders would cause "'vicious [C]entral American gangs'" and "jihadists" to push drugs, rape kids, and destroy lives (ibid.). He also boycotted a presidential debate on the Spanish-language network Univision, explaining that he would not "pander" to Spanish-speaking audiences because voters should be citizens and "[t]o be a citizen in this country you should know English" (ibid.). After he lost his bid for the White House, Tancredo called for reinstating literacy tests for voting, reasoning that President Obama won with the support of people who could not say or spell the word "vote" in English (ibid.).

The 2016 presidential election and its aftermath have also proven to be a trying time for the Latino community. Then Republican presidential candidate Donald Trump announced his campaign with the following words heard around the world:

> When Mexico sends its people, they're not sending their best. They're not sending you. They're not sending you. They're sending people that have lots of problems, and they're bringing those problems with us. They're bringing drugs. They're bringing crime. They're rapists. And some, I assume, are good people.
>
> (Yee Hee Lee 2015)

When confronted about this troubling rhetoric, Trump doubled-down on his comments and his poll numbers increased (Waldman 2015). In fact, his poll numbers and campaign following only escalated since the initial remarks, despite—or rather because of—his repeatedly expressed racial animosity and disdain toward Latinos and other communities of Color (Real Clear Politics 2015). For example, in December of 2015, Trump called for a ban preventing all Muslims from entering the United States and was rewarded with his highest approval rating, up to that date, in national polls (Gass 2015). Trump's repeated calls for building a wall between the United States and Mexico to keep out immigrants, and his disparaging comments about people of Mexican descent—like accusing a Mexican-American judge of being incapable of impartiality and fairness—have been rewarded with a formidable media presence, and now, the presidency (Smith 2016).

Anti-immigrant rhetoric such as that voiced by Tancredo, Trump, and others has solidified anti-immigrant movements across the country. From Minutemen groups and vigilantes who "guard" the Southwest border by "hunting immigrants" to mass deportations and discriminatory laws, anti-immigrant sentiment has gripped the nation (Price 2010). For example, in 2008, Anglo residents of Postville, Iowa, alarmed by the changing demographics of the agricultural town, sought to criminalize its Latino residents and supported the infamous Postville, Iowa raid (Ainslie 2015). During the raid, immigration officials rounded up 389 immigrants working at the local meat processing plant, arrested them by the busload, and detained them at a cattle exhibit hall. They did this while expediting their cases through a legal processing system that cut off their civil rights (Hincapié 2013). Hundreds of other immigrants escaped the raids by seeking asylum in churches, but the damage had already been done. The next day at school, "[h]alf of the school system's 600 [children] … including [90] percent of [its Latino] children," were absent from school because "their parents were … hiding" or detained (Hsu 2008). Ultimately, "[300] of the 389 workers served five month[s] [in] jail … before [being] deported" (Yu-Hsi Lee 2013). Many of those who were deported had no prior criminal convictions and had been residing in Iowa for years (Krogstad 2013; Yu-Hsi Lee 2013). Many similar raids have taken place since Postville, showing this country's disdain for Latino immigrant workers.

Similarly, recent English-only and anti-bilingual movements were born out of nativism. In fact, both movements "sprang up around the time that Latino immigration increased and gained national attention" (Delgado 2009, 308). More than half of the states, including California, have made English their official language (Schwarz 2014). But perhaps the most notorious anti-immigrant law in recent memory is Arizona's S.B. 1070, which, among other things, criminalized illegal presence in the United States by mandating that all immigrants carry documentation. The Supreme Court did not make a decision on the most contentious part of the law, which requires law enforcement officials to determine a person's immigration status if they have "reasonable suspicion" to believe the person is not in the country legally (*Arizona v. United States*, 2012). The Court clarified that the implementation of this law may raise constitutional questions related to unlawful search and seizure, yet it still did not invalidate this aspect of the law as unconstitutional (*Arizona v. United States*, 2012). In effect, the Supreme Court declined to fully enforce compliance with the Fourth Amendment's search and seizure provisions in arrests leading to removal proceedings (Cade 2013). Consequently, the Court left the door open for other states to enforce copycat laws. Indeed, dozens of states have attempted to implement laws modeled after Arizona's S.B. 1070, including California (Wessler 2011; National Immigration Law Center 2014). Certainly, anti-immigrant sentiment fosters anti-Latino discrimination and violence.

Hate Crimes and State Violence against Latinos

On April 18, 2015, five men in Jupiter, Florida, went "hunting" for Latino victims to rob and harass them (Carrigan 2015). The group made its way to the town's Latino community, where they came across 18-year-old One-simo Marcelino Lopez-Ramos who had stopped to meet with his brother and a friend on his way home from work (Fox News 2015; Jacobson 2015). The conversation between the two groups started friendly but soon turned violent, causing Lopez-Ramos and his friend to run away (Jacobson 2015). One of the aggressors threw a rock at Lopez-Ramos's head as he ran away, bludgeoning him to death (*Fox News* 2015).

Unfortunately, Lopez-Ramos's case is not uncommon. Approximately 60 percent of hate crimes motivated by race or ethnicity target Latinos (Thompson 2014). In fact, between 2004 and 2008, hate crimes against Latinos rose disproportionally to other hate crimes at a growth rate of 40 percent (The Leadership Conference 2016). Indeed, anti-Latino hate crimes have risen at an alarming rate over the past decade, with most of these crimes occurring in states with large Latino populations, like California and Texas (Costantini 2013). Although Latino victims targeted by hate crimes may very well number in the thousands, many Latinos, especially those who are undocumented, do not report crime to law enforcement authorities for fear of deportation or other law enforcement contact (ibid.).

Nativists groups who respond negatively to immigration have also grown over the last decade (ibid.). Indeed, many anti-Latino hate crimes occur in communities embroiled in anti-Latino tensions (Southern Poverty Law Center 2009). Studies have shown that incidents of anti-Latino violence are most common "in [areas] with high rates of [Latino] immigration" (Haglage 2014). For instance, one 2011 study explained that "[i]mmigration increased through 2002, dropped in 2003 and rose again in 2004"; and, similarly, "hate crime[s] ... against [Latinos] also fell through 2003 and rose again in 2004" (Long 2012). This period of time is also notable because it was marked by hate crime-inducing rhetoric from politicians and nativist groups (Southern Poverty Law Center 2009). A 2010 study found that a spike in the use of the word "illegals" in television programs corresponded with the passage of Arizona's SB 1070 and a number of racially motivated murders (Burge 2011). Specifically, from 2009 to 2010, the appearance of the word "illegals" quadrupled on television (Novoa 2011). Subsequently, 2010 saw a severe spike in anti-Latino violence (ibid.). In 2010, approximately 67 percent of racially or ethnically motivated hate crimes targeted Latinos, with a reported 747 victims (*Huffington Post* 2011).

This raises the question of how language can impact the rate of violence. While some individuals are explicitly racist and act violently on their racism, most are driven by implicit, or unconscious bias. Although implicit bias may not manifest in violent actions, it often alters the way people treat one another. Implicit bias works at the subconscious level, so while a person may reject stereotypes consciously, they may continue to adhere to negative unconscious associations or biases (Roberts 2011). Consequently, while explicit racial bias is controllable, implicit racial bias or common sense racism is generally not (Project Implicit 2016). Although 85 percent of Americans consider themselves to be unprejudiced, researchers have found that the majority of people in the United States are racially biased to some degree, although the bias may not be conscious or overt (Roberts 2011).

In the context of immigration and anti-Latino violence, implicit bias reveals itself in in-group (Americans/Anglos) versus out-group (immigrants/Latinos) thinking. Studies have documented in-group bias showing that people are more empathetic and generous with those in their perceived in-group than with those in the out-group (Sommers 2011). Specifically, one study found that individuals were more likely to remember the negative behaviors of people associated with an out-group than when that same negative behavior was exhibited by a member of their in-group (ibid., 223). In fact, this same study found that people actually expected more negative behavior from members of an out-group (ibid., 226). The study concluded that the "expecting and exaggerating of differences between categories is what opens the door for social stereotyping" (ibid., 226).

Further, social psychologists note that commonly, deeply-held emotions like jealousy, sympathy, and hope are generally denied to members of an out-group and are attributed to members of the in-group (Goff et al. 2008). This causes the in-group to dehumanize the out-group by negating their capacity to feel and express emotions, blocking empathy and prejudice-reduction toward the out-group (ibid.). Further, implicit bias operates in conjunction with media coverage to exacerbate prejudice. Media representations comparing Mexican immigrants to animals, like insects "swarming the border" or cockroaches "crawling under the fence," further dehumanize Latinos and shape people's opinions on immigration (ibid., 303). While a non-Latino person who is exposed to such media may not explicitly hate Latinos, the individual will likely subconsciously harbor prejudice and resentment toward those deemed to be part of the out-group. Further, media language reinforces the notion that members of the out-group are not fully human and thus do not share the same range of feelings as the media consumer. Consequently, the media consumer will likely show less empathy toward members of the out-group, Latinos, and may even be driven to take a hard line on immigration to keep the "pests" out.

Certainly, language matters. From Ronald Reagan's use of "welfare queens" to Bill Clinton's "super-predator" remarks encouraging tough-on-crime policies, politicians have mastered the art of racially coded appeals known as dog whistle politics. Dog whistling plays on people's implicit biases by creating racial animosity through coded language (Haney López 2014a). It allows politicians to act on White fear of racial others without explicitly mentioning race. For instance, in a 2005 memorandum, Republican consultant Frank Luntz encouraged Republicans to spread the unfounded narrative that undocumented immigrants commit crimes, drive without insurance, clog up hospital rooms, and are more likely to engage in anti-social behavior because immigrants believe that "breaking the law brings more benefit to them than abiding by it" (Haney López 2014b). Although hate crimes against Latinos rose by almost 35 percent between 2003 and 2006, covert messaging allows Republicans to counter that the plain language they used could not have incited racial violence (Mock 2007).

The racist and anxiety-driven conditions of the United States are conditions that lend themselves to individual and collective violence, including institutionalized violence (Ainslie 2015). For example, in August 2015, two Boston men, inspired by Donald Trump's anti-Latino vitriol, assaulted and urinated on a homeless, Mexican immigrant (Berman 2015). They later explained to arresting officers, "Donald Trump was right, all these illegals need to be deported" (ibid.). Since then, thousands of hate incidents have been recorded across the country. Trump has also influenced students across the country to use racial taunts to bully their classmates, leading many children of immigrants and children of Color to feel unsafe (Carroll 2016).

In the same vein, institutionalized violence is evident in the propensity for police officers to use excessive force on Latinos. In fact, the rising rate of police and Border Patrol killings of Latinos has coincided with the rising rate of hate crimes against Latinos (Nittle 2016). One recent study found that the New York Police Department, which already disproportionately and unjustly discriminates against African Americans and Latinos with its stop-and-frisk practices (Planas 2015) "almost exclusively shoots black or Hispanic suspects" (McKay 2014). In 2015, the police killed at least 195 Latinos across the country, which is likely an undercount considering that the data on Latinos are inconsistent and unreliable (Carrigan 2015). In Los Angeles, half of those who were killed in police encounters between 2007 and 2014 were Latino. Violence against Latinos is also institutionalized in this country's prison, jails, juvenile detention centers, and immigration detention centers, with the latter two becoming increasingly privatized. In fact, Immigration and Customs Enforcement (ICE) is Congressionally mandated to detain at least 34,000 in their facilities each night, leading to billion dollar windfalls for private companies who run most immigrant detention centers (Cartagena 2017).

Privatized immigrant detention has accelerated under the Trump Administration, whose draconian border policies have led to the unprecedented
expansion of child detention and deaths in custody.

Lynching by Another Name

Perhaps the most explicit example of state-sanctioned, institutionalized violence is found in the US criminal legal system, and capital punishment in
particular. The death penalty is riddled with racism and implicit bias at every
step of the process. Race matters from initial arrest to jury selection and
deliberation, to the prosecutor's decision to seek the death penalty. Latinos
have disproportionate contact with the criminal legal system beginning as
youth because they are more likely than their White peers to be arrested
(Rovner 2014). In addition, studies have shown that Latinos are more likely
than White people to be denied bail, required to pay bail, or obligated to
pay a higher bail to be released (Thomas Rivera Policy Institute 2016).
Perhaps the most damning research is the type suggesting that Latinos are
treated more harshly in the sentencing phase of a criminal proceeding. For
one, during plea bargaining, prosecutors are more likely to offer Latinos
punitive deals—which often include a custodial sentence—compared to
their White counterparts (ibid.).

A conversation about the role of juries is required to illustrate another
way in which Latinos are treated more harshly in the criminal legal
system. For example, juries are at the epicenter of death penalty trials, as
they ultimately decide whether to spare a convicted person from death
during the penalty phase of the person's trial. It is the defense attorney's
job to humanize his or her client during the penalty phase of the trial by
presenting mitigating evidence explaining why the client may have
committed the crime. This is a daunting challenge for several reasons:
overwhelmingly, jurors tend to be of a different race than the alleged
perpetrators of crimes; and jurors in death penalty cases, like all people,
are racially biased to some degree, especially when the victim is White
and the perpetrator is a person of Color. In opposition to the spirit of
the Sixth Amendment, people of Color rarely confront an "impartial
jury" of their peers in criminal trials. Although African Americans and
Latinos make up approximately 30 percent of the general population,
they comprise 58 percent of the prison population because these groups
tend to be over-policed and over-criminalized (Blow 2014). This feeds
the perception that African Americans and Latinos are inherently criminal. White people who associate crimes with African Americans and
Latinos are more likely to support punitive policies, such as capital
punishment (ibid.). On the other hand, African Americans and Latinos,
who experience crime at higher rates, are less likely than White people
to support punitive sentences (ibid.).

In California, as elsewhere around the country, prosecutors often strike African Americans and Latinos from the jury selection pool. Over the last two decades, the California Supreme Court has heard more than 100 cases involving juror discrimination and prosecutor strikes but only found unlawful discrimination in one (Sward 2014). The most recent case from the California Supreme Court to head to the United States Supreme Court was *Davis v. Ayala*, where the Latino petitioner sought relief in a federal habeas proceeding on the grounds that the prosecution's peremptory challenges that systematically and exclusively struck all African Americans and Latinos from the jury that ultimately sentenced him to death were impermissibly race-based under *Batson v. Kentucky* (*Davis v. Ayala* case a). *Davis v. Ayala* determined that once a defendant makes a prima facie case proving purposeful discrimination in jury selection, the State must come forward with a race-neutral explanation of why the juror was struck from the jury. Further, the petitioner claimed his case merited relief because the trial judge allowed the prosecution to disclose its reason for the strikes without the presence of defense counsel and concluded that the prosecution did indeed have race-neutral reasons for striking the jurors of Color (*Davis v. Ayala* case b). On direct appeal, in a case based on trial error, the Court explained that a petitioner must show "actual prejudice" that leads to substantial and injurious effect or influence in determining the jury's verdict (*Davis v. Ayala* case c). In this case, the Court conceded that "[t]he pattern of peremptory challenges was sufficient to raise suspicions about the prosecution's motives and to call for the prosecution to explain its strikes" (*Davis v. Ayala* case d). Yet, it concluded that the trial judge's determination that the strikes were race-neutral was "entitled to great weight" and that the exclusion of the defense attorney from part of the Batson hearing was a harmless error that did not play a role in the final outcome of the case (*Davis v. Ayala* case e). The petitioner's death sentence would stand.

The legal standard used to prove juror discrimination in death penalty cases is problematic because it does not leave room to account for the fact that jurors, like all people, are prone to "othering," or in-group bias. This in turn makes it easier for jurors to impose the death penalty when they do not share the same life experiences as the perpetrators and cannot identify with them (Leving 2015). Indeed, implicit bias studies suggest "interracial violence brings race to the top of jurors' minds" (Gershon 2014). In fact, the race of the victim remains the constant predictor of who will receive the death penalty. Generally, in California, there are more African American and Latino murder victims (Pierce and Radelet 2005). Yet, prosecutors and juries are more likely to find White-victim cases more deathworthy than African American or Latino victim cases (ibid.).

The extent to which the justice system values White lives over others is equally evident in the fact that those who kill Whites are four times more likely to be sentenced to death than those who kill Latinos (Anon 2005). Moreover, implicit bias studies show that when the victim is White and the perpetrator is a person of Color, jurors are triggered to "think about race as a relevant and useful heuristic for determining the blameworthiness of the defendant and the perniciousness of the crime" (Eberhardt et al. 2006). In Alberto Alvarez's case, the final death ruling was based almost entirely on the prosecution's proposed sentence (Bernstein-Wax 2016). The judge repeatedly referred to the murder as "savage," "brutal," and "vicious" (ibid.). The prosecutor called the crime one of the "most evil" crimes one can commit (Lee 2010). At final sentencing, at least one of the nine jurors appeared wearing a pin featuring a photograph of the deceased police officer (Bernstein-Wax 2016). Without doubt, when a juror is confronted with dehumanizing language in a court of law that already discriminates against people of Color, and the juror is bombarded with anti-immigrant and anti-Latino messages outside of the jury box, racial bias infects what should be a fair trial. Against the backdrop of historical anti-Latino racism in society and in the justice system, and given the fact that the Sixth Amendment fails to provide Latinos with a fair trial by a jury of their peers, Alberto Alvarez's death sentence in the courtroom is similar to the 1874 lynching of Jesus Romo in the street. Rather than confront the racism embedded in the death penalty process, the Supreme Court and the criminal justice system have used the death penalty as a neutral arbitrator used to determine who is deathworthy (*McCleskey v. Kemp*).

The overrepresentation of Latinos in the criminal legal system as defendants is also problematic because Latinos remain grossly underrepresented in positions of influence, including in the legal field. Latinos comprise just 9.7 percent of all federal judges and make up less than 4 percent of all barred attorneys in the US. These trends stand in stark contrast to the growing Latino population, which currently makes up approximately 17–18 percent of the total US population and is expected to reach 29 percent by 2050. As *Davis v. Ayala* demonstrates, in addition to diverse juries, the role of culturally competent judges and lawyers, who can also identify with defendants with backgrounds similar to their own, is critically important.

Conclusion

In this current racially-charged political climate, many of the conditions that fostered anti-Latino sentiment and violence in the nineteenth century still exist today. Such factors include economic insecurity, tension on the border, and explicit and structural racism endorsed by the government. Policymakers and political leaders need to combat these conditions and create a culture of inclusivity. Our leaders must also achieve meaningful criminal justice and police reform, as well as comprehensive immigration reform. These are just some suggestions from a long list of action steps we need to demand of our elected officials.

Although today's climate is tense, we must remember that we have been here before and have overcome. This period is difficult, but at the very least, it is motivating to see many well-intentioned people fighting for a more just world. I am right there with them, and hope you are too.

Notes

1 A shorter draft of this chapter was included as part of a dossier in *Aztlan: A Journal of Chicano Studies* (43(2), Fall 2018). That article drew parallels between lynchings of the past and hate crimes against Latinos today. This chapter describes how many of the factors that drove the lynchings of the past are the same drivers behind today's criminal legal system that is both punitive and violent against Latinos.

2 I will use "Mexican" in this chapter to describe Mexican nationals and Americans of Mexican origin. I will use Latinos to describe people of Latin American origin, which may also include Mexicans.

3 According to the California Penal Code Ann. (2016), ("'Lynching' came to mean the situation wherein a group of persons usurps ordinary government powers and exercises correctional authority over others. The word generally includes the infliction of summary punishment without benefit of trial or authority of law … ."),§ 405a. "[T]he taking by means of a riot of another person from the lawful custody of a peace officer is guilty of a felony … "). See codes.findlaw.com/ca/penal-code

4 After accounting for the smaller size of the Latino population in the US during the mid-nineteenth and early twentieth centuries, some researchers claim that the rate of African-American lynching and Latino lynching were in fact similar (Delgado 2009).

5 For an in-depth discussion of the "Latino Threat," see Chavez (2008).

References

Ainslie, Ricardo. 2015. "Latinos and the Death Penalty." Address at the University of Texas School of Law Symposium, Panel One, April 10, Austin, TX.

Alexovich, Ariel. 2008. "A Call to End Hate Speech." *New York Times*, online edition, February 1.

Anon. 2005. "Race and the Death Penalty in California." Death Penalty Information Center. Available at: www.deathpenaltyinfo.org/node/1534 (accessed September 3, 2016).

Associated Press. 2006. "Immigration Issues Draws Thousands into Streets." *NBC News*, March 25.

Attanasio, Cedar. 2015. "Latino Lynchings, Police Brutality, and the Challenges of Minority Law-Enforcement." *Latin Times*, online edition, February 10.

Berger, Maurice. 2012. "Lynchings in the West, Erased from History and Photos." *New York Times*, online edition, December 6.

Berman, Russell. 2015. "A Trump-Inspired Hate Crime in Boston." *The Atlantic*, August 20.

Bernstein-Wax, Jessica. 2016. "Judge Sentences Convicted East Palo Alto Cop Killer to Death." *Mercury News*. Available at: www.mercurynews.com/top-stories/ci-14361067 (accessed September 3, 2016).

Blow, Charles M. 2014. "Crime, Bias, and Statistics." *New York Times*, September 7. Available at: www.nytimes.com/2014/09/08/opinion/charles-blow-crime-bias-andstatistics.html

Burge, Laura. 2011. "Anti-Immigrant Hate Crimes Rise with Hateful Political Speech." *Care2i*, January 20.

Cade, Jason A. 2013. "Policing the Immigration Police: ICE Prosecutorial Discretion and the Fourth Amendment." *Columbia Law Review*, 113: 180–203.

California Penal Code. 2016. Desktop edition. Sacramento, CA: Thomson Reuters.

Carrigan, William. 2015. "Latinos and the Death Penalty." Address at the University of Texas School of Law Symposium, Panel One, April 10, Austin, TX.

Carrigan, William D. and Clive Webb. 2003. "The Lynching of Persons of Mexican Origin or Descent in the United States, 1848 to 1928." *Journal of Social History*, 37(2): 411–438.

Carrigan, William D. and Clive Webb. 2015. "When Americans Lynched Mexicans." *New York Times*, online edition, February 20.

Carrion, Kelly. 2015. "Jupiter, FL Police: Deadly Robbery Victim Targeted for Being Hispanic." *NBC News*, April 28.

Carroll, Rory. 2016. "'You Were Born in a Taco Bell': Trump's Rhetoric Fuels School Bullies Across U.S." *Guardian*, September 2.

Cartagena, Juan. 2017. "Latinos and the New Jim Crow: Untangling Convergences." Available at: http://latinojustice.org/civil_rights/New_Jim_Crow_Intro_Eng_final.pdf

Chavez, Leo R. 2008. *The Latino Threat: Constructing Immigrants, Citizens, and the Nation*. Stanford, CA: Stanford University Press.

Costantini, Cristina. 2013. "Anti-Latino Hate Crimes Rise as Immigration Debate Intensifies." *Huffington Post*, April 3.

DeFrancesco Soto, Victoria M. 2012. "Anti-Immigrant Rhetoric Is Anti-Latino." *Nation*, February 24.

Delgado, Richard. 2009. "The Law of the Noose: A History of Latino Lynching." *Harvard Civil Rights-Civil Liberties Law Review*, 44: 297–302.

Eberhardt, Jennifer L., Paul G. Davies, Valerie J. Purdie-Vaughns, and Sheri Lynn Johnson. 2006. "Looking Deathworthy: Perceived Stereotypicality of Black Defendants Predicts Capital-Sentencing Outcomes." *Psychological Science*, 17: 383–385.

Engler, Mark and Paul Engler. 2016. "The Massive Immigrant-Rights Protests of 2006 are Still Changing Politics." *The Los Angeles Times*, online edition, March 4.

Fox News. 2015. "Florida Cops Want Hate Crime Charges in Case of Guatemalan Bludgeoned to Death." April 28.

Gass, Nick. 2015. "Trump Hits a New High in National Poll." *Politico*, December 14.

Gershon, Livia. 2014. "MacArthur Fellow Jennifer L. Eberhardt Shines Light on Racism and Criminal Justice." *JSTOR DAILY*, September 19. Available at: http://daily.jstor.org/jennifer-l-eberhardt-shines-light-on-racism-and-criminaljustice/

Goff, Phillip Atiba, Jennifer L. Eberhardt, Melissa J. Williams, and Matthew Christian Jackson. 2008. "Not Yet Human: Implicit Knowledge, Historical Dehumanization, and Contemporary Consequences." *Journal of Personality and Social Psychology*, 94(2): 292–306.

Gonzales-Day, Ken. 2006. *Lynchings in the West*. Durham, NC: Duke University Press.

Haglage, Abby. 2014. "Hate Crime Victimization Statistics Show Rise in Anti-Hispanic Crime." *Daily Beast*, February 20.

Haney López, Ian. 2014a. Interview by Bill Moyers, February 28.

Haney López, Ian. 2014b. *Dog Whistle Politics: How Coded Racial Appeals Have Reinvented Racism and Wrecked the Middle Class*. New York: Oxford University Press.

Hincapié, Marielena. 2013. "What Shameful Postville, Iowa Immigration Raid Teaches Five Years Later." *Huffington Post*, July 13.

Hsu, Spencer S. 2008. "Immigration Raid Jars a Small Town." *Washington Post*, online edition, May 18.

Huffington Post. 2011. "FBI Hate Crime Statistics Report Finds Higher Percentages of Anti-Latino Hate Crimes in 2010." November 14.

Israel, Josh. 2013. "The Eight Most Xenophobic Stances of Tom Tancredo, Candidate for Colorado Governor." *Think Progress*, May 23.

Jacobson, Kate. 2015. "Men Accused of Killing Jupiter Man Targeted Him Because of Race, Police Say." *Sun Sentinel*, April 27.

Krogstad, Jens Manuel. 2013. "Iowa Raid Helps Shape Immigration Debate." *USA Today*, May 9.

The Leadership Conference. 2016. "The State of Hate: Escalating Hate Violence Against Immigrants." Washington, DC.

Lee, Henry K. 2010. "'Evil' Cop Killer Is Sentenced to Death." *San Francisco Gate*, online edition, February 9.

Leving, Maurice. 2015. "Latinos and the Death Penalty." Address at the University of Texas School of Law Symposium, Panel One, April 10, Austin, TX.

Long, Chrissie. 2012. "Impact of Immigration on Anti-Hispanic Hate Crime in the United States." *Journalist's Resource*, November 13.

McKay, Tom. 2014. "One Troubling Statistic Shows Just How Racist America's Police Brutality Problem Is." *MIC*, August 18.

Minsker, Natasha. 2010. "Time for California to Catch Up with the Death Penalty Decline." ACLU of California Center of Advocacy & Policy. Available at: www. aclu.org/…/mass-incarceration/time-california-catch-death-penalty-decline

Mock, Brentin. 2007. "Hate Crimes Against Latinos Rising Nationwide." Montgomery, AL: Southern Poverty Law Center.

National Immigration Law Center. 2014. "SB 1070 Four Years Later: Lesson Learned." Washington, DC.

Navarrette, Jr. Ruben. 2012. "Latinos Won't Forget Romney's 'Anti-Immigrant' Talk." *CNN*, January 31.

Negron-Muntaner, Frances. 2014. "The Latino Media Gap: A Report on the State of Latinos in U.S. Media." New York: Center for the Study of Ethnicity and Race, Columbia University.

Nittle, Nadra Kareem. 2016. "Racial Profiling and Police Brutality Against Hispanics." *ThoughtCo*, September 1.

Noriega, Chon A. and Francisco Javier Iribarren. 2012. "Social Networks for Hate Speech." Working Paper, UCLA, Chicano Studies Research Center.

Novoa, Monica. 2011. "Let's Turn Off the Hate Machine, in Arizona and Everywhere." *Colorlines*, January 14.

Passel, Jeffrey S., D'Vera Cohn and Mark Hugo Lopez. 2011. "Hispanics Account for More than Half of Nation's Growth in Past Decade." Washington, DC: Pew Research Center.

Pew Research Center. 2009. "Hispanics in the News: An Event-Driven Narrative." Available at: www.pewresearch.org

Pierce, Glenn L. and Michael L. Radelet. 2005. "The Impact of Legally Inappropriate Factors on Death Sentencing for California Homicides, 1990–1999." *Santa Clara Law Review*, 146(5): 36.

Planas, Roque. 2015. "Why the Media Pays Less Attention to Police Killings of Latinos." *Huffington Post*, February 24.

Price, Michelle. 2010. "Neo-Nazi Minuteman Hunts Arizona Immigrants." *Salon*, July 17.

Project Implicit. 2016. Frequently Asked Questions." Harvard University. Available at: https://implicit.harvard.edu/implicit/faqs.html (accessed September 2, 2016).

Real Clear Politics. 2015. "Republican Presidential Nomination." December 18.

Roberts, Hayley. 2011. "Implicit Bias and Social Justice." *Open Society Foundations*, December 18.

Rovner, Joshua. 2014. "Disproportionate Minority Contact in the Juvenile Justice System." *SENTENCING PROJECT*, 1:1–2. Available at: http://sentencingp roject.org/doc/publications/jj-Disproportionate%20Minority%2OCon tact.pdf

Schwarz, Hunter. 2014. "States Where English Is the Official Language." *Washington Post*, online edition, August 12.

Smith, Allan. 2016. "'I'm Building a Wall': Donald Trump and CNN's Jake Tapper Have Heated Exchange over Judge Attacks." *Business Insider*, June 3.

Snell, Tracy L. 2014. *Capital Punishment, 2013 – Statistical Tables*. Washington, DC: U.S. Department of Justice.

Sommers, Sam. 2011. *Situations Matter: Understanding How Context Transforms Your World*. New York: Riverhead Books.

Sommers, Sam. 2011. Situations Matter: Understanding How Context Transforms Your World. New York: Riverhead Books.

Southern Poverty Law Center. 2009. "Climate of Fear: Latino Immigrants in Suffolk County, N.Y." Available at: www.splcenter.org/sites/default/files/splc_suf folk_report.pdf

Southern Poverty Law Center. 2017. "Post-Election Bias Incidents Up to 1,372: New Collaboration with ProPublica." Available at: www.splcenter.org/hatewa tch/2017/02/10/post-election-bias-incidents-1372-new-collaboration-propublica

Sward, Susan. 2014. "A Question of Bias in Jury Selection." *Sacramento Bee*, January 5. Available at: www.sacbee.com/opinion/californiaforum/article2588019.html

Thompson, Nicole Akoukou. 2014. "¡Ya basta!: Violent Anti-Latino/Anti-Immigrant Hate Crimes Continues to Soar Nationwide." *Latin Post*, February 20.

Thomas Rivera Policy Institute. 2016. "Disparities in the Criminal Justice System: Racial and Ethic Disparities in Pretrial Detainment, Sentencing, and Incarceration." University of Southern California Available at: http://safeandjust.uscmediacurator. com/category/collections/disparities-system/ (accessed September 3, 2016).

Waldman, Paul. 2015. "Donald Trump Is on the Rise – and That's Very Bad News for the GOP." *Washington Post*, online edition, July 1. Available at: www.washingtonpost.com

Wessler, Seth Freed. 2011. "Bills Modeled After Arizona's SB 1070 Spread Through States." *Colorlines*, March 2.

Yee Hee Lee, Michelle Ye. 2015. "Donald Trump's False Comments Connecting Mexican Immigrants and Crime." *Washington Post*, online edition, July 8.

Yu-Hsi Lee, Esther. 2013. "How the Postville Immigration Raid Has Changed Deportation Proceedings." *Think Progress*, May 10.

Cases Cited

Arizona v. United States 132 S. Ct. 2492, 2509–10 (2012).

Batson v. Kentucky 476 U.S. 79, 97 (1986).

a *Davis v. Ayala* 135 S. Ct. 2187, 2193–2196, 2199 (2015).

b *Davis v. Ayala* 135 S. Ct. 2191.

c *Davis v. Ayala* 135 S. Ct. 2197–2198.

d *Davis v. Ayala* 135 S. Ct. 2208.

e *Davis v. Ayala* 135 S. Ct. 2208.

McCleskey v. Kemp 481 U.S. 279, 291–299 (1987).

People v. Jones 19 Cal. App. 3d 437, 443 (1971).

Chapter 2

Officer-Involved Shootings of Latinos

Moving Beyond the Black/White Binary

Robert J. Durán

National media attention has increasingly begun focusing on community protests, lawsuits, and public concern with deaths at the hands of law enforcement officers.[1] The Black Lives Matter Movement has galvanized residents to protest the deaths of a significant number of African American residents killed by police officers in communities across the nation, including victims such as Michael Brown, Eric Garner, Laquan McDonald, Tamir Rice, Walter Scott, and Alton Sterling. Historically, the extra-judicial practice of killing Blacks through lynching was perceived as a southern problem as the Jim Crow South enforced segregationist policies designed to ensure Blacks could never challenge White social control after slavery. However, in the post-civil rights era, the move toward color-blind racism has ensured the killing of Blacks continues, not through mob violence but rather through legalized policies allowing law enforcement officers the discretion to use deadly force. Public discussion has focused on the differences between Blacks and Whites, but where does the nation's largest minority group, Latinos, fit into such a discussion?[2] Do Latinos experience negative interactions with the police leading to a disproportionate use of excessive lethal force by police?

The social construction of race has been a long and contested political, economic, and social process in the United States. As the United States expanded westward into the previous colonies of Spain, public officials seemed confused as to where individuals of Spanish and indigenous descent stood along the Color line. Although a vast array of scholarship exists documenting these historical inequities (Gómez 2007; Mirandé 1985; 1987), the Black and White racial binary continues to limit how social power is manifested and described in U.S. society (Delgado 1997; Gómez 2007; Mirandé 1985; 1987; Perea 1995; 1997). Juan Perea notes:

> The Black/White binary paradigm, by defining only Blacks and Whites as relevant participants in civil rights discourse and struggle, tends to produce and promote the exclusion of other racialized peoples,

including Latinos/as, Asian Americans and Native Americans, from this crucial discourse *which affects us all.*

(Perea 1997, 167; emphasis in original)

Perea and other critical race scholars have pushed US society to broaden its understanding of race and racism that has historically existed on levels broader than can be captured by simply thinking in terms of the White or the Black experience.

For the past 20 years, I have been researching social groups, including gangs created in poor neighborhoods as well as law enforcement agencies designed to enforce social control. Gangs are primarily composed of marginalized members of society whereas the police are an institution that compels residents to follow laws created by the economic and political elite (i.e., upper-class Whites). Increasingly, law enforcement agencies have been forced to employ officers who reflect the demographics of the populations they serve (Sklansky 2006). In terms of social power, if a gang member was charged with murder, they were often found guilty and sentenced to prison. However, rarely were police officers charged with murder and if the case went to trial, they were often acquitted and allowed to continue to work as a member of law enforcement. In fact, rather than being punished, they were more likely to receive a medal of commendation for such violent actions.[3] Because of my background and experience as a former gang member, early on I began questioning the double standard and differential treatment of these groups.

I am a product of the Southwest, as my family lived in New Mexico before the colonization of the region both by Spain and the United States. As a gang member, I had also been regularly harassed by the police. Cops were as likely to point a firearm at me as rival gang members. While attending college, I decided one strategy to give back to the community and move beyond my past was to work in juvenile probation. This decision came with a law enforcement badge. Even then, I remained wary of calling a police officer in an emergency, but I was in a position where I monitored the behavior of youth on probation throughout the county. I made sure adjudicated youth were at home, school, work, or listed activities, and were not engaging in the use of alcohol or drugs. Later as a professor, I would teach students who were members of law enforcement or desiring to gain such employment and I had cultivated relationships where I regularly interviewed both gang members and law enforcement officers. I have, therefore, grown to learn both perspectives: one organization created from racial oppression whereas the other formalized to maintain mythical ideologies of democracy. The individuals involved reported a desire to protect their family, friends, and larger community. Both groups offered a high level of service for which only one provided a formal paycheck with benefits.

In this chapter, I use this background to interrogate why officer-involved killings remain understudied and pinpoint gaps where the discussion is ignored when the topic shifts to Latinos. My analysis, based on my previous research and experience, will remain critical of law enforcement officers possessing the authority and discretion to use deadly force. The reasons for this position should become clearer as I present the acquired research data. Firearms comprise most of these deaths and thus this chapter will focus specifically on actions resulting from law enforcement shootings. My research encompasses both fatal shootings and those resulting in injury. Firearm scholarship has emphasized that whether one lives or dies is more determined by the level of hospital care, medical emergency response, caliber of the bullet, and whether a vital organ is hit (Hemenway 2004). Cook and Goss (2014) reported that one in six gunshots will result in death and in the past three decades this has resulted in approximately one million deaths of US residents. I will first analyze the published research and news reports regarding officer-involved shootings along with incidents involving Latinos. Second, I will focus on some of the data I have collected in the Southwest region of the country. Finally, I will offer policy suggestions and recommendations.

My study was conducted in four different counties in the Southwest involving the states of Colorado, New Mexico, Texas, and Utah, with two of these states sharing a border with Mexico. Thus, a variety of agencies with jurisdictions at the local, county, state, and federal levels were included. My research has involved archival and ethnographic methodologies that compile insights regarding the past 18–30 years (1983–2017) of officer-involved shootings in these geographic areas, along with observations and interviews focused on police community interactions. A significant portion of my research has been enhanced through the study of Disproportionate Minority Contact (DMC), which uses comparative rates by race and ethnicity and these types of analyses will be incorporated into this chapter. The Office of Juvenile Justice and Delinquency Prevention (OJJDP), part of the U.S. Department of Justice, provides grants to state-administered programs to reduce racial/ethnic disparities in the juvenile justice system, yet no such effort has been devoted to officer-involved shootings. I will argue that officer-involved shootings exemplify color-blind racism in how legalized practices maintain colonial social control while at the same time denying the existence of inequality (Bonilla-Silva 2018).

The Existing Data

Historically, interactions between US law enforcement agencies and individuals of Mexican descent have been deeply conflicted. Sociologist Alfredo Mirandé (1987) described the criminal justice system as more similar to "Gringo Justice" since it reflected one standard for Anglos and another for

Chicanos. Mexicanos in the Southwest struggled to survive in a geographic landscape shaped by an ideology of Manifest Destiny and built on conquest. The Treaty of Guadalupe Hidalgo granted the option for the current residents to obtain U.S. citizenship but it still came with the social treatment of being non-White and unequal by a growing Anglo population. Law enforcement officers working for the Border Patrol and Texas Rangers were actively involved in maintaining differential treatment and the subordination of the Mexican population (Carrigan 2006; Hernández 2010; Samora, Bernal, and Peña 1979). Historian William Carrigan (2006, 175) reported the highest levels of violence in Texas occurred in south Texas where the Texas Rangers often joined Anglo aggression by going on a "brutal binge of retaliation, summarily killing hundreds of Mexicans without due process of law." During the period of increased federal efforts to professionalize the police, accounts such as the following could still be found:

> One reason the Mexicans carry guns is because of their relations with the police. The latter, especially in Indiana Harbor [East Chicago], shoot the Mexicans with small provocation. One shot a Mexican who was walking away from him, and laughed as the body was thrown into the patrol wagon. They are not bad as that in Gary.
>
> (Taylor 1931, 230)

The killing of a 12-year-old boy named Santos Rodríguez in July of 1973 by officer Darrell Cain reminded residents how Latino lives, whether past or present, could be destroyed based on the grossly negligent actions of law enforcement officers (Anchor 1978; Solis 2013). Officer Cain was questioning Santos and his brother about an attempted burglary of a soft-drink machine when he took out his .357 magnum handgun and spun the cylinder, warning Santos to tell the truth. Santos denied knowledge of the incident. Officer Cain's gun clicked when the trigger was pressed. Pulling the trigger a second time, the gun went off, killing the boy. Cain reported thinking the gun was empty and the police department suspended him for his actions. However, due to community protests, Officer Cain was eventually charged, convicted, and sentenced to five years in prison but only served half the amount of time. Meanwhile forensic evidence determined the brother's fingerprints did not match the attempted burglary. Solis's (2013) news article highlighted how even 40 years afterwards, the family continued to feel the pain from this murder.

My research on law enforcement has similarly documented problematic interactions between law enforcement and Latina/o citizens and non-citizens and how the inclusion of Latino/a police officers does not in itself change the institution of policing (Durán 2012; 2014; 2015). Contemporary research on Latino interactions with law enforcement lacks the depth of insight of similar research on Blacks or Whites, and researchers have questioned this omission (Carter 1985; Holmes 2000; Martínez 2007; Menjívar and Bejarano 2004; Mirandé 1987; Weitzer 2014). The best explanation offered is the lack of data collection, which has failed to separate Latinos from other racial groups. When data are gathered, researchers have noted differences in experiences and perceptions based on class, generational status, country of origin, region of the country, and demographic composition of the police force. One sociologist, Ronald Weitzer, went even so far as to critique the qualitative research on Latinos and the police, mostly conducted by Latinos, as "narrow in scope," "simplistic," and "one-dimensional," while never being self-critical for lacking insight into the Latino community and their interactions with the police (2014, 5). In sum, Weitzer outlined the complicated nature of conducting such research but felt comfortable outlining how Latinos appear to be in the middle ground between Whites and Blacks and therefore appear less alienated than Blacks.

One of the recurring problems with quantitative police research is that it often treats race or ethnicity as a dummy variable that can be controlled and manipulated statistically, while ignoring historical and structural context for which the data were produced. A second problem arises when thematic topics, such as policing, are applied to population groups in which the researcher may have little background, investment, or concern. Research that employs both quantitative and qualitative methods seems ideal, but there is great value as well in specific historical and qualitative case studies. Researchers attempting to study Latinos would be wise to consult the insights obtained from historians and ethnographers. Academia has often been challenged for its use of colonial scholarship, thus researchers should pay close attention to the lived experiences and research produced by members of similar racial and ethnic groups as the populations they study and work to produce insight collaboratively (Ladner 1973; Phillips and Bowling 2003). Sociologist Aldon Morris (2015), for example, outlined the career of W.E.B. Du Bois, which demonstrated the scholarship of people of Color is often neglected, co-opted, and deliberately suppressed in favor of White academics. To prevent replicating such practices requires deliberate awareness and effort.

Officer-involved shootings have been a research topic largely neglected prior to the shooting death of Michael Brown in 2014, yet several high-profile shootings had occurred prior to this incident, including the shooting death of Oscar Grant in 2009 and Amadou Diallo in 1999. As early as 1974, sociologist Paul Takagi critiqued the lack of research on police killings of Black citizens. He outlined patterns of racism, showing how Black men were killed by the police nine to ten times more often than White men, which only continued an institutionalized practice of genocide on Black citizens. Former police officer turned researcher, James Fyfe (1988; 2002), continued to critique the absence of research on police use of deadly force during his career and described it as a failure of a democracy that the country does not accurately report how often its own agents kill or injure its citizens. Fyfe (2002) outlined how the existing scholarship lacked systematic data and that at the time of his publication, noting that the *Washington Post* had done the best job accumulating information in several cities. To address this data gap, Fyfe believed the requirement of a federal mandate similar to the Uniform Crime Reports would be necessary to get law enforcement agencies nationwide to begin providing information.

As of 2017, the National Violent Death Reporting System (NVDRS), established by the Centers for Disease Control in 2003, was considered the most accurate data source regarding unjustified police killings (Barber et al. 2016). When the reporting system began, six states participated, but as of 2017 an additional 34 states had been added. The NVDRS is considered more accurate than previous measures of homicides committed by law enforcement officers that were gathered from the National Vital Statistics System and the Federal Bureau of Investigation's Supplementary Homicide Reports. But these data sources have been found to suffer from coverage, nonresponse, and measurement errors and thus were incapable of providing comparison between states (Loftin, McDowall, and Xie 2017). However, none of these assessment tools reaches the reporting levels offered by the *Washington Post*, the *Guardian*, or the internet site, Fatal Encounters, in which researchers are finding value in using newspaper reporting as a valuable tool for covering the gap between traditional data sources and actual rates (Miller et al. 2016). The *Washington Post* and *Guardian* have continued their efforts to document death at the hands of law enforcement begun by the Stolen Lives Project, but with greater resources and staff. Since 2015, the *Washington Post* has compiled data on officer-involved shooting fatalities and the *Guardian* has collected data on all forms of death due to law enforcement. The website Fatal Encounters is attempting to document all deaths due to law enforcement since 2000. In terms of access, logging onto the *Guardian*, the *Washington Post*, Fatal Encounters, and NVDRS websites to crosscheck my information, only the website Fatal Encounters was helpful. Searches of this website even added a few names but did not have the nonfatal shootings or the additional information obtained from multiple additional sources. There were also differences in terms of the categorization of race and ethnicity which my broader internet searches could assess.

Based on the difficulties in studying death and injury at the hands of law enforcement, it is reasonable to conclude that research studies which have attempted to sift through racial and ethnic disparities have also omitted Latinos. Black overrepresentation continues to be a common finding in the older (Fyfe 1981; 1982; 1988; Geller and Karales 1981; Takagi 1974) and newer studies (Barber et al. 2016; Brown and Langan 2001; Crosby and Lyons 2016; Miller et al. 2016). NVDRS data collected in 2013 found Blacks were killed by law enforcement at a higher rate (0.6 per 100,000 population) compared to Latinos (0.3 per 100,000) and Whites (0.1 per

100,000) (Crosby and Lyons 2016). Blacks and Latinos experienced a higher rate of law enforcement homicides than Whites for the years 2005–2012 (Barber et al. 2016). The data reported by the *Washington Post* on officer-involved shooting deaths documented that there was an average of 980 individuals shot by the police between 2015 and 2017. Demographically, the individuals shot and killed consisted of 48 percent White, 24 percent Black, and 17 percent Latino. Other racial and ethnic groups were categorized as other and comprised 4 percent of all shooting deaths. Based on these newer data, an argument developed that Latinos were killed at a rate equal to their proportion of the population whereas Blacks were over-represented and Whites were underrepresented.

Several mainstream news outlets such as the Public Broadcasting Station, the *Huffington Post*, and the *Los Angeles Times*, continued a line of questioning about why we don't hear about Latinos shot by the police as did alternative sources such as *Al Jazeera America* and Univision. A *Los Angeles Times* article similarly reported that over the past five years in Los Angeles County, Latinos made up about half the population and half of the people killed by police (Santa Cruz, Vives, and Gerber 2015). Despite Latinos having a history of tension with the police, the reporters noted Blacks experienced greater over-representation compared to their population numbers: Blacks make up only 9 percent of the population and represent 26 percent of those killed by the police. The individuals interviewed in these news articles reported a lack of attention due to differential organizing between churches attended by Latinos compared to Blacks, leadership gaps, and a lack of civil rights organizations. These all combined into media neglect. One study cited, *The Latino Media Gap: A Report on the State of Latinos in U. S. Media*, found fewer than 1 percent of news stories were devoted to Latinos (Negrón-Muntaner et al. 2014). Most of these news stories focused on crime or illegal immigration. Sympathetic or even in-depth stories of Latinos shot by the police do not seem to be of interest to TV producers.

Although the traditional approach of examining disparity is to compare incident numbers to the population, DMC researchers take these forms of analyses several steps further. For example, when examining juvenile case processing outcomes in Texas, several researchers found Latino youth were equally represented, however, multivariate analysis determined there was greater potential system bias against Latinos compared to Blacks and Whites (Carmichael, Whitten, and Voloudakis 2005). They reported how single-variable data may lead observers to conclude such inequity may not exist, however, multivariate modeling demonstrated how Hispanic youth progression in the juvenile justice system could not be explained by the same risk factors found for African American youth. Therefore, these researchers lacked an explanation for greater Latino case processing involvement other than ethnicity. They encouraged researchers to question whether proportionality can be the accepted indicator for equity.

DMC research determines disparity by not only examining whether the rate matches the population but whether it matches the comparison group, known as the Relative Rate Index (RRI). Therefore, in analyzing NVDRS data showing that Blacks were killed by law enforcement at a rate of 0.6 per 100,000 population compared to Latinos at 0.3 per 100,000 and Whites at 0.1 per 100,000, we would use Whites as the baseline, finding a pattern in which Blacks were killed at a rate six times higher than Whites and Latinos three times higher. We can also analyze the *Washington Post* data which has found an average of 980 individuals killed by the police with firearms, of which 48 percent were White, 24 percent Black, and 17 percent Latino. When compared to the population, non-Hispanic Whites were 62 percent of the population, Blacks 13, and Latinos at 18. Hence, explaining death at the hands of law enforcement, we observe a pattern of White under-representation and varying degrees of Black and Latino overrepresentation. The *Los Angeles Times* study reported an officer-involved shooting rate equal to the population, but when compared against Whites, it results in Latino overrepresentation. For these reasons, disparity data that involve a comparison group continue to provide important forms of analysis along with those incorporating multivariate analyses to determine whether certain characteristics, law enforcement agencies, or contexts may heighten victimization. In addition, the inclusion of various forms of analyses, both qualitative and quantitative, is necessary to determine whether single variable data alone may miss some of the larger patterns of discrimination.

Early Patterns from New Data

Nationwide data may not reveal the extent of police shootings of Latinos, since this ethnic group is more heavily concentrated in certain states and regions of the country. With the help of several of my graduate students, I therefore began putting together a database regarding officer-involved shootings in several counties in the Southwest where I could also follow up with ethnographic research in the communities to better understand the interactions of Latinos with the police.

Denver, Colorado (City and County)

My research on officer-involved shootings began in Denver after I witnessed the aftermath of a police officer shooting of an unarmed young Latino man named Michael Grimaldo in front of my apartment complex while my children were playing outside (Durán 2016). This shooting occurred in 2003 while I was a member of Denver Copwatch but the incident received very little local attention. After this incident, there were several additional shootings of Blacks and Latinos that made me curious as to what sociological patterns might emerge from analyzing the data and why protests differed in size. District Attorneys and police department officials continued to assert officers used their firearms only in self-defense or to save the lives of others. They maintained that the only observable pattern for these shootings was the reckless nature of "criminals" forcing law enforcement officers to make split-second decisions. The greatest benefit to studying this topic in Denver was that the District Attorney Office considered itself a national leader in having the most transparent officer-involved shooting protocol in the country. I reviewed decision letters from the District Attorney, reports from the manager of safety, and evidence files used to reach a conclusion as to whether to file criminal charges against an officer. These official reports were supplemented with newspaper articles and, when possible, conversations with victims, family members, protest leaders, and District Attorneys. I compiled a database of 218 shootings that had occurred during a 30-year-period from 1983 to 2012. Forty-eight percent of these shootings resulted in death. Individuals shot by the police were 42 percent Latino, 33 percent White, and 23 percent Black and 96 percent were male. Nearly 100 percent of these shootings were deemed legally justified after official review. As of 2016, the city and county of Denver consisted of 693,060 residents of whom 54 percent were White, 30 percent were Latino, 10 percent were Black, 4 percent were Asian, and 2 percent were Native American.

My first article published on these data in the *Du Bois Review* examined controversial shootings: police shootings of individuals who were unarmed, who were not the intended target, or who did not present a level of threat that would justify an officer firing his weapon (Durán 2016). There were also controversial shootings of Blacks, Latinos, and Whites; a later analysis of the data did not show statistical difference by race or ethnicity but since minority groups were shot more frequently overall, there was a larger number of controversial cases among minorities. There were a number of shootings of Latinos that could easily have become household names for serious questions as to why they were shot by a police officer. For example, law enforcement officers obtained a search warrant to conduct a drug raid of a duplex where a 45-year-old Ismael Mena was sleeping, prior to working his night shift (see Chapter 4). Officers broke through the door and fired eight shots at Ismael, resulting in his death. Officers found no drugs in the duplex or in Ismael's body. Afterwards a law enforcement tip to the media pointed out that the officers had raided the wrong house. Law enforcement officers justified their actions by reporting Ismael had fired a gun at officers, but numerous forensic studies countered claims of Ismael firing a gun or even possessing a gun. Ismael was but one of the 36 shootings coded as controversial and one of 15 who were Latino. Since Ismael was a citizen of Mexico and residing in the US through a temporary worker visa, the Mexican-Consulate General requested a federal investigation. The controversy behind this shooting was captured in a documentary by Alan Dominguez entitled *The Holes in the Door* (2007).

To get at the statistical disparity, I collaborated with my friend and colleague Oralia Loza of the University of Texas at El Paso. We examined Takagi's (1974) "two trigger fingers" thesis which holds that police officers have one trigger for Whites and another for Blacks (Durán and Loza 2017). We found support for the thesis in our data:

> The law enforcement finger was "looser" in terms of frequency with racial and ethnic minorities but more rigid in regards to how many officers fired their weapons and how many bullets were fired, partially because in our reading of the data [there were more] questionable events as towards determining the level of threat present. In other words, law enforcement officers were quicker to shoot Blacks and Latinos rather than delaying to gather additional information.
>
> (ibid., 21)

One of the interesting outcomes of this study was that characteristics of individual victims (i.e., age, gender, race, life or death outcome, foreign-born status, mental health status, and reported gang membership) were statistically different for Latinos and Blacks compared to Whites. However, officer characteristics and the contexts where shootings occurred showed less variation. Moreover, Latinos and Blacks were no more likely to engage in serious crime, to victimize another individual, or to injure an officer than Whites. This led my co-author and me to question why Blacks were shot at a rate four times greater than Whites and Latinos three times greater than Whites.

Based on the 42 percent of shootings involving Latinos, many of the factors mirrored Blacks and Whites who were shot by police officers. Some of the noted differences included the language used in the attempt to de-escalate the situation and whether primary Spanish-speaking victims understood primarily English-speaking law enforcement officers. There were cultural differences in terms of family expectations, celebrations, masculinity, and whether authority figures should be contacted to settle personal disputes. An increasing challenge arose in regard to pressurizing District Attorneys to scrutinize problematic cases when the individual was born outside of the United States. Since one of the most influential Chicano civil rights organizations, the Crusade for Justice, had been based in Denver, there were still former activists and new leaders who worked to pursue justice (Vigil 1999). Nevertheless, police shootings of individuals of all racial and ethnic backgrounds rarely sparked community protests, even controversial cases were difficult to increase community awareness as to why they were problematic.

Ogden, Utah (Weber County)

One major obstacle encountered in every city and county I studied after Denver was that records on officer-involved shootings were not made publicly available for review. I, therefore, had to rely on newspaper searches through *Newsbank Access World News* and internet searches in order to construct a timeline of shootings. In Ogden, Utah, where I had lived as a teenager, my research found disproportionate minority contact at the point of arrest, a lack of Latino police officers, and higher rates of incarcerations for Latinos compared to whites (Durán 2013). These ongoing social problems (i.e., residential, labor, and educational segregation) were largely neglected and blamed on Black and Latino community members themselves. From 1999 to 2017, there were 31 officer-involved shootings, of which 65 percent resulted in death. All the shootings were of males. Based on various assessments, at least 55 percent of the individuals shot were White, 29 percent were Latino, and 3 percent were Black; the racial/ethnic identity of 16 percent could not be determined. In 2016, the population of Weber County, with 247,560 residents, was 77 percent White, 18 percent Latino, 2 percent Black, and 2 percent Asian.

Contrary to many law enforcement agencies around the nation being criticized for shooting Black residents, the low proportion of Blacks living in Utah and their overall low number of shootings did not result in the same level of backlash. Despite a higher proportion of Latino residents being shot by the police, these shootings did not generate a heightened level of public attention or response, perhaps because of the relative absence of effective Latino community groups and political organizations like the Crusade for Justice in Denver and the Justice for Mena Committee. Ironically, the shootings that did generate criticism and public response were those of White residents. For example, one officer-involved shooting that produced a tremendous amount of debate was of a 37-year-old, White, military veteran named Matthew Stewart, who encountered a drug raid by law enforcement officers on his home. It was reported that during the raid, the veteran shot and killed one officer and injured three others before being shot and arrested. His defense argued how he had just woken up from sleep to begin working a graveyard shift when plainclothes men armed with guns began firing at him. Fearing a robbery, Matthew fired back in self-defense. This case along with the incidents involving Whites gave me the opportunity to begin exploring Derrick Bell's (1980) concept of interest convergence, which posits that change in practices will occur when they benefit Whites. If the White community experienced the negative impact of officer-involved shootings, would greater rules and regulations develop to control such discretion? In this manner, the statewide review seemed more critical and policy-oriented. A 2014 *Salt Lake Tribune* news article included the headline "Killings by Utah police outpacing gang, drug, child-abuse homicides" (Alberty 2014). It reported that the newspaper had reviewed nearly 300 homicides since 2010 and found use of force by police was the second-most common reason after intimate partner violence for why Utahns kill one another. Almost all of the shooting deaths had been considered legally justified. The reporter interviewed several sources to discover why law enforcement officers in Utah killed so many people. Shortly after, a documentary entitled *Peace Officer* followed this line of reasoning when a retired law enforcement officer conducted his own investigation into the shooting incident of Matthew Stewart. His examination of the facts led him to a very different conclusion than the one provided by the police department and he questioned whether the officer killed was actually killed by friendly fire. In response to this shooting, advocates have been working to end "knock-and-announce" search warrants.

Officer-involved shootings of Latinos seemed to be reported with terms such as criminal, gang member, hoodies, and the presence of guns which left officers no other choice than to use deadly force. Such rationale was used in Denver for Blacks and Latinos. Since Weber County, along with other law enforcement agencies in the state of Utah, do not make officer-involved shooting data publicly available, I intend to follow up with Government Records Access and Management Act (GRAMA) of the 31 officer-involved shootings which have occurred since 1999 to understand how best to reduce these incidents and prevent them from occurring in the future.

The Borderlands: Las Cruces, New Mexico, and El Paso, Texas (Doña Ana County and El Paso County)

The major difference I observed when I first moved to Las Cruces in Doña Ana County, New Mexico, was the presence of Hispanic police officers and a community in which Hispanics were the majority of the population, and many of my college students sought careers in law enforcement.[4] These border communities have some of the lowest rates of violence in the country. In terms of homicides, El Paso has continuously ranked as the safest or one of the three safest large cities in the United States. In my book entitled *The Gang Paradox: Inequalities and Miracles on the U.S.-Mexico Border*, I explain that marginalized youth in gangs were involved in a portion of the violence that occurred in these communities but law enforcement violence added an almost comparable proportion. From 1999 to 2017, 37 individuals were shot by law enforcement officials in Doña Ana County. Sixty-eight percent of these shootings resulted in death and all the shootings were of males. Sixty percent of the shootings were of Latinos, 16 percent White, 5 percent Native American, 3 percent Black, and 16 percent unknown. These numbers compared to a county population of 214,207 residents, of whom 68 percent were Hispanic, 28 percent White, 2 percent Native American and 2 percent Black. During the time frame, El Paso County had 49 officer-involved shootings. Sixty-three percent of these shootings resulted in death and all the shootings were of males. Proportionately, 80 percent of the shootings were of Latinos, 6 percent White, 4 percent Black, and 10 percent unknown. El Paso County, Texas, has 837,918 residents, of whom 82 percent are Hispanic, 12 percent White, and 4 percent Black and 1 percent Native American.

Similar to the other counties included in this chapter, the shootings of Latinos in the border region of Southern New Mexico and West Texas did not garner media attention with regard to officer bias or societal racism. The individuals who were shot were blamed for their actions. Some of the individuals shot were even military veterans like Matthew Stewart, who were reported to be suffering from PTSD. A lot of the information shared from the media appeared secretive as the officer involved and even the name of the individual shot were not readily provided. In Texas, all officer-involved shootings were taken before a grand jury where the information remained secret. Several civil rights advocates calling for transparency encouraged this practice to be discontinued. Most shootings in both counties were considered legally justified. There were a couple of shootings in El Paso where the officer was fired but then reinstated into the police force. Thus, despite questionable and/or controversial evidence and video footage, these officers remained law enforcement officers. Shootings of Mexican nationals often resulted in the Mexican Consulate stepping in to make sure there was increased attention, but the outcome was nevertheless the same.

One difference that existed along the US-Mexico Border was whether there were legal consequences for an officer for shooting someone from the US side standing in Mexico. One of the most controversial cases involved 15-year-old Sergio Adrian Hernandez-Guereca who was shot and killed by a Border Patrol agent after allegedly throwing rocks in 2010. Video footage shows some of his friends throwing rocks but not Sergio. The case was submitted for review to the US Supreme Court on the issue of whether the family of a person standing in Mexico is able to sue a federal agent on US soil. The Supreme Court remanded the case back to the Court of Appeals, which decided in a 13–2 decision that the family could not sue. The photograph image of the youth lying in blood while his family members mourn continues to be an enduring image in my mind as many critics question why law enforcement officers possess so much discretion and why there is no recourse for victims of police use of excessive force.

Conclusion

A much-needed dialogue has begun about the killings of Blacks by police, thanks largely to the Black Lives Matter Movement and nationwide protests, but the murders of Latinos also deserve increased attention. The long and difficult history of colonization did not end when several states became territories and then states, it has persisted into the post-civil rights era where a Black/White binary dominates the discussion. The country recalls slavery and the Civil War but fails to examine the violent seizure of indigenous lands. An expanded version of history could serve to challenge strongly held ideologies regarding nativism and immigration. The colonization of half of Mexico granted Mexicans living in the newly acquired territory the option to become citizens (White), while at the same time treating these residents as foreigners (non-White). When the law and how it is practiced treats one group more favorably it infringes on rights guaranteed by the US Constitution.

Deaths at the hands of law enforcement officers deny victims their constitutional due process protections. Individuals shot by the police do not receive judicial review and the adversarial process that normally determines innocence or guilt and the subsequent punishment. Law enforcement officers do not possess the information, the expertise, or the authority to make snap judgments about an individual's guilt or to determine the required punishment. First impressions are often shaped by bias. Latinos, like Blacks, are often profiled through local, state, and federal wars on drugs, gangs, and processes of criminalization. Early research on police shootings mostly neglected to study Latinos and newer studies suggest they are shot in proportion to their population numbers. However, such analysis requires us to compare these incidents to those involving other racial groups. In the counties where I conducted research, Latinos were numerically the largest minority group. My data consistently show Latino overrepresentation in victimization compared to Whites and occasionally the number of officer-involved shootings is greater than justified proportionally by the population numbers. As pointed out in the research by Carmichael, Whitten, and Voloudakis (2005), proportionality alone may not be the best indicator of inequality. Nevertheless, officer-involved shootings in the Southwest highlight a situation where Latinos are shot at a rate greater than Whites. The comparison with Blacks varied due to African Americans often being a low proportion of the population. Law enforcement shootings of Latinos need to consider language, citizenship status, and whether a shooting of this ethnic group is scrutinized by media and public officials in the same manner as those conducted against Blacks or Whites. The data I have collected indicate the shootings of Latinos were not criticized in the same manner as those of Blacks or Whites. The one exception was if they were non-U.S. citizens and then consulates worked to provide greater clarity for family members and friends.

The pattern nevertheless holds that when someone is Latino, it increases the chance of a law enforcement officer interpreting his behavior as dangerous and responding with the use of deadly force. Latinos will be blamed for causing their own death and law enforcement officers may even receive praise and even formal commendation. The shooting will not garner increased media attention and even when very controversial, it will be very difficult to develop national interest similar to Whites or Blacks whose stories are more regularly covered in the news media. Most of the reporting will simply reinforce stereotypes while providing little insight into how we can prevent the greatest source of loss of life at the hands of the State.

Policy Suggestions

Officer-involved shootings are a public health concern that has largely gone unnoticed. Latino overrepresentation in these shootings compared to Whites has largely been lost in a dialogue involving a Black and White binary. As an increasing number of research studies have begun investigating the differences between the communities in which Blacks, Latinos, and Whites live, we are beginning to gain more understanding as to how life chances based upon the social construction of race continues to shape outcomes. Based on an analysis of 87 cities nationwide, Peterson and Krivo (2012) found Blacks live in neighborhoods with extreme disadvantage, Latinos in disadvantaged neighborhoods, and Whites in more advantaged neighborhoods. Continuing the paradox argument, researchers have sought to explain the reasons why Latinos have lower rates of violence despite living in disadvantaged communities (Martínez 2015). Such a discussion could also be important in determining why Latinos experience a higher number of officer-involved shooting than Whites but less than Blacks in some settings.

Since my previous research emphasized individual characteristics as being more important to police decision-making than law enforcement characteristics or the context where the shooting occurred, we may begin to inquire how the structure of bias is replicated in the outcome of a structured decision to use deadly force. Primarily, this will involve the importance of improved data sources, access to review information, and the ability to engage in comparison across different geographic areas and among racial and ethnic groups. In some of these geographic areas, Latinos and not Blacks encountered greater disproportionality. It is also important when coding for researchers to point out when an individual is of mixed racial and ethnic heritage, such as White and Latino or Black and Latino, which could result in the undercounting of Latinos. More research is required in understanding colorism and how dark- and light-skinned individuals may provoke a different reaction from law enforcement officers. Moreover, surnames require greater assessment as to whether they mark ancestry. Another understudied issue is the role of English language fluency and comprehension in the encounters between Latinos and the police.

In 1974, sociologist Paul Takagi advocated disarming the police, but he argued that by itself such a requirement will not get at the causes of police misconduct. Based on my data coding in Denver, 35 percent of the shootings appeared legitimate, leaving the remainder (65 percent) as questionable or problematic. For this reason, we may ask whether the ability to control a small proportions of the population who present possible harm to others supersedes the civil rights of the majority who fail to receive justice through an adversarial court process. It is time that we begin to question what it means to live in a society where nearly 1,000 homicides per year are committed by those we trust to protect and serve. Moreover, we should also question why certain groups in society, such as Latinos, can be killed at rates much higher than Whites and receive very little attention. Moving beyond the Black and White binary allows for greater forms of collaboration in eradicating laws that deny human rights.

Notes

1 An earlier and much shorter draft of this chapter, "Latinos and the Police: A Critical Analysis of Officer Involved Shootings," was previously published in *Aztlán: A Journal of Chicano Studies* 4(2) (2018). The original piece was 5,700 words whereas this version was substantially revised and expanded to 8,364 words. Changes include added discussion on the Black/White binary, the early history of officer-involved shootings of Latinos, along with added information regarding police shootings in Utah, New Mexico, and Texas.

2 Several terms will be used interchangeably. Latino will be used to denote individuals of Latin American descent and as an umbrella term. Chicano is used to signify persons of indigenous and Latin American descent along with political connotations of the term specific to individuals of Mexican descent. Hispanic will be confined to regions that use this term. It too is an umbrella term. Individuals encompassed by these terms can vary in terms of skin color, language ability from English or Spanish only to bilingual, and citizenship status, ranging from first generation to fifth or sixth generation. These groups are also racially diverse and may identify with any of the racial categorizations outlined by the United States Census.

3 Officer-involved shootings are gendered. Most police officers are male, as are most persons shot by police. Additional research could focus on shootings of females specifically in addition to the impact shootings of males have on mothers and families.

4 Hispanic instead of Latino is the preferred identity term in Southern New Mexico.

References

Alberty, Erin. 2014. "Killings by Utah Police Outpacing Gang, Drug, Child-abuse Homicides." *Salt Lake Tribune*, November 24.

Anchor, S. 1978. *Mexican Americans in a Dallas Barrio*. Tucson, AZ: University of Arizona Press.

Barber, Catherine, Deborah Azrael, Amy Cohen, Mathew Miller, Deonza Thymes, David Enxeb Wang, and David Hemenway. 2016. "Homicides by Police: Comparing Counts From the National Violent Death Reporting System, Vital Statistics, and Supplementary Homicide Reports." *American Journal of Public Health*, 106(5): 922–927.

Bell, Derrick A. 1980. "Brown v. Board of Education and the Interest-Convergence Dilemma." *Harvard Law Review*, 93(3): 518–553.

Bonilla-Silva, Eduardo. 2018. *Racism Without Racists: Color-blind Racism and the Persistence of Racial Inequality in America*. Lanham, MD: Rowman & Littlefield.

Brown, Jodi M., and Patrick A. Langan. 2001. *Policing and Homicide, 1976–98: Justifiable Homicide by Police, Police Officers Murdered by Felons*. Washington, DC: U.S. Department of Justice.

Carmichael, Dottie, Guy Whitten, and Michael Voloudakis. 2005. "Study of Minority Over-Representation in the Texas Juvenile Justice System. Final Report." Submitted to the Office of the Governor Criminal Justice Division College Station, TX: The Public Policy Research Institute, Texas A&M University.

Carrigan, William D. 2006. *The Making of a Lynching Culture: Violence and Vigilantism in Central Texas 1836–1916.* Urbana, IL: University of Illinois Press.

Carter, David L. 1985. "Hispanic Perception of Police Performance: An Empirical Assessment." *Journal of Criminal Justice,* 13(6): 487–500.

Cook, Philip J. and Kristin A. Goss. 2014. *The Gun Debate: What Everyone Needs to Know.* New York: Oxford University Press.

Crosby, Alex E. and Bridget Lyons. 2016. "Assessing Homicides by and of U.S. Law Enforcement Officers." *The New England Journal of Medicine,* 375(16): 1509–1511.

Delgado, Richard. 1997. "Book Review: Rodrigo's Fifteenth Chronicle: Racial Mixture, Latino-Critical Scholarship, and the Black-White Binary." *Texas Law Review,* 75: 1181–1201.

Dominguez, Alan. 2007. The Holes in the Door. Documentary. Loco Lane Filmworks.

Durán, Robert J. 2012. "Policing the Barrios: Exposing the Shadows to the Brightness of a New Day." In Martin G. Urbina (Ed.), *Hispanics in the US Criminal Justice System: The New American Demography.* Springfield, IL: Charles C. Thomas, pp. 42–62.

Durán, Robert J. 2013. *Gang Life in Two Cities: An Insider's Journey.* New York: Columbia University Press.

Durán, Robert J. 2014. "Borders, Immigration and Citizenship: The Latino Experience with Gringo Justice." In Martin G. Urbina (Ed.), *Twenty-First Century Dynamics of Multiculturalism: Beyond Post-Racial America.* Springfield, IL: Charles C. Thomas. pp. 59–80.

Durán, Robert J. 2015. "Mexican American Law Enforcement Officers: Comparing the Creation of Change versus the Reinforcement of Structural Hierarchies." In Martin G. Urbina and Sofia Espinoza Álvarez (Eds.), *Latino Police Officers in the United States: An Examination of Emerging Trends and Issues.* Springfield, IL: Charles C. Thomas, pp. 128–147.

Durán, Robert J. 2016. "No Justice, No Peace: Examining Controversial Officer Involved Shootings." *Du Bois Review: Social Science Research on Race,* 13(1): 61–83.

Durán, Robert J. and Oralia Loza. 2017. "Exploring the Two Trigger Fingers Thesis: Racial and Ethnic Differences in Officer Involved Shootings." *Contemporary Justice Review: Issues in Criminal, Social, and Restorative Justice,* 20(1): 71–94.

Fyfe, James J. 1981. "Who Shoots? A Look at Officer Race and Police Shooting." *Journal of Police Science & Administration,* 9(4), 367–382.

Fyfe, James J. 1982. "Blind Justice: Police Shootings in Memphis." *Journal of Criminal Law and Criminology,* 73: 707.

Fyfe, James J. 1988. "Police Use of Deadly Force: Research and Reform." *Justice Quarterly,* 5(2): 165–205.

Fyfe, James J. 2002. "Too Many Missing Cases: Holes in Our Knowledge about Police Use of Force." *Justice Research and Policy,* 4: 87–102.

Geller, William A. and Kevin J. Karales. 1981. "Shootings of and by Chicago Police: Uncommon Crises: Part I: Shootings by Chicago Police." *Journal of Criminal Law and Criminology,* 73(Winter): 331.

Gómez, Laura E. 2007. *Manifest Destinies: The Making of the Mexican American Race.* New York: New York University Press.

Hemenway, David. 2004. *Private Guns: Public Health.* Ann Arbor, MI: University of Michigan Press.

Hernández, Kelly Lytle. 2010. *Migra: A History of the U.S. Border Patrol.* Berkeley, CA: University of California Press.

Holmes, Malcolm D. 2000. "Minority Threat and Police Brutality: Determinants of Civil Rights Criminal Complaints in U.S. Municipalities." *Criminology*, 38: 343–367.

Ladner, Joyce A. 1973. *The Death of White Sociology.* New York: Random House.

Loftin, Colin, David McDowall, and Min Xie. 2017. "Underreporting of Homicides by Police in the United States, 1976–2013." *Homicide Studies*, 2(2): 159–174.

Martínez, Ramiro. 2007. "Incorporating Latinos and Immigrants into Policing Research." *Criminology and Public Policy*, 6(1): 57–64.

Martínez, Ramiro. 2015. *Latino Homicide: Immigration, Violence, and Community.* New York: Routledge.

Menjívar, Cecilia and Cynthia Bejarano. 2004. "Latino Immigrants' Perceptions of Crime and Police Authorities in the United States: A Case Study from the Phoenix Metropolitan Area." *Ethnic and Racial Studies*, 2(1): 120–148.

Miller, Ted R., Bruce A. Lawrence, Nancy N. Carlson, Delia Hendrie, Sean Randall, Ian R. H. Rockett, and Rebecca S. Spicer. 2016. "Perils of Police Action: A Cautionary Tale from US Data Sets." *Injury Prevention* [online first].

Mirandé, Alfredo. 1985. *The Chicano Experience: An Alternative Perspective.* Notre Dame, IN: University of Notre Dame Press.

Mirandé, Alfredo. 1987. *Gringo Justice.* Notre Dame, IN: University of Notre Dame Press.

Morris, Aldon D. 2015. *The Scholar Denied: W. E. B. Du Bois and the Birth of Modern Sociology.* Oakland, CA: University of California Press.

Negrón-Muntaner, Frances, Chelsea Abbas, Luis Figueroa, and Samuel Robson. 2014. "The Latino Media Gap: A Report on the State of Latinos in U.S. Media." New York: The Center for the Study of Ethnicity and Race Columbia University. Available at: http://docs.wixstatic.com/ugd/73fa65_e8b1b4ec675c41b3a06f351926129cea.pdf

Perea, Juan F. 1995. "Ethnicity and the Constitution: Beyond the Black and White Binary Constitution." *William and Mary Law Review*, 571(2): 571–611.

Perea, Juan F. 1997. "The Black/White Binary Paradigm of Race: The Normal Science of American Racial Thought." *California Law Review*, 85(5): 127–172.

Peterson, Ruth D. and Lauren J. Krivo. 2012. *Divergent Social Worlds: Neighborhood Crime and the Racial-Spatial Divide.* New York: Russell Sage Foundation.

Phillips, Coretta and Benjamin Bowling. 2003. "Racism, Ethnicity and Criminology: Developing Minority Perspectives." *British Journal of Criminology*, 43: 269–290.

Samora, J., J. Bernal, and A. Peña. 1979. *Gunpowder Justice: A Reassessment of the Texas Rangers.* Notre Dame, IN: University of Notre Dame Press.

Santa Cruz, Nicole, Ruben Vives, and Marisa Gerber. 2015. "Why the Deaths of Latinos at the Hands of Police Haven't Drawn as Much Attention." *Los Angeles Times*, July 18.

Sklansky, David Alan. 2006. "Not Your Father's Police Department: Making Sense of the New Demographics of Law Enforcement." *The Journal of Criminal Law and Criminology*, 96(3): 1209–1243.

Solis, Dianne. 2013. "40 Years After Santos Rodriguez's Murder, Scars Remain for Family, Neighbors and Dallas." *Dallas News*. Available at: www.dallasnews.com/news/news/2013/07/21/40-years-after-santos-rodriguezs-murder-scars-remain-for-family-neighbors-and-dallas

Takagi, Paul. 1974. "A Garrison State in Democratic Society." *Crime and Social Justice*, Spring/Summer: 27–32.

Taylor, Paul S. (1931). "Crime and the Foreign Born: The Problem of the Mexican."In *Report on Crime and the Foreign Born*. Washington, DC: GPO, National Commission on Law Observance and Enforcement.

Vigil, Ernesto B. 1999. *The Crusade for Justice: Chicano Militancy and the Government's War on Dissent*. Madison, WI: University of Wisconsin Press.

Weitzer, Ronald. 2014. "The Puzzling Neglect of Hispanic Americans in Research on Police-Citizen Relations." *Ethnic and Racial Studies*, 37(11): 1995–2013.

Chapter 3

Interest-Convergence Theory and Police Use of Deadly Force on Latinos

A Case Study of Three Shootings

Roberto Rivera

Since the 1991 police beating of motorist Rodney King in Los Angeles and the subsequent acquittal of the officers involved and more recent incidents that have garnered public attention, there has been increased concern with the high level of lethal force in officer-involved shootings and the victimization of people of Color by police. Unfortunately, little attention has been paid to the killing of Latinas/os by police officers or to the police response to violent events within Latina/o communities. This chapter, based on qualitative ethnographic field research and participant observation, describes three unrelated police shootings of Latinos in a California community and critically evaluates a community policing program that emerged in response to the shootings.[1] Although trained as a social scientist, this case study offers not a detached and objective analysis but one that centers my experience as a Latino police officer and my role in developing and implementing the program.

The events described took place in "Corozal City" (pseudonym), a medium-sized city in California of about 100,000 residents, 42 percent of whom are Latino and 48 percent White. The research is centered on "El Cibuco Park" (also a pseudonym), a 1-square-mile barrio whose residents are 85 percent Latino, primarily immigrants and Spanish speakers. The "Move Forward Project" (heretofore "MFP," or "The Project") as I call it, was initiated by law enforcement in Corozal City with the aim of promoting positive engagement, mutual trust, and respect between the police and the Latina/o community. To protect the identity and privacy of the parties involved, I use anonymity and pseudonyms, not only for the barrio and larger community but also in relation to dates, locations, news sources, and internal documents. Except as noted, my information comes from participant observation or from sources who asked to remain anonymous.

The Project was launched in response to rising community-police tensions and the racial profiling of Latinas/os by police officers in Corozal City. Tensions came to a head during a five-day period in the mid-2000s, when three unrelated fatal shootings took place in the community. Significantly, all the police officers involved in the shootings were White, while all three victims were Latino. The fact that three separate fatal shootings of Latinos took place within such a short period and that they were all committed by White officers from the same department suggested a broader pattern of abuse. Prior to the shootings, there had been little communication or collaboration between the community and police, and the three shootings sharpened the distrust of police that already simmered among Latina/o residents. In the following days and months, thousands of residents came out to protest, deteriorating an already strained relationship with police. The lack of communication appeared to have increased the racial divide, promoting an "us versus them" standoff between community residents and law enforcement.

The Move Forward Project was initiated to promote a more positive engagement between the police department and the Latina/o community: one with mutual trust and respect. In critically evaluating the Project, this chapter draws specifically on Derrick Bell's Interest Convergence Theory (ICT). An analysis of propositions as markers and angles is used to examine the success of the Project.

In assessing the attitudes of Latinas/os toward law enforcement (McCluskey, McCluskey, and Enriquez 2008), previous studies have found that the racial division that exists between Latinas/os and White officers is impacted by a number of factors, including community residents' fear of deportation and procedural unfairness (Messing 2015). Latina/o perceptions of police performance have been generally poor since the *Tennessee v. Garner* (1975) decision, which, overturned the common law doctrine and state statutes which allowed police officers to use lethal force to apprehend a fleeing felon. Although *Garner* held that deadly force could only be used when there was a threat to the life of the officer or the lives of others (Blume 1984; Carter 1985), this precedent-setting case has been misinterpreted as allowing officers to use lethal force if they believe that the victim has a weapon, even if the belief is unreasonable, mistaken, or unwarranted. This interpretation favors police officers and ironically has led to an increase in officer-involved shootings (Katz 2015).

An additional factor impacting police/community relations and how officers approach patrolling is social identity and cooperation, where Latina/o residents share similar values and concerns with police (Bradford 2014; Reck 2014). These characteristics include residents avoiding police officers, being fearful, not sharing information when contacted by police, and not reporting crimes as they occur (Martinez et al. 2010).

In response to civil and racial unrest in the 1960s, police departments across the United States started looking for ways to improve race relations and the relationship between the police and minority communities. In the 1980s, police departments began implementing Community Oriented Policing and Problem Solving (COPPS) initiatives, and by the 1990s approximately 100,000 police officers were federally funded to support such projects. The Violent Crime Control and Law Enforcement Act of 1994 provided funding to improve policing in urban areas by adding or redeploying more police officers. The initial intent of community policing was to make the nation's streets safer, as studies suggested that police departments that were transparent and worked to improve trust were better able to collaborate with community interests and reduce conflict between the police and residents (Glaser and Denhardt 2010).

This chapter attempts to shed light on two reasons why police-sponsored initiatives that seek to increase community trust are often unsuccessful. First, it argues that such programs tend to be either short-sighted and geared to short-term, limited goals that do not consider the community's real aspirations, or, second, that they are aimed at advancing the interests of White police administrators and a residential White majority in power rather than the interests of community residents.

This chapter draws on Derrick Bell's Interest-Convergence Theory (ICT), which argues that Whites will generally endorse projects that are designed to benefit minorities only largely to the extent that such efforts are also perceived as being beneficial to members of the dominant group (Bell 1980). Although Bell was concerned mainly with relations between Whites and Blacks, his theory can also be applied to relations between White police officers and Latina/o residents.

In retrospect, it is clear that the leadership of the Corozal City Police Department promoted the Move Forward Project because it was perceived as serving the interests of the police and the White power structure in the community, whose members sought to ease tensions just enough to stop the protests. I conclude that the program was discontinued after only two years, not because it lacked effectiveness but because once the protests stopped and crime declined, the project was no longer seen as serving the interests of the dominant group.

Methods

The data were collected based on participant observation, my own hands-on experience, and ethnographic fieldwork. Additionally, archived newspaper articles, television news reports, District Attorney reports and a U.S. Department of Justice report on the three shootings are included. Attempts at contacting the local District Attorney's office to gain permission to review files on the three officer-involved shootings were unsuccessful. However, I personally knew the officers involved in the three shootings, and I was consulted for my experience during my career as a police officer. My reflections on how my position as an officer shaped people's behavior around me, as well as my access to settings, resulted from my assignment to Corozal City.

To implement a Community-Oriented Policing and Problem Solving (COPPS) project in 2006, as an officer with Corozal City, I wrote a grant in cooperation with the local university. The project brought in M.A. graduate students from the local university to examine the relationship between the Corozal City officers and Latino residents. Five graduate students from various disciplines, including sociology, business, and marketing, participated in police ride-alongs with officers over a 4-month period. The students ranged in age from 22 to 28 and rode with police officers for a minimum of 8 hours a week. The students kept monthly progress reports and logs, and wrote a final paper in response to what they saw and heard regarding the attitudes of officers toward Latino residents. They shared a research question, "Which is more of a barrier to improve police relations in Corozal City, the Mexican culture or Spanish language?" During the time of the student research, the department had begun a Spanish language immersion program where 12 officers from the Corozal City station were selected to learn Spanish over a 10-week period.

In addition, I kept departmental emails from high-ranking police officials that highly praised the Move Forward Project. Each month, Corozal City leaders and city government officials evaluated the project. I also gave COPPS monthly reports on the Move Forward Project to Sergeant Carrillo. The Move Forward Project had ten goals, as outlined below. Eight of the 10 goals were met. One of the two items not met, to develop a boxing team, was in process and nearly completed when the project was canceled. The project was ostensibly canceled due to the El Cibuco Park COPPS unit being transformed to a gang unit led by a new Sergeant. Plans to develop a high school mariachi troupe from two rival high schools also never materialized. As the project was implemented, there were increasing media reports of improved police/Latino community relations measured by perceptions of increased trust, as well as by a decrease in the number of protests. There was also an increase in Latina/o involvement with the Corozal City Police Department.

I examined government reports that reviewed the trio of shootings in Corozal City. For instance, in 2008, the County District Attorney's office which oversaw Corozal City and adjacent cities issued a report that evaluated the use of force. The U.S. Department of Justice also issued a report in 2008 justifying the use of lethal force in the trio of shootings that took place during the period examined. Additionally, archived newspaper reports on the Corozal City shootings and their aftermath were collected until my transfer out of the Corozal City station. Finally, Corozal City reports of the shootings were examined, which gave detailed accounts of the three residents who were killed, as well as the actions of the officers involved in the shootings.

A few methodological limitations must be noted. For one, determination of the nationalities of the three Latino residents killed in the incidents with police was based on media accounts from the internet, archived newspaper sources, and past TV news segments. Additionally, though I can be considered an insider because of a former assignment to Corozal City, at the time of the three officer-involved shootings, I was assigned to another station in the area.

Interest-Convergence Theory: An Overview

Law professor and foundational Critical Race Theory (CRT) scholar, Derrick Bell based his Interest Convergence Theory (ICT) on the landmark 1954 case *Brown v. Board of Education* (Bell 1980; 1985). In critically assessing the impact of this case, Bell concluded that the much-heralded decision outlawing de jure segregation was issued not because it advanced the interests of Blacks but rather because it also favored the interests of White Americans, particularly industrialists who saw segregation as detrimental to economic progress (Bell 1980). He argued that the interests of Whites typically diverged from the interests of people of Color, making integration unfeasible unless Whites also benefitted from the change. In other words, racial equality was accommodated generally only when it converged with White interests (ibid.). More generally, ICT argues that policies that benefit communities of Color, including Latina/o communities, generally are enacted only when they also serve to advance the interests of White Americans (Alemán and Alemán 2010).

African Americans have historically lacked trust in White citizens and White police officers, a distrust rooted in the Jim Crow-era segregation and the violent White response to desegregation. This was seen, for example, in 1957 at Little Rock Central High School in Arkansas, where nine African American students had to be protected by the National Guard from Whites who were violently protesting integration of the school. In the community under study, there has long been a high level of distrust as well between disadvantaged Latina/o residents and the White officers who hold positions of power over them. In assessing the attitudes of Latinas/os toward law enforcement, previous studies have found that the racial division that exists between Latina/o citizens and White officers is often exacerbated by Latina/o fear of deportation and procedural unfairness (McCluskey, McCluskey, and Enriquez 2008; Messing et al. 2015). Latina/o residents are generally distrustful of White officers, while White officers often do not trust their Latina/o peers in the police department.

While desegregation was not the issue for Corozal City, Latino residents had more officer contacts and higher arrest rates than White residents, and the community had a history of violence by White officers against Latinas/os. In the four months prior to the trio of shootings, two other shootings had taken place in Corozal City. As was the case in the trio of shootings, all the officers in the earlier cases were White, and the victims were Latino males. Furthermore, none of the officers assigned to patrol in Corozal City were fluent in Spanish. The officers' inability to communicate contributed to intense racial conflict, which often manifested in excessive force. It was not until the Latina/o community began to protest that White residents of Corozal City took notice of the problem. At that point, public pressure from White residents prompted the police department to act.

Community policing efforts have generally been based on a Black/White racial binary, as has Critical Race Theory (Delgado 2015). This chapter argues that ICT can be applied successfully to cases involving Latinas/os and Whites. In this way scholars can expand the theory beyond the racial binary while also assuming an intersectional perspective (Crenshaw 1989), which focuses not only on race but also on other factors such as language, culture, citizenship, and real or perceived immigration status (Mirandé 2013).

"Los Tres Disparos": Three Police Shootings

The case study provides a unique opportunity to examine multiple police shootings in a Latina/o community and the police response to the shootings. Prior to these events, there were no documented cases of multiple officer-involved shootings within such a short time frame, neither in Corozal City, nor in the surrounding counties and cities. By focusing on these case studies, this study seeks to critically examine why police initiatives are implemented, and more importantly, why seemingly successful programs are discontinued. By applying ICT, I argue that such programs will be advanced and continued only to the extent that they are perceived as benefiting the dominant community and advancing White interests.

The media and community residents believed the succession of shootings to be the first such incident for the Corozal City Police Department, and possibly all of California. In the aftermath of the shootings, mass protests erupted within the predominately Latina/o community and continued for two years. Barrio residents decried the shootings and the police department's failure to recruit Spanish-speaking officers who could communicate more effectively with the community they represented. At the time of the shootings, none of the city's 49 officers were fluent in Spanish. A cultural divide existed because of the department's failure to address the Latina/o community's needs and assuage their fear and distrust of police.

The string of shootings began on a summer day in the mid-2000s as officers responded, for the third time in 24 hours, to a domestic disturbance call in a Corozal City neighborhood. The officers reported confronting a Latino male who had allegedly threatened other people and attacked a deputy with dumbbells. He was described by officers as "unfazed" by pepper spray. Two officers subsequently fired, and the man died at the scene. The shooting was deemed justified under the state's penal code, which defines shootings as justified if necessary to overcome resistance to the discharge of a lawful duty or if in defense of others. Subsequent to the shooting, there was no record of community outreach by the police department to the residents of the area, nor any attempt to understand what took place, or for the department to issue a report to the family about the man's death.

The next day, Friday, a deputy spotted a Jeep suspected of having been involved in an armed robbery. The officer stopped the vehicle and chased an unarmed Latino male who ran from the scene. The officer fired three shots at the man; the final volley of shots penetrated the man's body as he was lying on his back. The District Attorney's audit report, released in the year after the shooting, stated that the officer shot the man when the suspect reached into his clothing. Once again, the family was not given any explanation as to why the suspect was killed.

This event added to the community's safety concerns about police-involved shootings. Residents had to rely on the media for information about the killing; the police department also did not provide a mental health liaison or make any other personnel available to explain what took place or to help community members process the emotions they experienced as a result of the incident. Latina/o leaders vocalized their feelings of alienation, further increasing the level of distrust between the community and the police.

The following Monday, officers tried to stop a Latino man who was said to "fit the description" of a suspect in a reported car theft. The man ostensibly "ran." Officers chased him, and one deputy shot him as he reportedly reached for a "Leatherman-like tool" in a pouch on his hip. At this point, with three shootings of Latino men within a five-day period, the community became even more enraged and fearful of local police officers. Again, there was no community outreach or explanation from the department given to the family about the man's death. Incredibly, all three shootings were subsequently ruled to have been "justified" by the local District Attorney's office overseeing the police department, as stated in the audit reports.

Significantly, but not surprisingly, all of the officers involved in the shootings were all White males with military backgrounds. The officers spoke no Spanish, while the victims were Latino males who spoke little or no English. There was no specific examination of the language barrier to assess whether the men might not have responded to the officers' demands because of their lack of English fluency.

The national political climate during the period of these shootings was contentious, with public hysteria over immigration policy and control of the US-Mexico border. As these heated conversations were taking place, a new vigilante group was gaining momentum at the border and throughout the Southwest. The Minutemen and their members were primarily White males (Yoxall 2006). While protests by local Latinas/os over the three shootings were taking place, the Minutemen aligned themselves with Immigration and Customs Enforcement (ICE) officers and the Border Patrol in the roundup of undocumented Latina/o immigrants to combat the "Latino threat" (Chavez 2013; Holmes et al. 2008). Meanwhile, the presence of Latino day laborers looking for work was also becoming increasingly contentious not only in Corozal City but elsewhere in the Southwest (Varsanyi 2008). In addition to focusing on the police shootings, Latino protestors came to the defense of the immigrant day laborers.

I was a police officer in another city at the time of the shootings and was transferred back to Corozal City about 15 months later, as tensions continued to build. At the first protest where I was assigned to provide security, I witnessed hundreds of people supporting the Minutemen and their anti-immigrant sentiment, as well as hundreds of protestors on the opposing side, who were supporting Latina/o immigrants and day laborers. As the protests were taking place, leaders of the Minutemen were meeting with the Captain of the Corozal City Police Station to promote a proposed city ordinance that would have required those hiring day laborers to register with the city.[2]

As Latinas/os were protesting the officer-involved shootings, the Minutemen were fomenting anti-immigrant rhetoric and propaganda that were distracting for the city, yet were openly and tacitly supported by its police command. This sent mixed messages to residents and officers alike. The fact that the Captain in charge, for example, was working in concert with Minutemen and ICE was troubling to members of the Latina/o community, especially in the aftermath of the shootings. The Minutemen clearly had a voice in determining local police practices involving illegal immigrants. ICE agents were made available to officers from Corozal City during police traffic stops and police calls for service. For Latina/o officers like myself, it was troubling to hear the term "noncitizen" used interchangeably with "Hispanic" in conversations between federal agents and police officers. It was even more startling to hear "NHI"—no human involved—applied to police contacts with persons suspected of being undocumented. This fueled mistrust of police officers on the part of the Latina/o community, as well as mistrust among officers themselves (White versus Latino officers). It mirrored a past narrative of questionable police actions aligning with White interests (Mirandé 1987). The Minutemen were later determined to be a White supremacist organization and movement by the Southern Poverty Law Center (Sandoval 2010).

The Move Forward Project: A Pilot Program in Community-Police Engagement

Declining community trust in local law enforcement came through clearly not only in residents' comments at public events such as community forums, Spanish-speaking PTA meetings, local English immersion classes, and media interviews but also in my conversations with local residents. Latinas/os were reluctant to call our department to request assistance or report an emergency, deterred by language and cultural barriers and wary of the possibility of arrest or deportation. Indeed, many Latina/o residents feared the officers who patrolled the area. Above all, residents wanted law enforcement to be held accountable for the trio of shootings, which illustrated a discrepancy between the stated intentions of law enforcement to enforce justice and the community's perceptions of injustice. Given the loss of trust, the police department sought a middle ground between the desires of protestors for restorative justice and the desire of Corozal City officials to see the protests come to an end.

Move Forward was initiated in response to conflict between barrio residents and law enforcement; its main purpose was to end the protests and alleviate tensions in the community. The disproportionate number of Latinas/os shot and killed by police called into question attitudes and behaviors that had been institutionalized. The mutual mistrust and perception of threat held by law enforcement agents and people in the barrios created group dynamics that reinforced in-group solidarity and intergroup conflicts that would not typically occur in more affluent areas (Holmes and Smith 2012). This perception took hold not only on the streets, where the three officer-involved shootings took place but also in discussions behind closed doors between more progressive law enforcement officers and community residents who sought a more humane resolution to the conflict.

After being transferred to Corozal City, I was recruited along with Sergeant Leo Carrillo to lead law enforcement efforts to formally address community-police conflicts. A COPPS storefront office was set up in El Cibuco Park to increase officer presence and visibility as well as make contact with barrio residents. I was assigned to the storefront station because of my Hispanic heritage, my proficiency in Spanish, my prior experience with civic engagement, and first-hand knowledge of the city's Latina/o community, acquired through previously having patrolled the area.

While assigned to the COPPS unit, I created the Move Forward Project, an initiative to address the cultural divide between the Latina/o community and the police. The project sought to develop community trust through collaboration and team building. The ten-point program involved leadership recognition, partnership with a local newspaper, and collaboration with Latina/o community residents. In town hall meetings and face-to-face interactions, residents had consistently expressed their lack of trust in law enforcement officers. Distrust was especially intense when it involved conflicts between police and youth in the barrio.

One solution was to address the language barrier between police officers and the Spanish-speaking residents. I opted to walk door-to-door to listen to the community's concerns. Bilingual staff and community leaders also reached out to barrio residents to encourage further discussion with me and other officers. As trust among Latinas/os in the community grew, residents in the local neighborhood gradually began to cooperate with law enforcement and to provide information on criminal activities. For example, when a canine handler was involved in a foot pursuit in an alley, a teenage resident of El Cibuco Park pointed the officer in the direction that the person had fled. The officer later told fellow officers that he had "never witnessed" such cooperation before. I was later able to share the information with city officials, detectives, and street-level officers. By including all community partners, I found a holistic means of policing that made it safer for residents to come forward with ideas for solutions. Residents would drop by the local storefront station to offer suggestions on ways to improve police-community relations. This created buy-in and allowed some residents to be a part of a new collective policing structure. It may have also set the parameters for what some authorities would categorize as a new culture that emerged with this new partnership.

The Move Forward Project also included the recognition of good citizenship and leadership achievements, with a "Champion in the Community" program where each month a member of the Latina/o community would have lunch with the police captain and receive a certificate from the police department. The person was also profiled in the local newspaper and photographed with the police captain. Additionally, The Project identified Latina/o leaders to participate in a Latino Roundtable with police officials. This group worked together to address the community's mistrust of police due to excessive use of force. The captain organized simulator shooting training for the Latino Roundtable members and facilitated agreements to continue future collaborations between the community and the police department. By working as a team, the Latino Roundtable members modeled unity between the community and the police.

My efforts proved successful in building rapport between residents and police officials. For example, I staffed a team-building event called Soccer Fest, which was attended by 2,000 persons. The event included a soccer match between local officers and rival high schools. The self-esteem of the student players was bolstered, as evidenced by their jubilant on field celebration of their 11-to-1 triumph over the officers. Additionally, representatives of 25 community social service agencies attended the games, along with other residents. The residents learned about services offered by the agencies and could seek volunteer and paid employment opportunities. On the soccer field, the Latina/o residents benefitted from seeing officers in a more engaging, humane context.

A Christmas dinner was also organized to serve about 800 people from the barrio, with 200 turkeys given out to residents. The donated dinners were served by officers and command staff from the police department, while I dressed as Santa Claus and gave out candy and gifts donated by local merchants to children. In addition, the visual arts department of a local university produced a video targeting single Latina mothers and provided information on community resources. The aim of the video was to inform the young mothers about behaviors in children that could be indicative of potential gang activity. A former member of the Mara Salvatrucha (MS13) gang was also invited to the event, speaking to Latino children in several middle schools and appearing in the anti-gang video. A second video targeted children between the ages of 8 and 12 and was distributed within the community. A preventative anti-gang game was also designed to reach younger children between the ages of 6 and 8. In the game, children had opportunities to make good life choices that demonstrated good citizenship. The Move Forward Project also reached out to a local elementary school, where officers and detectives read to primarily Spanish-speaking first graders to enhance their reading skills and promote literacy. The outreach was well received by school administrators, teachers, individual family members, and the community at large.

Following the opening of the storefront office, the community experienced, over time, a significant reduction in violent crime. This was confirmed by both the police department and outside sources. For example, over the two years that The Project was up and running, the national FBI violent crime index showed that violent crime in Corozal City declined by 20.9 percent. Unfortunately, this drop in violent crime also resulted in a reduction of the local police department's funding, making it impossible to sustain the new efforts. As a result, the Move Forward Project was abruptly terminated by the Corozal City Police Department, even though other high-ranking administrators called it successful. Instead, the local police department turned to the traditional model of community policing, discussed by Richard Alvarado in Chapter 6 of this volume, which uses the broken-windows theory to increase reported crime rates in order to obtain more funding (Sampson and Raudenbush 2004).

From an ICT perspective, a major problem with the Move Forward Project was that the funding received by police departments from the Department of Homeland Security was based on increased or high crime rates. Ironically, when a community experiences a large drop in crime, it may lose the funding it needs for officers, equipment, and training, making it difficult to sustain the gains. Though it seems counterintuitive, it is more advantageous for the department's funding situation to have a high crime rate than a low one. It is therefore not in the best financial interest of police departments to reduce crime.

In sum, the Move Forward Project employed alternative and successful methods to address the lack of trust in law enforcement by people of Color. The holistic strategies that were implemented during my tenure in Corozal City raised the Latina/o community's level of trust in barrio policing and led to greater cooperation between Latina/o residents and the police. The attempt to promote positive police-community relations was clearly reflected in the interactions of police officers with Latino residents. During this period, the city received fewer complaints against officers. Although proving cause and effect is difficult, department personnel were convinced—and expressed in numerous internal emails and other communications—that the trust-building project was instrumental in bringing about the community's drop-in crime, one of the largest-ever one-year reductions of crime for Corozal City. Although there was no formal external evaluation of the project by any outside agency or academic institution, the department considered the project successful because the protests ended during its period of activity. Despite, or perhaps because of, the project's success, it was ultimately terminated. Though the department saw the initiative as a crime reduction program, in truth, the department wanted to end the protests, not to reduce crime, but fearing they would lose officers as a result of the ensuing decrease in federal funding.

During the period of implementation, there were no officer-involved shooting incidents. The initiative resulted in the community going out and participating in various phases of the project. Additionally, Latina/o residents began walking into the COPPS field office, addressing community concerns, and reporting local crimes. The Spanish immersion program had only one deputy who passed the final exam. The same deputy had some prior Spanish proficiency. Of the five university students, their results all reported finding that "culture" was more of a barrier than language. The most common theme was the racial divide between officers and Latinas/os in the El Cibuco area. Recommendations from the students included that the department hire Spanish-speaking officers and that they institute culturally sensitive training. Through the department administrators and the station Captain, I received a commendation letter, and numerous departmental emails from high-ranking superiors praising both officers involved in the Move Forward Project.

Move Forward addressed these concerns by giving community members a sense that they had an equal footing with the police officers. From the perspective of the community, trust is not granted automatically to law enforcement, but must be earned through the actions of police officers and public officials. As the program progressed within the Latina/o community, there were observed changes in the attitude of the command staff at the police station. Despite the positive efforts that were uniting community residents together and rebuilding trust, there was an obvious increase in numbers of Border Patrol agents at the station and a pushback from officers from the Corozal City station. Additionally, an ICE agent was assigned to assist officers in the field. Double talk by the station Captain that ICE was not working in Corozal City was given at the Latino Roundtable meetings during this period. Once again, a racial division was becoming more evident between the White officers and city leaders and those who were primarily Brown and Spanish speakers

Despite the efforts of the Move Forward Project personnel, many officers continued to demonstrate an adversarial attitude toward Latinos. This phenomenon was witnessed in the interaction of the ICE agents assigned to patrol stations with the police officers in the area (Armenta 2017). Once again, a color line was emerging where those who did not appear to be US citizens were seen as "them." There was also evidence of biased behavior, as White officers were more prone to call for ICE or Border Patrol agents to determine the deportation status of those who might fit the description of illegal immigrants.

In retrospect, the primary achievement of the Move Forward Project was the development and implementation of a holistic model of policing that included the voice of the citizens of Corozal City. By doing so, the project improved community-police relations and reduced police violence. The following is a brief description of holistic policing developed from the Move Forward Project, on how future law enforcement agencies can improve upon this initiative.

Holistic Policing

Language barriers created divisions between relationships that were crucial in devising a system that met the needs of the community and of the officers to maintain law and order. Even more so, those who see this racialized group as the "other" or an enemy had to learn a more humanistic and integrated approach when working with people of different cultures and languages. This alternative policing method examines and evaluates hiring practices, academy instruction, police attitudes, and behaviors through social identity theories of individual perceptions within policing structures.

A humanistic and integrated approach could be designed as a method of policing to solve conflicts with Latinas/os and other minority groups; an approach that focuses on human potential and achievement and not on social disorder or social control. This methodology would embrace face-to-face interactions, develop a community forum of leaders to solve problems, conduct education outreach, and reward positive behaviors that contribute to community collaboration and harmony. Such a holistic approach would promote trust, peace, unity, and compassion within communities with large proportions of people of Color. It would also promote police authorities working with these communities as a unified team with a common goal—to create trust by incorporating all the components listed above. Additionally, a holistic model of policing could be further examined to improve trust of police by Latinas/os and decrease the use of excessive and lethal force by police.

The Move Forward Project holistically addressed the needs of the Latino community by recognizing that they were part of the solution in their policing and not part of the problem. The proposed holistic model would invite residents of good standing to be included within the structure of its police departments. The model would be reflective of the demographics of the city and would move away from aggressive, confrontational, and punitive police tactics.

I learned through retrospective research that analysis of data from the past can shed light on current events. The advantage of this type of research is the ability to revisit past events and recreate them through analysis by those who had a connection. This type of research cannot be duplicated unless an actor from that period existed to direct and connect the dots, say, for example, by access to the information. By creating timelines and managing the supporting data, it was easier to reconstruct the events and climate surrounding the trio of shootings and the subsequent implementation of the Move Forward Project. The problem is that, due to the nature of the events, I had no access to the actual police reports in the trio of shootings, nor was I able to speak to the officers involved. It was also difficult to obtain interviews that could have expedited this study. In short, holistic policing seeks to expand on the restorative justice movement.

Conclusion

This case study sought to demonstrate how Interest-Convergence Theory can be used to assess the relationship between local law enforcement agencies and Latina/o residents by examining how a primarily White police force benefits by maintaining stratified police practices and high crime rates. It also demonstrated that ICT can be expanded beyond a Black/White race binary. Consistent with ICT, this study showed that an in-group/outgroup racial division exists between the White power structure, including the police, and Latina/o residents. The theory can be applied to the events in Corozal City by critically assessing whether the interests of the police and of Whites aligned with those of the Latina/o community.

The theory also suggests that the events in this community were a continuation of the historical subjugation of Latinas/os by non-Latinas/os, rather than representing significant change. It was not until the protests began that the police department was moved to respond to residents' hostility toward the department and the White officers involved in the trio of shootings. Significantly, the Captain of the Corozal City Police Station and his ten superiors were all White males. Furthermore, the dominant power structure was maintained by the department's leadership and the nearly all-White police force, continuing a divisive "us versus them" framework that lacked Latina/o input on policing. Although members of the Corozal City Police Station believed that the Move Forward Project was successful in reducing violent crime, the project was disbanded because the drop-in crime ultimately led to a reduction in federal funding of the city's police. Consistent with ICT, the Move Forward Project was discontinued because the project's success no longer advanced White interests.

Institutional inertia is a powerful force preventing change within police agencies, as police departments resist changing discriminatory practices. Many of the apparent changes that I witnessed were undermined by officers and department heads who wished to maintain past practices despite the harm these outdated methods caused the community. These police practices were designed in an era when minorities constituted a small percentage of the population. As the demographics changed and the Latina/o population grew, the biased nature of those practices became more apparent. The interests of the Latina/o community did not converge with the interests of the dominant White power structure until the three shootings occurred and triggered widespread protests. Once the protests stopped, it was no longer in the interest of the police department to maintain the Move Forward Project or to create other outreach initiatives to improve trust with Latina/o residents.

Despite the apparent success of the Move Forward Project, the issue of police accountability was constantly called into question by the Latina/o community. It was quite common at Spanish-speaking PTA meetings to hear residents say they did not understand the need for sustained police presence in the community. It appears that these attitudes reflect the reality in that the Move Forward Project may have brought about cosmetic changes, but it never changed the reality of police brutality. The questionable behavior of the officers involved in the three shootings tore down the fabric of trust. It was challenging for social activists from Corozal City and neighboring areas to have leaders within the community navigate the deep-rooted structures of policing culture.

Corozal City was recognized as a site for federal funding, including funding by the Department of Justice, based on the city's crime rate, which was higher than that of neighboring cities. Future research should examine the impact of federal funding to police departments based on higher levels of crime. More research is also needed to analyze trust-building community-police initiatives within Latina/o communities. ICT can hopefully be used to better understand how police violence benefits Whites and continues to marginalize ethnic communities. The findings of this study suggest that the Move Forward Project was a short-term fix focused on improving community-police relations rather than a long-term solution to the perennial problem of the use of excessive deadly force by police in communities of Color.

Notes

1 An earlier, shorter draft of this chapter was published in *Aztlan: A Journal of Chicano Studies* (43(2), Fall 2018). The article focused on a trio of officer-involved shootings and the impact on community levels of trust. This chapter expands the discussion theoretically and applies Derrick Bell's Interest Convergence Theory as well as the

concept of "Brown and Out" in driving out Latinas/os from locations and spaces. In addressing police use of deadly force, the chapter also proposes and expands on the concept of Holistic Policing as an alternative to traditional policing.

2 For a discussion of the rise of police as immigration enforcement, see Armenta (2017).

References

Alemán, Enrique, and Sonya M. Alemán. 2010. "Do Latin@ Interests Always Have to 'Converge' with White Interests? (Re)claiming Racial Realism and Interest-convergence in Critical Race Theory Praxis." *Race, Ethnicity, and Education*, 13(1): 1–21.

Armenta, Amada. 2017. *Protect, Serve, and Deport: The Rise of Policing as Immigration Enforcement*. Oakland. CA: University of California Press.

Bell, Derrick. 1980. "Brown v. Board of Education and the Interest-Convergence Dilemma." *Harvard Law Review*, 93: 518–533.

Bell, Derrick. 1985. "Foreword: The Civil Rights Chronicles." *Harvard Law Review, 99* (1): 4–83.

Blume, John H. 1984. "Deadly Force in Memphis: Tennessee v. Garner." Ithaca, NY: Cornell Law Faculty Publications.

Bradford, B. 2014. "Policing and Social Identity: Procedural Justice, Inclusion and Cooperation Between Police and Public." *Policing and Society*, 24(1): 22–43.

Carter, D. L. 1985. "Hispanic Perception of Police Performance: An Empirical Assessment." *Journal of Criminal Justice*, 13(6): 487–500.

Chavez, Leo R. 2013. *The Latino Threat: Constructing Immigrants, Citizens, and the Nation*. Palo Alto, CA: Stanford University Press.

Crenshaw, Kimberlé. 1989. "Demarginalizing the Intersection of Race and Sex: A Black Feminist Critique of Anti-Discrimination Doctrine, Feminist Theory and Anti-Racist Politics." *University of Chicago Legal Forum*, 1: 139–167.

Delgado, Richard. 2015. "Why Obama? An Interest Convergence Explanation of the Nation's First Black President." *Law and Inequality: A Journal of Theory and Practice*, 33 (2): 345–369.

Glaser, Mark, and Janet Denhardt. 2010. "Community Policing and Community Building: A Case Study of Officer Perceptions." *American Review of Public Administration*, 40(3): 309–325.

Holmes, Malcolm, and Brad W. Smith. 2012. "Intergroup Dynamic of Extra-Legal Police Aggression: An Integrated Theory of Race and Place." *Aggression and Violent Behavior*, 17(4): 344–353.

Holmes, Malcolm D., Brad W. Smith, Adrienne B. Freng, and Ed A. Muñoz. 2008. "Minority Threat, Crime Control, and Police Resource Allocation in the Southwestern United States." *Crime and Delinquency*, 54(1): 128–152.

Katz, Walter. 2015. "Enhancing Accountability and Trust with Independent Investigators of Police Lethal Force." *Harvard Law Review*, 128(6): 235–245.

Martinez, R., J. I. Stowell, and M. T. Lee. 2010. "Immigration and Crime in an Era of Transformation: A Longitudinal Analysis of Homicides in San Diego Neighborhoods, 1980–2000." *Criminology*, 48(3): 797–829.

McCluskey, John D., Cynthia Perez McCluskey, and Roger Enriquez. 2008. "A Comparison of Latino and White Citizen Satisfaction with Police." *Journal of Criminal Justice*, 36(6): 471–477.

Messing, Jill Theresa, David Becerra, Allison Ward-Lasher, and David Androff, 2015. "Latinas' Perceptions of Law Enforcement Fear of Deportation, Crime Reporting, and Trust in the System." *Affilia*, 30(3): 328–340.

Mirandé, Alfredo. 1987. *Gringo Justice*. Notre Dame, IN: Notre Dame University Press.

Mirandé, Alfredo. 2013. "Light But Not White: A Race/Plus Model of Latina/o Subordination." *Seattle Journal for Social Justice*, 12(3): 947–982.

Reck, P. 2014. "The Influence of Community Characteristics on Police Officers' Approaches to Patrolling Latinos in Three Towns." *Race and Justice*. Available at: doi:10.1177/2153368714537524

Sampson, Robert J., and Stephen W. Raudenbush. 2004. "Seeing Disorder: Neighborhood Stigma and the Social Construction of 'Broken Windows.'" *Social Psychology Quarterly*, 67(4): 319–342.

Sandoval, Claudia. 2010. "Citizenship and the Barriers to Black and Latino Coalitions in Chicago." *NACLA Report on the Americas*, 43(6): 36–39.

Varsanyi, Monica W. 2008. "Immigration Policing through the Backdoor: City Ordinances, The 'Right to the City,' and the Exclusion of Undocumented Day Laborers." *Urban Geography*, 29(1): 29–52.

Yoxall, Peter. 2006. "The Minuteman Project, Gone in a Minute or Here to Stay? The Origin, History and Future of Citizen Activism on the United States–Mexico Border." *University of Miami Inter-American Law Review*, 37(3): 517–566.

Cases Cited

Brown v. Board of Education, 347 US 483 (1954).
Tennessee v. Garner 471 U.S. 1 (1975).

Chapter 4

Killing Ismael Mena
"The SWAT Teams Feared for Their Lives..."

Ernesto Vigil

Introduction

On September 30, 1999, the news media reported that Denver's SWAT had killed an unidentified man in a drug raid at 3738 High Street in Northeast Denver, vaguely claiming he shot at them or pointed a gun. Those who knew the neighborhood assumed he was Mexican or African American, but drug dealers of any color seldom have gunfights with police. When it was revealed that Ismael Mena, the victim, was an undocumented Mexican,[1] some thought public interest would fade and wondered what remained to be known.

Reporters generally rely on the police for the details when killings occur so the official story of Mena's death began with Detective Dave Neil's affidavit obtained for the second search warrant used in the raid. Neil, who wasn't present at the raid, claimed SWAT officers "moved towards a bedroom ... on the first floor" (it was actually on the second floor) when they "were *confronted* by a *suspect* ... kneeling [in a] three-point stance and pointing a pistol at the officers. The *threatened* officers began yelling 'police' and 'policia,' ordered him to lower his weapon," but Mena purportedly "refused [and] continued pointing [the gun] at the ... officers who *eventually* felt ... their lives and/or the lives of other occupants [or] officers were in danger and fired" (Ensslin and Gutierrez 1999). Although Neil described Mena as a *suspect* who *confronted* police with a *pistol* and was killed when they *eventually* felt their lives were in danger,[2] neither Neil's affidavit nor the DPD revealed that SWAT had raided the wrong house or that police never said he *fired* a gun until two months *after* they killed him, initially claiming he "brandished a gun, but have not commented on whether he fired at officers" (Kass 1999).

The following account of the shooting shows the roles of Denver's District Attorney, Manager of Safety, Police Chief, Internal Affairs Bureau, and to a lesser extent, the judiciary, when police kill people in questionable circumstances. The house where drugs were allegedly sold, a "crack-house," was in fact 3742 High Street, next to Mena's residence. In fact, it took an anonymous policeman to reveal that SWAT had raided the wrong house, a blunder hidden from the public for over two months. Two search warrants were used in the raid, the first a "no-knock" warrant for "immediate entry," but police needed a second warrant after realizing the first was faulty, though they never explained how they realized it.

Additionally, for Neil to ignore that a suspect's gun was fired was odd, especially in view of his own history. In 1977, Neil and other officers killed two men in a public park near a crowded swimming pool because one was wanted on assault charges and police said he tossed a gun to the other man as police approached, so they killed them both. Civilians, however, said the men were drunk and had passed out when police drove their cruisers onto the lawn near the men, got out with guns drawn while yelling at them not to move, then killed the startled men when they did. State law considered a .100 blood alcohol content (BAC) level as being intoxicated. One man had a .290 BAC and the other's was .140 *after* 13 blood transfusions. Neil, the only cop indicted in the incident was charged with manslaughter, but acquitted.[3]

SWAT Anatomy of a Murder

SWAT teams are special police units patterned after US counter-insurgency teams used in Vietnam. Three SWAT teams confronted Ismael Mena around 2 p.m. at 3738 High Street on September 29, 1999, after an informant reportedly made a $20 cocaine purchase *in the alley behind Mena's house* six days earlier. One team bashed in the front door and "cleared" the first floor, another "covered" the back door, as Captain Vincent Di Manna's team charged upstairs and killed Mena. No drugs were found. Di Manna's team included Lt. Anthony P. Iacovetta, Officers Ken A. Overman, Mark Haney, Thomas S. Lahey, Frank J. Vessa, Sr., and Jimmy J. Gose.[4]

When Di Manna's team found adjacent bedrooms with closed doors on a short, second-floor hallway, Haney and Gose tried to kick open Mena's door, claiming they yelled "Police! Policia!"[5] None of the highly-trained SWAT gunmen would say they *saw* or *knew* Mena shot at them, although Iacovetta was so close he said he considered grabbing Mena's gun. Instead, they killed Mena with an H&K M5 submachine gun and .45 Glock with hollow-points. The public didn't know these details, either, but some became suspicious after reading—two month later—that police were still "trying to determine whether [Mena] fired his handgun." Many critics doubted Mena had a gun and wondered how the police could not know whether he was armed. One victim's family was awarded a settlement in civil court (Guy 2000). No drugs were found.

In a letter to a conservative national news program, James Kearney, a former FBI agent, wrote that Overman, "armed with a fully automatic MP-5 sub-machinegun," was positioned "within five feet of the door and took careful aim," as Gose and Haney, "standing left of the door," each kicked Mena's door, "which immediately became ajar as the top door hinge broke … and the bottom hinge loosened," opening the door "a foot or two," but it "became hung-up on the carpet and [stood] in place partially tilted" (Kearney, email, November 15, 2002).

In videotaped statements later that day, Di Manna, Iacovetta, and Overman said Mena pointed a gun at them. Haney heard others yelling, "Drop the gun!" saw the gun in Mena's right hand and shot him, yet "couldn't tell if [Mena] was or was not firing" (Author's Notes). Overman, who said the hallway was "well lit," saw Mena raising his gun to eye level, so he shot him, yet didn't *know* if Mena fired, only *thought* he heard a shot, or *maybe* saw a flash of gunfire.

Since no drugs were found at the scene (or during Mena's autopsy), the lack of a definitive police statement raised questions among observers who knew the respective histories of Di Manna, Iacovetta, Haney, Lahey, and others as shown in news articles and court records. Observers also recognized the names of non-SWAT officers who "investigated" the killing at the scene and/or at headquarters: Capt. Marc Vasquez, Ken Chavez, Tim Leary, Dave Abrams, John Wycoff, Martin Vigil, and Jonathan Priest.[6]

The Informant and the Police Cover-Up

The only other civilian present during the raid was Antonio Hernandez, a tenant. When interviewed, Hernandez said he feared for his life, thinking the men who charged into his room dressed in black with ski masks were robbers. They never identified themselves. "I was ready to tell them, 'Take my television; take my watch. I got $100 in my wallet. Take that, too, just please let me live'" (Gutierrez 1999). Additionally, "Hernandez ... told Kearney that minutes after the initial burst of shots, he heard several more shots in the vicinity of Mena's bedroom, [but] did not give this information to police because he [feared] retaliation" (Herdy 2003).

In fact, Hernandez was the only one interviewed at all who wasn't a SWAT officer, because "at the time of the raid, *District 2 officers were told to steer clear of the area* [and] no non-SWAT witness interviewed recalled hearing shots, except for [Hernandez]." Additionally, the best record of what happened after gunfire erupted were SWAT's radio broadcasts which were tape recorded (and later disappeared).

Hernandez' account was unknown until December 18, 1999, and would have remained unknown except for an anonymous cop, who called Brian Maas, an investigative reporter at Channel 4, a CBS affiliate. The caller, who seemed troubled and may have been drinking, urged Maas to investigate a recent police shooting, but would give no details. Maas inquired, but DPDHQ revealed nothing until the whistle-blower gave details in a second call, allowing Maas to report on November 29, 1999, that SWAT had raided the wrong house. Interestingly, the day after Maas' revelations, police only claimed Mena "brandished a gun, but have not commented on whether he fired at officers" (Kass 1999). Additionally, the Denver District Attorney's office knew "there are questions surrounding ... the warrant and [whether it] was accurate," but nothing showed the DA did anything to investigate the killing until Maas' revelations.

In fact, journalists were told "some police commanders [who weren't named] wanted to treat any problems … as 'training issues' and not open them up to investigation." When questioned why police found no drugs at Mena's residence, DPD spokesperson Mary Thomas replied that drug raids sometimes failed to find them. In contrast, Mena's neighbors told reporters that people at the raided house often sold "corn on the cob, strawberries, popsicles, and Spanish-language cassettes. [Neighbors] remembered Mena and other residents often worked in the evening doing cleaning and maintenance jobs. 'I thought there were very humble people,'" said one neighbor (Ensslin and Gutierrez 1999).

Another article reported that "[Officer] Joseph Bini stated that a previously reliable informer using a marked $20 bill purchased a rock of cocaine from two men at the house," and officials assured journalists that "as a result of the shooting, police … added an extra step of having a supervisor check warrants," which was meaningless. After all, when police shot an innocent woman in her home in 1981, 16 years previously, city attorney Chuck Lepley instructed police to "*independently corroborate* confidential informers' information *especially if they are planning a no-knock raid*" (Flynn 2000; Flynn and Kilzer 2000) and the lead detective in that raid was also involved in the Mena raid (as was Lepley), but the detective blamed his informant for the blunder. And the DA prosecuted the informant.

When interviewed in December 1999, Capt. Di Manna said SWAT was concerned about allegations that they *might have* raided the wrong house, saying, "We do everything we can to protect the officers and the innocent" (Ensslin and Gutierrez 1999), but didn't say they all knew they went to the wrong house shortly after killing Mena. Similarly, and despite official comments from September 1999 to January 2000, Chief Tom Sanchez, the first minority police chief in Denver's history, knew his boys had raided the wrong house the day it happened.

Lastly, when it was known that SWAT had raided the wrong house, the Denver District Attorney transferred whatever investigation existed of Mena's death to District Attorney Dave Thomas's office west of Denver in Jefferson County. The Denver DA, after all, wanted to avoid the appearance of a conflict of interest since Mark Haney shot Ismael Mena in the neck, killing him, and Haney's brother was an investigator for the Denver DA. However, the Denver DA failed to mention Dave Thomas previously worked for the Denver DA's office.

Public Outrage over "No-Knock" Search Warrants

The unique circumstances of Mena's killing, especially the whistle-blower's revelations, moved journalists to closely examine the case, including some angles that had been neglected all along. No-knock search warrants, for example, had no authority under federal law in the twentieth century until the GOP seized power in Congress and the White House with Ronald

Reagan's and George H. W. Bush's election in 1980. Such raids were thereafter given legal authority by Congress and Supreme Court conservatives appointed by Richard Nixon and Reagan, whose law-and-order administrations were tainted by scandal and corruption, the historical context absent from most reporting.

US Marines trained America's first SWAT teams at Camp Pendleton for LAPD in 1967, shortly before Nixon's 1968 election. Like Robo-cops, SWAT teams were supposed to handle the crimes that were beyond the ability of normal police officers and protect the public with military efficiency (and military weapons) against violent kidnappers, hostage-takers, snipers, terrorists, and barricaded evil-doers in the "wars" on crime, gangs, drugs, terrorism, or other pseudo-wars of convenience.[7] At the time of Mena's death, SWAT teams conducted over 80 percent of no-knock raids nationwide, mostly arresting minor drug dealers and users.

The *Denver Post* found that judges granted 97 percent of all local no-knock warrants, but experts said this "approval rate is too high and indicative of a blanket-approval process, which is unconstitutional" (Migoya 2000b), so the front-page headline bluntly stated: "Judges rubber-stamp no-knocks." David Lane, a prominent attorney, said "judges are generally rubber stamps for the police in signing warrants [and] this is certainly a Fourth Amendment violation ... an unreasonable search" (Migoya 2000c). Further, "nearly all no-knock warrant requests ... were approved merely on ... assertions that a regular search warrant could be dangerous for [police] or that the drugs they were seeking could be destroyed" (Migoya 2000b). The *Denver Post*, however, found 19 search warrant applications that lacked the criteria to grant them, yet judges approved them anyway.

According to George Mannerbino, a former presiding judge, "It certainly raises questions of whether judges are paying enough attention, not just to the facts, but what the police are asking in the first place" (Migoya 2000c). Police routinely claimed they needed these warrants because they believed weapons were present, but none were found in 81 percent of the raids, and "nearly a third of the warrants were ... never reviewed by an assistant district attorney" (ibid.), although Chief Sanchez claimed police policy involved a prosecutor's review of each warrant.

The racial and class disparities in Ismael Mena's killing also manifested the sexism of Denver's police culture as will be shown in another related allegation, and it should be noted that these disparities persisted in a decade when Denver had its first Mexican and African American mayors, Federico Pena and Wellington Webb, respectively. In fact, Mayor Webb appointed Tom Sanchez as Denver's police chief and Fidel "Butch" Montoya as Manager of Safety, the first "Hispanics" in those positions.[8] Montoya, Sanchez' nominal superior, would be paid $106,000 yearly and had been a TV cameraman and news director, presumably with his media skills at the mayor's service. If so, he failed badly, as did Sanchez.

By the time Brian Maas revealed SWAT had raided the wrong house, Chief Sanchez had transferred the Mena matter to the Internal Affairs Bureau (IAB) where internal complaints and civilian complaints about officers are handled. "We don't publicize internal affair cases" (Vaughan 2000b), Sanchez explained with an attitude reflecting institutional arrogance. "What if we publicized it and the allegations turn out to be false? You've probably done some major damage to somebody's career and you can't put toothpaste back in the tube" (ibid.). Institutional arrogance, however, has consequences.

At the height of the Mena controversy, a federal judge sent US Marshals to seize IAB records after the IAB failed to obey his order to provide them to attorneys for an African American man police beat unconscious after a traffic accident. One of the victim's attorneys, for example, waited two hours for a room to view IAB files although an empty room was in sight and then found 60 of 100 files to be reviewed were missing (McPhee 2000; Prendergast 2000). The IAB also printed copies of some documents in ways that obliterated a "significant portion of the contents," pages that were "crucial to the [victim's] case claiming that Denver police conspire to cover up brutality." Chief Sanchez and the head of the IAB, Kirk Hohn, were among those "accused of conspiring to cover up the assault" (*Denver Post* 2000b) when

> [the] incensed federal judge ordered US Marshals to confiscate volumes of [IAB] files ... fined the city and its attorneys [Halaby,[9] Cross, and Schluter] $10,000 for interfering with court orders," telling them, "Your arrogance is exceeded only by your petulance."

The city of Denver settled the case for $160,000 a few days later.

The growing public outrage led Mayor Webb to dismiss Chief Sanchez in February 2000 after Sanchez and various command officers, along with their wives, were filmed boarding a flight to Hawaii to spend *several* days at a *three-day* conference. Webb phoned Sanchez who immediately returned to Denver and was soon demoted. Later, in June 2000, Mayor Webb would appoint another Manager of Safety after demoting Montoya over earlier and subsequent revelations, one being that Montoya personally influenced the admission to the Police Academy of a candidate who had been rejected by 19 police departments, including the DPD. Journalists reported Webb would have supported Montoya's election as mayor after Webb left office, but Montoya's career apparently died with Ismael Mena.

Meanwhile, Patrolman Joe Bini was suspended on February 4, 2000, and later charged with forgery for false claims in his search warrant's affidavit that "he received information that 3738 High Street ... was a crack house, that he saw [his] informer go to the house ... with a suspect, [and] a drug buy happened at the house" (Migoya 2000a),[10] none of which happened. Few noticed, additionally, that Capt. Vasquez and Capt. Di Manna were transferred to headquarters, i.e., away from reporters, after a subordinate lodged a serious complaint against Vasquez before Sanchez's demotion. Activists later learned that Di Manna was put in charge of the DPD Intelligence Bureau (DPDIB) and Vasquez now handled various police projects, e.g., the Professional Standards Bureau, and also devised policy.

In early February 2000, Jefferson County DA Dave Thomas made claims he knew were not true, using the article on Bini's suspension to do so. Thomas blamed Mena and Bini's informer for Mena's death by mistaking "which home was a supposed crack house" (Migoya 2000a), asserting Mena "wouldn't have been in *a gunfight*" with police if the informer had given the right address, using the word "gunfight," a word even SWAT didn't use, as if proclaiming a "gunfight" occurred in order to exonerate SWAT. After saying the informer "miscounted the houses and remembered it wrong," ignoring that no raid would have happened without Bini's falsified affidavit, Thomas then said, the "officers were justified in gunning down Mena ... because he pointed and fired a ... handgun at police [and] may have had the gun to protect the drug dealing ... next door" (Migoya 2000a).

Had he been asked, Thomas could not have justified his claim that Mena had a gun to protect the "drug dealing next door," because no evidence from police, informers, or Bini's affidavit linked Mena to his neighbors, as was well known by Thomas. Additionally, when SWAT raided the crack house *behind* which their informer bought cocaine in September 1999, they did so two months after killing Mena, arresting an African American man and a boy in a raid prompted by an anonymous call that "individuals as young as 11 and 12 [were] selling crack at 3742 High Street [and] handguns were in the crawl space."[11] According to this search warrant's affidavit, "The caller also said people at the home 'would go to war with the police.'"

When Denver DA Bill Ritter was questioned about the wisdom of raiding a house when children were present, he replied:

> [This] isn't about a 12-year-old. There may be information ... that weapons are in the house or ... the evidence ... is easily destructible. The people who suffer ... are ... in their community. Their quality of life is very much affected.

Ritter's concern for the quality of life in a neighborhood where he didn't live ignored the fact that the quality of Mena's life ended when SWAT killed him in that community, something about which Ritter did nothing. He also did not mention Alfredo Gonzales who owned the home where Mena was killed, his tenants who were afraid to return, or the $25,000 dollars in damages incurred after police ransacked his house looking for drugs (or a gun?) to justify the raid (Gutierrez 2000).

Ritter, moreover, never mentioned Minnie Clark, a 71-year-old African American woman whose home was ransacked by the SWAT team hours before they killed Mena. "[The SWAT team has] been here six times," said Mrs. Clarke. "They said somebody snitched, but they ain't found no drugs" (Flynn and Kilzer 2000). Bini was pressuring Mrs. Clarke's daughter to become an informer ("or I'll take your momma to jail") (Migoya 2000b),[12] and although it's unclear if his informer was used in both raids, both warrants had "*identical wording* [and] were written *six days before* the twin raids [when] Judge Raymond Satter," an African American, "signed both warrants at … 12:35 p.m., Sept. 23."

On January 29, 2000, two months after the police confessed to raiding the wrong house, Susan Scott, an African American officer, revealed that she "was pressured by superiors to fabricate evidence" with a police computer "to make it appear … there was a history of trouble … where a man was killed in a 'no-knock raid'" (Vaughan 2000a). Scott had 20 years of police experience, was "well-respected among her peers," and complained that "supervising officers" wanted her "to make it look as if there had been a history of complaints about … 3738 High Street where Mena was living." Her supervisors, although the article didn't name them, were Michael Quiñones and Capt. Marc Vasquez, in whose district Mena was killed.

An official with the local National Association for the Advancement of Colored People chapter praised Scott, saying it would be easier for her to do what she was asked [by Capt. Vasquez] than stand up and file a report with [the] Internal Affairs [Bureau]."

> [Scott's] charges triggered shock inside the police department and criticism outside it. Detective Manny (Manuel) Alvarez said he "felt sick after hearing the allegations … You think about something like that happening in New York or Los Angeles [but] you don't think about something like that happening at home."
>
> (Vaughan 2000a)

Chief Sanchez promised a vigorous investigation after Scott's allegation was publicized and quickly dumped the problem in DA Dave Thomas' lap for disposal. Thomas, in turn, exonerated the SWAT team in February 2000 for killing Mena, no charges were filed against Capt. Vasquez, and activists viewed Bini as the DPD's sacrificial lamb. Nevertheless, Detective Alvarez's criticism provides a rare example of a Mexican detective publicly criticizing a high-ranking Hispanic[13] for pressuring an African American woman to fabricate evidence for White men who killed a Mexican while raiding the wrong address.[14]

The Justice for Mena Committee ("JMC")

In December 1999, Ben and Elsie Mecillas, relatives of Ismael Mena in Denver, contacted LeRoy Lemos, a former student activist working at a non-profit agency. Lemos, along with Cynthia Gallegos, the Mecillas couple, and others, formed the Justice for Mena Committee (JMC). On February 23, 2000, police threatened to arrest JMC activists leafleting in downtown Denver after a security guard claimed skyscraper tenants complained about noise from the JMC bullhorn. When a reporter later asked Det. Mary Thomas if threatening arrests violated protester's First Amendment rights, she replied, "If there's a complaint, the First Amendment doesn't apply,"[15] prompting one editorial to denounce the arrest threat as "outrageous conduct" for which the "police owe an apology" to the protesters.

On March 17, 2000, after meeting with Manager of Safety Montoya, the JMC criticized city officials, lambasting DA Thomas for absolving police for killing Mena. The JMC declared "DA Thomas' farce was used to justify further inaction [by] Denver officials" and described no-knock warrants and SWAT raids as needless "police state methodology" that only resulted "in 3 felony convictions in over 140 'no-knock' raids" in operations that were a "recipe for disaster."[16] The JMC also declared that

> the culture of violence ... in the police ranks infects officers of color as well. Certain Black and Brown officers are among the most brutal and an honest investigation ... leading to [their] punishment ... is obviously needed.[17]

The JMC then distributed leaflets critical of Capt. Vasquez and Capt. Di Manna, noting that in 1974, Di Manna and his partner Tim Leary were removed from District 2 after Truman Cole, an African American attorney, sought their transfer over their "violence and brutality" (Rocky Mountain News 1974a). Cole addressed four traffic stops from "January to May 1974" involving "Di Manna ... and 7 [African American] civilians, including 3 women. Old newspaper articles record the results: 4 beatings, 3 hospitalizations, and ... racist name-calling: 'black bitch,' 'whore,' 'niggers,' 'nigger-loving bitch,' and 'black son of a bitch.'" DPD Chief Art Dill, indeed, transferred Di Manna and Leary for "their own protection," as well as the community's, after they beat up Nathaniel Bailey.[18]

> Bailey claims Di Manna called [Bailey's white girlfriend] a "nigger-loving bitch" and made several ... racial slurs, [but] Bailey concedes, "the cop got so abusive I spoke up and said, 'Man, if you're going to arrest us, just take us to the station and leave us alone.'" In response, Bailey [said], Di Manna turned, called him a "black son of a bitch" and hit him on the forehead with a nightstick.

Di Manna's conduct with non-Whites, interestingly, differed from his conduct in White suburbia in the April 1999 Columbine High School massacre five months before Mena was killed. Two students, Eric Harris and Dylan Klebold, killed several students before committing suicide ending a 40-minute shooting spree. Di Manna and George Gray, another SWAT cop in the Mena raid, were among 1,000 officers at Columbine, including 120–150 SWAT officers "from 10 local and federal agencies [who] entered the school in two groups,"[19] and Di Manna, "parent of a Columbine student," was among "the first officers to enter," but "declined to comment."

Harris and Klebold shot at police from inside the school shortly after noon, then committed suicide minutes later. Di Manna and others entered the school, but one hour later. Police, because they proceeded slowly, found wounded teacher Dave Sanders three hours after the shooting ended. He lingered a few minutes, then died. Ironically, the excuse Di Manna, SWAT, and the others had for killing Mena was the same one for entering Columbine too late to save Dave Sanders – the officers feared for their lives.

The JMC leaflet on Capt. Vasquez was more detailed, but merely captioned, "Who Is Captain Marc Vasquez?"

Captain Vasquez commanded District 2 where unarmed Ismael Mena was killed in a drug raid at the wrong house. [Vasquez] urged Officer Sue Scott to falsify records to portray Mena's residence as a target of community complaints. The DA decided not to prosecute Vasquez for obstruction of justice [but he] will now be investigated by the ... Internal Affairs Bureau [although he] is married to another ... cop [assigned to the] Internal Affairs [Bureau].[20]

The leaflet also noted Vasquez' role in a 1981 no-knock raid

when a snitch said a drug dealer lived on 9th and Irving. Police raided Juan and Leilani Lucero's home ... Mrs. Lucero was wounded when Detective Vasquez and Officer Ken Chavez fired their weapons. It was natural for Captain Vasquez to cover up for the cops who killed Mena. [Vasquez] had a lot of practice [with cover-ups].[21]

Police, led by Vasquez and Ken Chavez,[22] shot their way into a home from where the suspect moved two years earlier, shooting Ms. Lucero when her husband fired once at the men in civilian clothes who broke into their home at night with guns, firing at least 15 times at the couple. Vasquez' informant was indicted for giving "false information to a police officer," (Hulse 1981), but the DA "declined to file criminal charges against the officers [because they] acted within the law."

The leaflet also noted that Vasquez and Officer Robert Silvas, his brother-in-law, killed Joey Rodriguez, 16, in 1979 after they saw Rodriguez and Richard Sandoval sniffing paint and pursued them.

[Silvas chased] Rodriguez into Mary Rojas' apartment and killed him. Ms. Rojas saw the body, [but] saw no gun [on or near] Rodriguez. [Witnesses] saw Richard Sandoval drop a gun when Vasquez chased him [and] Sandoval confessed to having the gun. A woman admitted loaning [it] to Sandoval [but the officers] said Joey Rodriguez ... had the gun.[23]

The JMC's educational leafleting ended after Ismael Mena's family accepted a $400,000 settlement from Denver in late March 2000. Stephen Nash, a JMC supporter, issued a statement on March 24, 2000, declaring, "The ... settlement [is] the highest amount ever paid by the city over a wrongful death ... by the police," but this "in no way diminishes the deep-set problems [in] the Denver Police Department, the District Attorney's office, or the administration."[24] Despite the settlement, the JMC organized a June 6, 2000, rally at the location where Mena was killed.

"Settled but Not Solved": Aftermath of the Shooting

Despite the settlement of the case, a leaflet announcing the rally declared that "police allowed [the] loss of vital physical evidence," referred to "new evidence of police wrongdoing," declared there was "new info on the .22 [revolver] Mena is alleged to have fired," and revealed that "Mena's body was moved after his death." The turnout was small because the case was settled, although not *solved*. For example, the tapes of SWAT's radio transmissions during the raid had somehow disappeared, but the media ignored these details, and when they were published in 2003, it was too late to make a difference. And as was eventually reported, "No fingerprints were found on the revolver police say they took from Mena's hand nor on the ammunition [although District Attorney] Thomas said he still believes the shooting [was] justified. *The officers were in fear for their lives*, he said, and protected as such by Colorado law" (Herdy 2003).

It should be noted that Burgo revolvers like the one Mena allegedly fired are made with cheap metal alloy and are known for their poor quality. With time, the cylinders and barrels often misaligned, ejecting residue and lead fragments sideways when fired, dangerous to bystanders and those firing them.[25]

According to a laboratory report, gunshot residue found on Mena's hand did not match the .22-calibre Burgo police say he fired. Rather, one Denver homicide lieutenant said in a sworn statement [that] *the residue was consistent with a submachine gun used ... to shoot Mena.* [Jefferson County DA] Thomas said he was unaware of the lab test results when he released his findings.

(ibid.)

The residue on Mena's hand indicates he was shot while trying to hold his bedroom door shut as Overman and Haney shot through the wall, door, and open gaps because the door was partly off its hinges.[26] Haney fired twice, missed once, but his other .45 hollow-point severed Mena's carotid artery. According to James Kearney, the "shots by Overman were easily discernible in a five-shot pattern stretching horizontally, starting in the left palm of [Mena's] left hand, to the left side of his cheek, and ending in the victim's right arm,"[27] breaking bones in Mena's left hand and wrist and his right arm.

Haney's work was also "easily discernible ... one fatal shot to the right side of the victim's neck," and "the sequence ... placed the victim slumping to the floor [after] Haney fired." But how could Mena sustain an attack by the SWAT team after falling to the floor when his carotid artery was cut? In fact, Mena's ferocity puzzled Overman years later. "I'd say he was definitely injured," Overman noted, "He probably had sustained enough injuries to be fatal, but *he just wouldn't stop moving*, I mean he wouldn't stop his aggressive actions toward us" (ibid.).

On the other hand, DPD documents held by the Denver and Jefferson County District Attorneys on the fearsome .22 Burgo showed it had a "crane retaining screw [that] is missing; thus the cylinder will not stay in the frame of the firearm when the cylinder pin is freed. The firearm, cartridges, and casings were fingerprinted with negative results."

Additionally,

> Steve Evans, an investigator working for [District Attorney] Thomas ... concluded from physical evidence at the scene that Mena's body was moved at least 18 inches immediately after the shooting [and] must have been moved by SWAT members, he said in a deposition ... after Thomas' findings were released ... In [their] depositions, SWAT team members all swore they did not move the body.

Unfortunately, the examination of physical evidence halted with the 2000 settlement of Mena's case, possibly saving SWAT members from indictments for perjury and fabricating evidence, but leaving key questions unanswered. Overman, for example, said Mena fell when he shot him, as was apparent by the large pool of blood at the foot of the door. Further from the door, i.e., where SWAT moved Mena's body, was a second—but far smaller—blood stain *under Mena's back* where two bullet slugs were recovered. Additionally,

> An autopsy [showed] two [of Overman's] bullets ... were not fired at an upward angle. In a videotaped statement [Overman] said he was lying on a staircase outside Mena's bedroom [when] shooting [but] months later [said] he stood up during the final shots, but [Capt. Di Manna] said he stepped over a prone Overman after the shooting stopped.

Although Overman said Mena fell after being shot, he "then tried to get up with gun in hand,"[28] so Overman shot him again. Mena again fell back, but again tried to rise, so Overman blasted him yet again, and then—because Mena's body was still "fidgeting" after Overman entered the room—he stepped on Mena's right hand, which held the gun. But why were no fingerprints found on the gun and why did the last bullets enter Mena's body at a different angle than the first? In James Kearney's opinion, "Officer Overman fired [these] two rounds at close range into Mena's chest, unlike his other five rounds, [and] would travel through Mena's body leaving a clear shot pattern to the carpet padding and flooring which were devoid of blood" (Kearney, email, November 15, 2002).

Had the public seen Chuck Lepley and others interview SWAT members at DPDHQ hours after they killed Mena, they would know Di Manna physically demonstrated *twice* how Mena held a gun in both hands. Iacovetta, however, said Mena held it *one hand*, the right hand, no, maybe the left, he wasn't sure, but he saw enough to scream, "He's gotta gun, he gotta gun! He has the gun cocked, he has the gun cocked!" (ibid.). Although Iacovetta *thought* Mena fired, he didn't see it, and only spoke of *one* shot by Mena. When questioned on this, Iacovetta seemed puzzled by Lepley's helpful question, so just replied he *thought* Mena "fired *one* round," i.e., not *three*.

If one anonymous cop had not called Bryan Maas, the DPDHQ would have had its way and the inconvenient facts herein would have remained unknown, except to those who killed Mena. But thanks to that cop and Maas, Denver's Mexican consulate retained attorney Robert Maes who on December 30, 1999, sent private investigator James Kearney, a retired-FBI agent with 25 years experience (20 of them in New York) to the crime scene where Mena was slain.

A few days later, Kearney met with DA Dave Thomas and Denver FBI Agent Robert Espinoza. As an article belatedly reported two years later, Kearney "recovered two spent slugs … found by Mena's landlord after police cleared the scene," slugs that "had been embedded in the carpet padding," slugs that SWAT's depositions "could not explain" (Herdy 2003). Kearney turned them over to DA Thomas and Agent Espinoza, along with "photographs of the carpet-padding showing bullet holes" and "the underlying linoleum showing bullet marks."

As described by Kearney, "A blood pattern [was] found on the carpet padding and flooring where the victim first lay bleeding profusely, but not on the other carpet padding and flooring to where [Mena] had been moved" (Kearney, email, November 15, 2002). specifying elsewhere that

> Overman's final two shots … entered Mena's chest a few inches apart [which] traveled through his body [and] created … two bullet holes approximately 2 inches apart … straight into the carpet padding and …

into the linoleum beneath the carpet padding [which] aligned perfectly with the two bullet holes fired *vertically* into Mena's chest.[29]

Kearney, in outrage, and against attorney Maes' direction, openly charged the police with a cover-up, and the two did not work together thereafter.

It should be noted that not all police were complicit in the cover-up and that many rank-and-file cops were unhappy with the DPD hierarchy and, in 2004, one anonymous officer asked the rank-and-file for a vote of no confidence in their command, writing:

> This is an extreme measure that has been effective in the past … It is widely known that several command officers who have stars on their collars have been involved in very questionable shootings [and] have retained their careers due to cover-ups … [A no confidence vote is one] of the methods [for] officers to express their grievances to Chief Gerald Whitman.[30]

The anonymous cop, ignoring his duty to enforce the law, didn't want the "widely known" commanders punished although they committed felonies if his charges were true, but was only angry because he felt they were pandering to civilians demanding reforms and accountability (Gutierrez 2004). Additionally, by 2004, the DPD was being sued over revelations in 2002 that the DPD Intelligence Bureau (DPDIB) had conducted a *massive, prolonged,* and *unauthorized* domestic spying campaign since the 1950s and JMC members learned in 2002 that the DPDIB used informants to spy on them.

> Captain Marc Vasquez … received information [that Ernesto] Vigil was an associate of LeRoy Lemos with the JUSTICE FOR MENA COMMITTEE and [Capt. Vasquez] needed to be careful. The [informer] indicated [Lemos and] Vigil were capable of anything … [On January 3, 2000] Vigil along with Chief Gerald Whitman and District Attorney Bill Ritter attended a public forum … on Channel 12. Ernesto Vigil indicated he was [with] the [JMC] and was going to hold the police department accountable.[31]

Postscript: Police Policing Themselves

Ismael Mena's death is not simply a tale about bad people doing bad things without being punished, although this was a big part of the formula. Joe Bini, for example, pled guilty to a misdemeanor over his falsified affidavit, was only suspended a few months without pay, then left the DPD. He was later arrested for sex offenses involving homeless adolescent females and is now a registered sex offender (Pankratz 2008; Shikes 2008). Mena, however, wasn't killed because Bini was a sexual predator, but because there is no effective way to protect civilians from police abuse and/or punish guilty officers.

Police abuse is not a new phenomenon, locally or nationally, and the police use of deadly force has been exhaustively researched, but one study of the police use of deadly force in five Latino communities found 12 characteristics in such incidents,[32] and five are found in Mena's case: (1) killings in situations where police should not have been present anyway; (2) killings, or beatings, by an officer[s] with a long-standing reputation[s] for using excessive force; (3) killings involving a controversial unit or precinct; (4) killings in which police showed an utter disregard for others' safety; and (5) killings manifesting an enormous overkill. History, however, gives the context for understanding why such killings persist.

The Denver Public Library maintains a large file card index where newspaper articles on the police are indexed as far back as the late 1800s. Some cards refer to grand jury investigations of the department in the 1940s and 1950s, but the articles are seldom incisive. The DPD's problems, however, led to some reforms, one reform being the establishment of the Internal Affairs Bureau (IAB),[33] but unfortunately one staffed entirely by police to the frustration of the public that has complained of abuses for decades.

In 1955, the year attorney William Geer became Manager of Safety, Capt. Tom Branch wrote to Mayor Bill Nicholson complaining about loose discipline in the DPD, the details of which are unknown. The Mayor gave Branch's letter to the Manager of Safety who gave it to Chief Walter Johnson who quickly suspended Branch. As Branch recalled,

> My phone was tapped and I had to use a public phone four blocks away or a neighbor's phone to call Joe [his attorney]. At one time we were fearful that Joe's phone was also tapped. Officers who called me or stopped by were plainly told not to do it again – or else.
>
> (Vigil 1999, 12–13)

Branch was sent to walk a beat in Five Points, an African American and Mexican neighborhood, saying, "The idea was that exertion or perhaps a physical attack would kill me [before] they finally gave up on that plot and reassigned me" (ibid., 12–13).

Manager of Safety Geer created the Internal Affairs Bureau in July 1958 after his California visit with LAPD Chief William Parker (ibid., 12–13),[34] who inspired Geer's structural "reform," an IAB in which only policemen investigate police abuses. The problems in the lower ranks of authoritarian structures, however, imperil the careers of those in the supervisory ranks, as Capt. Branch demonstrates. The IAB was never independent of the chief and initially was only to investigate cases he—and only he—assigned them, and while authoritarian structures concentrate at the top, all ranks will circle their wagons when their careers are at stake, but the culture of denial has consequences.

In 1960, two years *after* the IAB's creation, the DPD garnered national headlines over a scandal the IAB apparently never detected, much less prevented, a massive police burglary ring. In a force of slightly over 700 officers, more than 100 men were implicated (14 percent), 53 were suspended, confessed, or found guilty, a dozen more "resigned," and others entered no contest pleas, were disciplined in administrative hearings, or were immune because statutes of limitations expired (ibid., 11–13). Of the 30 who were found guilty or confessed, the highest ranking was a sergeant, suggesting the command staff was oblivious, complicit, or lucky.

The reality is that police bureaucracies expand and police chiefs accept credit for their underlings' successes, but generally dodge responsibility for their failures, so bad policies and self-serving bureaucratic practices become institutionalized as chiefs, managers of safety, and mayors move on. In fact, DPD's history of denial and its growing political power allowed both to remain in place to fail again when Ismael Mena was killed.

Police departments are not democracies, but authoritarian paramilitary organizations that can threaten civil liberties and public safety when lacking strict *departmental* supervision under *civilian* control, responsibilities frequently undermined by the cronyism of urban politics. Indeed, these reforms have been demanded, and undermined, for decades. Columnist Tom Gavin, for example, wrote about the voters' anger with Tom Currigan, a Democrat voted into office after promising to create a civilian review board to investigate complaints against police in 1964.

> In fairness to both the officer and the citizen involved in such a complaint, it would seem that a body completely separated from the police department could receive and hear grievances with greater detachment than a unit of the police force. I would strongly urge the creation of such a board in Denver and feel that it would not only protect the policeman from unfair charges, but give the public an opportunity to present grievances against improper police action. [Mayor Tom Currigan's] promises to the ... groups involved have not been kept and these people are justifiably angry.[35]

However, once elected, Currigan immediately reneged on the promise.

Effective civilian oversight of the police requires the power to issue subpoenas for testimony and DPD files on officers accused of abuse, a power that immediately outrages police, their unions, attorneys, and socially conservative supporters. In November 1978, for example, Denver police allies, calling themselves the Committee for Professional Law Enforcement, helped raise $55,000 to defeat Charter Amendment A, which called for a review board patterned after the Los Angeles Police Commission. Three police groups raised money as well: the Police Protective Association (PPA), the Police Union, and the Police Brotherhood (the PPA alone raised

$30,000).[36] Supporters of Amendment A only raised $3,000 and lost by a two-to-one margin and the DPD has remained a power in city elections.

Unfortunately, the legacy of the DPD's refusal to go beyond cosmetic "reforms" saddled the department with flawed policies, half-baked bureaucratic dodges, and the recycling of flawed personnel from its ranks, including those who climbed into leadership positions and were given undeserved power. If police killings are to be seen as more than tales of bad men (or women) doing bad things without punishment, the confluence of flawed people, bad policies, and authoritarian structures needs to be examined.

After Brian Maas' revelations in late 1999, Capt. Marc Vasquez was transferred to DPDHQ by Chief Sanchez in 2000, then worked for Chief Gerry Whitman on various police programs and policy matters after Sanchez was demoted. By September 2000, Vasquez' responsibilities included collecting "policies and procedures from around DPD"[37] to devise the policy governing the DPD Intelligence Bureau's new computer system. When this task remained incomplete in 2001, Vasquez called upon Capt. Di Manna, who was in charge of the Intelligence Bureau, to join Vasquez' "Project Team" and devise the intelligence-gathering policy.[38]

The policy, however, remained incomplete when Vasquez took charge of the Internal Affairs Bureau and Civil Liabilities Bureau in 2002, before his appointment by Whitman to Commander in 2003, a new rank directly under the chief and the most powerful rank except for the chief. Unfortunately, but not surprisingly, no one could find any intelligence-gathering policy when the DPD's political surveillance scandal erupted in February 2002. As far as DPDHQ could show, there had been no policy for years, but having no policy didn't mean the DPD's command staff didn't exercise their authority. Here again, Vasquez' example serves to show the consequences of having authority without a policy or strict guidance when he implemented policy in the field as District 2's captain.

According to TV reporter Julie Hayden in a February 2000 meeting with the author and Gene Cisneros,[39] District 2 officers were angry with Vasquez for ordering them to recruit informers so his district could tally more drugs raids than other districts because Vasquez wanted a promotion to Commander, a new rank in the hierarchy. Officers worried that they were untrained for the task and feared something would go wrong, and it did, so while Ismael Mena's death is more than a tale of bad people doing bad things without punishment, it is clear that many people involved in killing him escaped its consequences.

It should also be noted that the year after the case was settled, *Denver Post* reporter Bruce Finley wrote a February 14, 2001, article captioned, "Widow: Mena killed a man," reporting that Ismael Mena killed a young man five years previously in a family clash with relatives of a youth who impregnated his 16-year-old daughter. Police knew of the killing, Mena left Mexico as a consequence, as Mena's widow confirmed, but Mexican police took no action to arrest him on the occasions he returned to see his family. The reason for their inaction was unknown to Finley's sources, so that question remains.

It is conceivable, however, that Denver's new police chief, Paul Pazen, might contact his counterpart in Jalisco to ask questions, but it might be awkward if he is questioned in return. Pazen, after all, was in one of the SWAT teams that raided Mena's home and might be asked what he *heard, saw, and did after he heard 15 shots erupt* in Mena's second-floor bedroom.

The manner of Mena's death deserves full disclosure, and the fact that an anonymous cop had to reveal that SWAT raided the wrong address should prove that point, and the fact that he never identified himself shows the department's power to hide the truth, silence critics, or ignore their criticism, as shown with Susan Scott's charge of being urged to fabricate evidence. The mechanisms in place to report, review, and punish police misconduct—and to protect the public—are ineffective and show the functional bankruptcy of the mechanisms now in place. Ismael Mena's life was taken by men in an institution that doesn't admit it is wrong and therefore cannot change, but society has never treated all classes of people equally. The underlying economic system creates the disparities of which police abuse is one evil among many, and the communities most affected by police abuse will remain abused until they are as organized as the police, and free of illusions that politics serve them in the same way they serve the powerful.[40]

Notes

1 See Hector Gutierrez (2000a) who notes that police killed Miguel Angel Ochoa, saying he was shot in the chest while reaching for a gun. The coroner's report showed Ochoa was shot in the back; the city of Denver paid a $35,000 settlement.

2 Court rulings acquit police in controversial killings if officers encounter people who made them "fear for their lives." Government attorneys and/or private law firms lecture at police and sheriffs' academies explaining the law allows officers to kill someone if at the moment they shoot they "fear for their life," but often fail to mention that the fear must be reasonable or justifiable.

3 One victim's family was awarded a settlement in civil court (Vigil 1999, 341–342). See also Steve Garnass (1985).

4 Other SWAT members included Paul M. Pazen, George A. Gray, Kenneth Padget, Steven W. Panck, James R. Smith, Douglas Braden, and Jesus Quinones, i.e., numerous White cops and one Hispanic.

5 Author's Notes of March 13, 2000, Jefferson County District Attorney's office, hereafter "Author's Notes." I reviewed SWAT members' September 29, 1999, statements videotaped at Denver Police Department headquarters. Quotes are from statements by Di Manna, Overman, Haney, Iacovetta, Vessa, and Gose as I viewed them with Gene Cisneros, an interpreter for Robert (Bob) Maes, the Mena family's attorney.

6   SWAT officers' names are taken from a civil suit against them by James Kearney, a former FBI agent who worked as a private investigator on the Mena case.

7   See Haberman (2014) and Kraska (2001). The LA SWAT team's first highly-publicized incident was an attack on the Los Angeles Black Panther's headquarters on December 8, 1969, who used informants and provocateurs to target the LA Black Panther chapter as part of the FBI's Black Nationalist-Hate Group Counter-intelligence Program.

8   Denver's Manager of Safety, an appointed position that oversees the police and fire departments, is the nominal superior to the police and fire chiefs.

9   Ted Halaby was Dave Neil's defense attorney in the 1977 death of Artie Espinoza.

10 Bini's phrasing indicates police used boiler-plate affidavits and judges were as negligent as the DPD in performing their duty. Bini remained free on a personal recognizance bond on a felony charge with a potential maximum sentence of six years in prison. Few civilians receive such leniency.

11 For additional details of both SWAT raids, see Alan Prendergast (2000). The article starts on page 20, but is captioned, "Unlawful: The high price of Denver's drug war: Lies, bad busts, cops in harm's way – and the death of an innocent man," different from the cover page.

12 The SWAT team dumped a gallon of paint on Mrs. Clarke's basement floor after the raid (Migoya 2000b).

13 In 1990, Detective Alvarez questioned a city employee about a Denver event commemorating a peaceful protest in Los Angeles on August 29, 1970, that was attacked by LA sheriffs and police, killing three people. When questioned why he was gathering intelligence, Alvarez down-played his inquiry as an insignificant favor for DPDIB detectives gathering information for the LAPD Intelligence Division. When pressed as to why he ran errands for the DPDIB when the LAPD Intelligence Division had no jurisdiction in Denver anyway, Alvarez slowly and uneasily began answering questions to which most cops would react with hostility, denial, deception, and/or contempt. Alvarez said he respected the activism of Colorado's Mexican ("Chicano") community in the 1960s and 1970s when it was known for its militancy, including frequent protests against police abuses. He later said this movement benefited communities of Color, crediting his own employment to a Colorado federal court case by attorney Kenneth Padilla over racial and gender discrimination in the police force. Its 1972 ruling required the DPD to hire a woman or person of Color for every White male hired until reaching an acceptable level of parity. Alvarez had been a policeman in Pueblo, Colorado, when he applied to the DPD and spoke of a White officer to whom he was assigned who refused to speak to him at all. He confided he was born in Mexico and was not a US citizen, but a Permanent Resident. It was not surprising to read his comments on Susan Scott's charge against Capt. Vasquez.

14 For accuracy's sake, three SWAT teams raided Mena's residence and one Hispanic was among them, Quinones, but all those who killed Mena were White.

15 Peter G. Chronis, "Denver police squelch protest over fatal raid," February 23, 2000. See also, "Respecting protesters' rights" (Rocky Mountain News 2000): "Government officials have authority, in limited ways, to regulate protests … but they may not make rules, or apply the ones they have differently, based on the content of the signs, the leaflets and the speeches."

16 Minutes of JMC meeting, by author, including verbatim portions of JMC press release of same date.

17 Minutes of JMC meeting, by author, including verbatim portions of JMC press release of same date.

18 "Two policemen in black district are reassigned" (Rocky Mountain News 1974b). The main target of the allegations that led to Di Manna's removal from District 2 involved Off. Tim O'Leary, his long-time partner, but Truman Cole's complaint called for Di Manna's removal as well. One article noted Di Manna and Leary

> work nights in a largely black precinct [and they] have been partners since [March 1973]. Both were born in November 1951, within a week of each other [and] joined the force in November 1972; Leary's badge ... is 72–113 [and Di Manna's is 72–114].

See Ceil Jones and Jeff Rosen, "Stories differ in four violence cases," *Rocky Mountain News*, May 26, 1974.

19 For Denver PD SWAT officers Di Manna and Gray at the Columbine massacre, see "No second-guessing SWAT" (Denver Post 2000a).

20 Justice for Mena Committee leaflet, captioned "Bulletin # 1," undated, but written in March 2000.

21 For the shooting of Leilani Lucero, see Jane Hulse, "Lawsuit filed in 'no-knock' raid on home," *Rocky Mountain News*, March 31, 1981.

22 For Ken Chavez, who shot at least 6 people, see Mike O'Keeffe, "Cop linked to other shootings," *Rocky Mountain News*, April 4, 1996. Chavez killed 25-year-old Jeff Truax, a White male, as he and his friend drove from a bar's parking lot after a fight. Chavez and Andrew Clarry, another off-duty officer, claimed the car struck Clarry so they fired 25 times into the car because they feared for Clarry's life. Denver lost a civil suit in Truax death and paid a $500,000 award. See Tony Perez-Giese, "Same as it ever was," *Westword*, March 18, 1999.

23 The JMC leaflets were written from articles in Denver newspapers. For the death of Joey Rodriguez, see Ernesto B. Vigil (1999, 344–346). The Rodriguez killing was the first case in which Marc Vasquez and Robert Silvas came to my attention. Silvas has killed at least five people in his career.

24 Steve Nash's statement was on behalf of End the Politics of Cruelty. To clarify possible confusion over the awards in the Truax and Mena cases, Mena's family settled out of court for $400,000, but Truax' family was awarded $500,000 in a federal civil suit.

25 Burgo revolvers were made in Germany before World War II with cheap metal alloys when Germany had limited access to raw materials and were of poor quality. As parts wore out, the guns often malfunctioned because cylinders holding the bullets did not align with the gun barrel, causing some to blow up when fired. The sale of Burgo handguns was curtailed by legislation banning the importation of "Saturday Night specials." The Burgo Mena allegedly fired was completely untraceable.

26 The ignition of gunpowder propels a bullet through the gun's barrel, but its residue can be found in "striplings," i.e., in a wound's exposed flesh, if someone is within 3 feet of the barrel when shot.

27 James Kearney, letter to Fox News, 1211 6th Avenue, New York, New York, November 15, 2002. Kearney called the SWAT team a "terrorist group."

28 Author's Notes.

29 Courtesy copy of a draft of a civil action complaint sent to Leroy Lemos of the JMC on January 22, 2003, by plaintiff James Kearney in the United States District Court for the District of Colorado against defendants Vincent Di Manna,

13 other SWAT members, 10 other DPD personnel in the Police Protective Association, at least 8 others.

30 See http://thebrokenbadge.com/7%united_we_must_stand.htm (accessed 22 October 2004).

31 Some JMC members knew they were under surveillance and one, the author, unsuccessfully sued the city of Denver over the DPDIB spying. The DPIB's stilted jargon insinuates I threatened the DPD on TV by claiming I would "hold the police department [and Capt. Vasquez?] accountable," a stupid remark for anyone to make.

32 The National Council of La Raza, a lobbying group, conducted a study in five cities during the Carter administration. The study, originally entitled "The Police Use of Deadly Force in Hispanic Communities," was essentially shelved when Ronald Reagan became president. I draw from early drafts of the study.

33 The IAB's name was once changed briefly to the Staff Inspection Bureau, but the IAB's evolution has not solved the pro-police bias that prevails against civilians.

34 Chief Parker and FBI Director J. Edgar Hoover, the nation's foremost law enforcement figures, apparently had so much in common that each detested the other.

35 *Viva!*, an early activist publication, founded by Rodolfo Gonzales and a community group called Los Voluntarios (The Volunteers) thanked Gavin in "Hats off to Tom Gavin," in its May 20, 1964, issue.

36 Charter Amendment A lacked support due to a rift between its City Council sponsor and community activists. A former-policeman-turned-activist-law-professor, Prof. Jose Sandoval, noted Amendment A would create a committee like the Los Angeles Police Commission and would not eliminate the problems about which communities complained. See, Rocky Mountain News, July 15, 1978a. See, also, Rocky Mountain News, July 23, 1978b; Delsohn, July 31, 1978; Ashton, August 8, 1978; Kilzer, September 2, 1978; Schlesinger, November 8, 1978; and Rocky Mountain News, August 31, 1979.

37 Note from Gerry Whitman, Chief of Police, to "Marco," January 9, 2000.

38 Vasquez DPD email to Vince Di Manna and five others, January 2, 2001.

39 Gene Cisneros worked as an interpreter for Robert Maes, the Mena family's attorney.

40 For a striking parallel to Denver's situation that suggest these problem are national, see Adam Serwer, "Something went wrong in Chicago," *Atlantic Monthly*, October 5, 2018.

References

Ashton, John. 1978. "[District Attorney] Tooley Rips Police Commission Plan." *Rocky Mountain News*, August 8.

Chronis, Peter G. 2000. "Denver Police Squelch Protest over Fatal Raid." *Denver Post*, February 23.

Delsohn, Gary. 1978. "Police Plan Assailed At [Activist] Rally." *Rocky Mountain News*, July 31.

Denver Post. 2000a. "No Second-Guessing SWAT." March 12.

Denver Post. 2000b. "Editorial." March 23.

Ensslin, John and Hector Gutierrez. 1999. "Police Defend Raid that Took Lethal Turn." *Rocky Mountain News*, December 1.

Flynn, Kevin. 2000. "Wrong House in No-Knock Wasn't the 1st." *Rocky Mountain News*, February 16.

Flynn, Kevin. 2001. "Group Demands Facts in Mena Shooting." *Rocky Mountain News*, February 22.

Flynn, Kevin and Lou Kilzer. 2000. "Mena Raid 2nd of Day to Find No Drugs." *Rocky Mountain News*, February 17.

Gutierrez, Hector. 1999. "Immigrant Thought Cops Were Robbers." *Rocky Mountain News*, December 19.

Gutierrez, Hector. 2000. "Tenants Seek Compensation After Raid." *Rocky Mountain News*, April 4.

Gutierrez, Hector. 2004. "Denver Cops Get an Earful." *Rocky Mountain News*, March 18.

Guy, Jr., Andrew. 2000. "No Knock Resonates a Year Later." *Denver Post*, September 29.

Haberman, Clyde. 2014. "The Rise of SWAT Team in American Policing." *New York Times*, September 7.

Herdy, Amy. 2003. "Findings Complicate Mena Case Raises Questions Over 1999 Denver Police Shooting." *Denver Post*, January 23.

Hulse, Jane. 1981. "Lawsuit Filed in 'No-Knock' Raid on Home." *Rocky Mountain News*, March 31.

Jones, Cecil and Jeff Rosen. 1974. "Stories Differ in Four Violence Cases." *Rocky Mountain News*, May 26.

Justice for Mena Committee. n.d. Who Is Captain Mark Vasquez? Bulletin # 1." leaflet.

Kass, Jeff. 1999. "Warrant that Ended in Killing Being Scrutinized." *Rocky Mountain News*, November 30.

Kilzer, Louis. 1978. "Policemen Oppose Commission." *Rocky Mountain News*, September 2.

Kraska, Peter B. (Ed.). 2001. *Militarizing the American Criminal Justice System*. Boston: Northeastern University Press.

McPhee, Mike. 2000. "Police Play Hide and Seek." *Denver Post*, March 23.

Migoya, David. 2000a. "Cop Charged in No-Knock Raid." *Denver Post*, February 5.

Migoya, David. 2000b. "No-Knock Raids Used as Leverage." *Denver Post*, February 19.

Migoya, David. 2000c. "Judges Rubber-Stamp No-Knocks." *Denver Post*, February 27.

O'Keeffe, Mike. 1996. "Cop Linked to Other Shootings: Officer Investigated in Killing of Nightclub Patron Cleared in 2 Earlier Cases." *Rocky Mountain News*, April 4.

Pankratz, Howard, 2008. "Affidavit: Ex-Cop Held Girls Against Will." *Denver Post*, June 4.

Perez-Giese, Tony. 1999. "Same as It Ever Was." *Westword*, March 18.

Prendergast, Alan. 2000. "A Death on High Street: The Address Wasn't the Only Thing Wrong with the Drug Raid that Killed Ismael, Mena." *Westword*, February 24–March 1.

Rocky Mountain News. 1974a. "Suspension of Denver Patrolman Is Sought." June 6.

Rocky Mountain News. 1974b. "Two Policemen in Black District Are Reassigned." June 8.

Rocky Mountain News. 1978a. "Mayor's Panel Opposes Civilian Control of Police." July 15.

Rocky Mountain News. 1978b. "Mayor Opposes Police Commission." July 23.

Rocky Mountain News. 1979. "Mayor in No Rush to Create Proposed Safety Commission." August 31.

Rocky Mountain News. 2000. "Respecting Protesters' Rights." February 23.

Schlesinger, Andres. 1978. "Police Commission... Defeated." *Rocky Mountain News*, November 8.

Serwer, Adam. 2018. "Something Went Wrong in Chicago." *Atlantic Monthly*, October 5.

Shikes, Jonathan. 2008. "Joe Bini's Squalorous Fall." *Westword*, June 4.

Vaughan, Kevin. 2000a. "Cop's Allegation Brings Swift Action." *Rocky Mountain News*, January 29.

Vaughan, Kevin. 2000b. "Police Brass Silent on No-Knock Error." *Rocky Mountain News*, February 10.

Vigil, Ernesto B. 1999. *The Crusade for Justice: Chicano Militancy and the Government's War on Dissent*. Madison, WI: University of Wisconsin Press.

Part II

The Youth Control Complex

Chapter 5

The Street Terrorism and Enforcement Act

A New Chapter on the War on Gangs

Alfredo Mirandé

Cain and Abel

Adam made love to his wife Eve, and she became pregnant and gave birth to Cain. She said, "With the help of the Lord I have brought forth a man." Later she gave birth to his brother Abel.

Now Abel kept flocks, and Cain worked the soil. In the course of time, Cain brought some of the fruits of the soil as an offering to the Lord. And Abel also brought an offering—fat portions from some of the firstborn of his flock. The Lord looked with favor on Abel and his offering, but on Cain and his offering he did not look with favor. So Cain was very angry, and his face was downcast.

Then the Lord said to Cain, "Why are you angry? Why is your face downcast? If you do what is right, will you not be accepted? But if you do not do what is right, sin is crouching at your door; it desires to have you, but you must rule over it."

Now Cain said to his brother Abel, "Let's go out to the field." While they were in the field, Cain attacked his brother Abel and killed him.

Then the Lord said to Cain, "Where is your brother Abel?"

"I don't know," he replied. "Am I my brother's keeper?"

The Lord said, "What have you done? Listen! Your brother's blood cries out to me from the ground. Now you are under a curse and driven from the ground, which opened its mouth to receive your brother's blood from your hand. When you work the ground, it will no longer yield its crops for you. You will be a restless wanderer on the earth."

(Genesis 4, New International Version)

This chapter is a case study of 17-year-old identical twin brothers, Marcos and Mario Mercado, who, along with their first cousin, Junior Díaz,[1] were jointly charged with attempted murder under California Penal, §186.22, better known as the Street Terrorism Enforcement and Prevention Act (STEP). The STEP Act is an aggressive piece of anti-gang legislation drafted by prosecutors and law enforcement personnel that makes "active participation" in a criminal street gang a separate criminal offense punishable independently of the underlying felony and provides for numerous enhancements if the felony is committed for the benefit of, in associating with, or while actively participating in a gang. The Act also severely limits the court's discretion by imposing enhancements for specified serious and violent felonies, mandating variable "minimum to life" sentences if they are committed for the benefit or in association with any criminal street gang.

Since I was Marcos' attorney, I provide a first-person account of the case, as well as discussing the significance and implications of the STEP Act. Because Marcos and Mario were virtually inseparable, it is difficult for me to talk about one twin without talking about the other, or about their cousin who was raised with the twins. The three were affectionately referred to by the family and friends, not as gang members but simply as "The Boys." Before detailing the case and the STEP Act, I attempt to put it in historical perspective by looking at the War on Gangs that took place in Los Angeles during the 1940s.

The War on Gangs in the 1940s: Sleepy Lagoon and the Zoot-Suit Riots

The STEP Act, heralded as the beginning of a new war on juvenile delinquency and youth gangs by police and law enforcement, can be seen more as the continuation of a domestic war on barrio youth that was initiated in the 1940s with the infamous Sleepy Lagoon case and the Los Angeles Zoot-Suit Riots. I argue that Sleepy Lagoon and the pachuco hysteria that was prevalent in this era were important historical precedents that marked the beginning of the current war on barrio gangs and the hyper-criminalization of Chicana/o youth.

Sleepy Lagoon: The 38th Street Boys

The Sleepy Lagoon case emerged in the aftermath of a fight between the 38th Street boys and a rival gang during a party at the Delgadillo home on the Williams Ranch, about a quarter of a mile from a reservoir and popular Lovers Lane spot known by local youth as the Sleepy Lagoon (Mirandé 1987, 157). Widely publicized, the case resulted in the conviction of 17 young Chicanos, alleged members of the 38th Street gang, for conspiring to kill José Díaz on the night of August 2, 1942, after he had left a drinking party at the Delgadillo home (Sleepy Lagoon Defense Committee 1942; Endore 1944).

On the evening of August 1, 1942, a birthday party was held honoring Mrs. Amelia Delgadillo at her home. The party was attended by her husband, members of her family and some 20 or 30 other invited guests. The court record indicates that some 8 or 11 uninvited persons were also in attendance, including some of the Downey boys who had been involved in a fight earlier in the evening with some of the 38th Street boys (66 Cal. App. 2d 174).

The group, consisting of some of the boys who later became defendants in this case and their girl companions, had been at Sleepy Lagoon earlier in the evening when they were attacked and beaten up by another group identified only as "boys from Downey" (66 Cal. App. 2d 175). They returned later in the evening to confront the assailants and went to the Delgadillo home in search of the Downey boys (66 Cal. App. 2d 175).

The conviction was obtained despite the fact that there was no evidence linking the defendants to the alleged murder of José Díaz. Members of the entire group were arrested, and charged with conspiracy to commit murder, even though it was never established that they were in fact a gang or that they had conspired to commit murder. Each defendant was charged with murder, irrespective of whether he was in fact involved in the killing of José Díaz (Figure 5.1).

The defendants were also repeatedly referred to as a "gang" by the prosecution and the judge during the trial. Guy Endore, who worked closely with the Sleepy Lagoon Defense Committee and authored several pamphlets on the incident, noted that the defendants referred to each other as "the bunch" or "the crowd" but they were simply friends and not really a gang (Endore 1944, 14). However, the judge, "in a statement to the jury deliberately linked the horror of Chicago gangsterism with the boys" (ibid., 14).

Figure 5.1 Arraignment of the "Sleepy Lagoon" murder suspects. Herald Examiner Collection/Los Angeles Public Library.

Alice Greenfield (McGrath), Executive Secretary of the Sleepy Lagoon Defense Committee and a staunch supporter of the Sleepy Lagoon Defendants, in an interview with the author also did not see 38th Street as a gang. Alice repeatedly referred to them as "the boys."

> I would strongly disagree with anybody who would call them a gang ... Groups, you know, were referred to as "gangs," even if they sort of hung out on the same corner, and gang was a word that didn't mean anything. *Our* gang was our group ... and you would hear people talking about our gang goes to this or our gang goes to that. They don't mean gangster at all. The kids who lived on 38th Street were said to belong to the 38th St. gang [group] ... but it didn't mean at all, anything like what was inferred by people and was implied by the newspapers.
>
> (Greenfield, interview with author, December 8, 1986)

Alice had a very close intimate relationship, with Henry Leyvas, who was viewed as the leader of the 38th Street gang, and acknowledged during the interview that if someone were to beat up on Henry that he might get his friends to say, as was alleged in this case, "Well, the next time we see them, we'll get even" but it wasn't as structured and 38th Street didn't go around defending their turf (Greenfield, interview, December 8, 1986).

Even though Presiding Judge, Fricke, was recognized as an expert on criminal procedure and touted himself as a mentor to attorneys in his courtroom, the case represented a gross miscarriage of justice and the denial of significant due process rights to the defendants. For example, the boys were in jail for over three months and were not allowed to get haircuts or a change of clothes during the trial, because the state argued that their distinctive appearance was evidence of their guilt. The prosecution maintained that "their style of haircut, the thick heavy heads of hair, the duck tail comb, the pachuco pants and things of that kind" were important evidence (Endore 1944, 31). Despite repeated objections by defense lawyers, the prosecution also continually called attention to the ethnic origin of the defendants. Because the judge was confused as to the identity of the defendants, each one was asked to stand up every time that his name was mentioned, creating the impression that this was an admission of guilt.

> The witness might, for example, be asked: "Did you see Padilla fighting?" And Padilla would be asked to stand up. And whether this particular testimony was torn to pieces or not by the lawyers, the one memorable picture that is left in the mind is that of Padilla standing up as the witness testifies against him.
>
> (ibid., 31)

Judge Fricke also prevented the defendants from consulting with their lawyers by his actions, prohibiting the defendants from sitting with or communicating with counsel. The judge further instructed that the bailiff take the defendants to the prisoners' room and that they not be allowed to consult with their attorneys during court recesses. One of the Sleepy Lagoon defendants' attorneys, Mr. Shibley, objected to the fact that the defendants were not allowed to sit or to confer with their attorneys, while prosecution witnesses were allowed to sit with the district attorney throughout the trial. Shibley protested vigorously,

> If your Honor please, I object on the grounds that this is a denial of the rights guaranteed all defendants, and each one of them, both by the Federal and state constitution. I think their right to consult and be represented by counsel at all stages of the proceedings demands that they have a right to come to their counsel during the proceedings and speak to them.
>
> (ibid., 32)

Although 17 of the boys were convicted, the defense was ultimately successful in appealing the convictions and on October 4, 1944, they were reversed by the District Court of Appeals. The main reason for reversing the conviction was that "there was no substantial evidence to support the claim that when the defendants left the vicinity of Vernon and Long Beach" to confront the Downey boys "they had 'murder in their hearts' or even that they had then formed any intent to go to the Delgadillo home" (*People v. Zammora* 1944, 66 Cal. App. 2d 176). In fact, the evidence

> strongly supports the theory that some of the defendants were intent upon meeting the 'Downey boys' and engaging in a fist fight with them in retaliation for the attack made upon some of the defendants, including Henry earlier that night.
>
> (*People v. Zammora* 1944, 66 Cal. App. 2d 176)

It was only after the defendants learned that the objects of their search had left Sleepy Lagoon that they decided to go to the Delgadillo home (*People v. Zammora* 1944, 66 Cal. App. 2d 176). In short, the court ruled that there was not support for the theory that

> [crashing the] Delgadillo party was the result of a collective intent upon the part of the defendants to commit murder, and that the conduct, behavior and actions upon the part of the defendants at the party manifested a conspiracy to commit murder or assaults with intent to commit murder.
>
> (66 Cal. App. 2d 176–177)

At most, according to the Court of Appeal, the defendants had a common intent to find the Downey boys and to engage in disorderly conduct, breach of the peace, or battery (66 Cal. App. 2d 177).

Another basis for overturning the conviction was that during the course of the trial, the defendants did not have the opportunity to confer with their attorneys during the examination of witnesses. The Court of Appeal noted,

> the right to be represented by counsel at all stages of the proceedings, guaranteed by both the federal and state Constitutions, includes the right of conference with the attorney, and such right to confer is at no time more important than during the progress of the trial ... If he be deprived of his life or liberty without such right to appear and defend, such deprivation would be without that due process of law required by the Constitution.
>
> (66 Cal. App. 2d 235)

The Zoot-Suit Riots

Although Sleepy Lagoon preceded the 1943 Zoot-Suit Riots, anti-pachuco sentiment was rampant long before the riots erupted. In fact, as early as August 17, 1941, Los Angeles newspapers began to run sensationalized stories of zoot-suit crime after a crime at a party-crashing incident in the Rose Hill Section. Patricia Adler noted, "Both gangs were composed of Mexicans—as the papers called them without distinction as to their individual citizenships—and some of the boys were dressed in the bizarre style favored for 'jive' dancing, the 'zoot-suit'" (Adler 1974, 145). Adler insightfully described the clash between Chicano youth and American servicemen as but "a brief episode in a long conflict" (ibid., 145).

The Zoot-Suit Riots were in fact a misnomer since it was American servicemen and not the zoot-suiters who were rioting, so it would be more accurate to have described them as the "U.S. Servicemen's Riots" (Mirandé 1987, 166). While the riots only lasted from June 3 to June 10, 1943, "they were the culmination of a vicious and intense campaign waged against Mexican residents of Los Angeles by the press, the police, and the public at large" (ibid., 166). Ultimately, the so-called Zoot-Suit Riots proved to be a form of state-sanctioned violence and extra-judicial vigilantism. Historian Carey McWilliams described the key elements involved in inciting the riots:

> first, the much publicized "gangs," composed of youths of Mexican descent, rarely over eighteen years of age; second, the police, over-whelmingly non-Mexican in descent, acting in reliance on the theories of Captain Ayres;[2] the newspapers, caught in a dull period when there was only a major war going on, hell-bent to find a local scapegoat, an internal enemy ...; fourth, the people of Los Angeles, Mexican and

non-Mexican, largely unaware that they were sponsoring, by their credulity and indifference, a private war; and fifth, the men of the armed services stationed in or about the city, strangers to Los Angeles ...

(1968, 238–239)

While the riots began on June 3, 1943, as several off-duty policemen undertook a vigilante hunt for zoot-suiters who had allegedly attacked several servicemen in the Mexican district (Mirandé 1987, 167), conflict between sailors and zoot-suiters had been building up since the beginning of 1943 and was prevalent throughout Los Angeles County (Jones 1969, 20). In fact, in April 1943, marines and sailors entered Black and Mexican areas in Oakland and "cleaned up on" some 200 zoot-suiters (ibid., 20).

The Lick Pier Incident took place in May 1943. The move to end discrimination in public facilities had opened areas previously off limits to Mexicans, such as amusement parks and dance venues. The public recreation area in Venice had become a popular hang-out for Chicano youth. In May 1943, a group of Venice high school boys went to the Venice Amusement Pier to "clean up" on the zoot-suiters (ibid., 20).

It is worth noting that prior to the riots the wearing of the zoot-suit was not an exclusively Mexican phenomenon. In fact, peg bottoms and long coats had been popular in Los Angeles and other large cities and were worn by Whites, Blacks, Filipinos, and other youth of certain economic and social status (Tuck 1946, 315). According to Ruth Tuck,

> The wearing of exaggerated clothing as a means of achieving distinction and recognition denied in other fields is a well recognized phenomenon. "High rise" trousers and bell bottoms were worn by the same groups a few years ago, but no mention was made of a high rise crime wave. Until June 13, 1943, the Los Angeles Times had for many months run a comic strip which glorified the wearer of a zoot suit as sort of a superman.

(ibid., 315)

Penal Code §186.22: Legislative History, Overview, and Implications

Just as the 38th Street boys and so-called pachucos in the 1940s were declared guilty and criminalized because of their style of dress, demeanor, and the persons they associated with, so is the STEP Act a mechanism for criminalizing and labeling contemporary barrio youth based on their lifestyle, attire, argot, monikers, and associations. The First Amendment to the United States Constitution, as applied to the states via the 14th Amendment, in addition to protecting freedom of speech and religion against government intrusion asserts "the right of the people peaceably to assemble, and to petition the government for a redress of grievances" (First Amendment, U.S. Constitution). While most people take the freedom of association constitutional protection for granted, in California, the Street Terrorism Enforcement and Prevention Act severely threatens this right because, as in the Sleepy Lagoon Case and the Zoot-Suit riots, a defendant can be found guilty by simply associating with persons believed to be members of a street gang or flashing their gang signs. By analogy, while the Patriot Act threatens to erode constitutional rights because of fear of terrorism, the STEP Act erodes constitutional protections because of a fear of juvenile crime, gangs, and so-called domestic terrorism. Under the Act, persons like Marcos can find themselves guilty of a crime if they simply associate and actively participate in any criminal street gang with knowledge that its members engage in or have engaged in a pattern of criminal gang activity.

Attorney Killain Jones (2011) graphically illustrates the dangers of the STEP Act. He provides an example of a person who has a number of close friends who spend a lot of time together, so that everyone identifies the person and his friends as a cohesive group, and gives then a nickname like "The Good Old Boys" [GOB]. Let's further assume that some of these friends come upon hard times and start selling drugs to pay the bills (ibid.).

> Since GOB is like a family unit, the new found prosperity of one friend (let's call them members from now on) inspires that friend to invite the others in on the new way to make a few extra dollars. Like any business, competition is not usually welcomed and you find that GOB is having to stick up and protect their fellow member. In the process things get out of hand and people get hurt. What would you classify this group of friends as: buddies? Best friends? Bros? Well, under the California Street Terrorism Enforcement and Prevention Act (the STEP Act; Pen. Code, § 186.20 et seq.) this could be considered a criminal street gang (§ 186.22, subd. (a)).
>
> (ibid.)

Initially known as the Gang Violence and Juvenile Crime Prevention Act of 1998, it was overwhelmingly approved by voters as a ballot initiative and added to the California Penal Code on March 7, 2000, by a vote of 62.1 percent "Yes," to 37.9 percent "No" (Ballotpedia 2017). Proposition 21 made various changes to California's law relative to the treatment of juvenile offenders. According to the CA Legislative Analyst (2000), Proposition 21 did the following:

- required that more juvenile offenders be tried as adults;
- required that certain juvenile offenders be held in local or state correctional facilities;
- changed the types of probation for juvenile felons;
- reduced confidentiality protections for juvenile offenders;
- increased penalties for gang-related crimes;
- required convicted gang members to register with local law enforcement agencies;
- increased criminal penalties for certain serious and violent felonies.

Crafted by prosecutors, police, and law enforcement, Proposition 21 reflects a War on Juvenile Crime and Gangs approach. Per Penal Code 186.21, in order to combat a serious gang threat in several cities throughout the state of California, its state legislature finds that:

> The State of California is in a state of crisis which has been caused by violent street gangs whose members threaten, terrorize, and commit a multitude of crimes against the peaceful citizens of their neighborhoods. These activities, both individually and collectively, present a clear and present danger to public order and safety and are not constitutionally protected.
>
> There are nearly 600 criminal street gangs operating in California, and that the number of gang-related murders is increasing. The Legislature also finds that in Los Angeles County alone there were 328 gang-related murders in 1986, and that gang homicides in 1987 have increased 80 percent over 1986.
>
> It is the intent of the Legislature in enacting this chapter to seek the eradication of criminal activity by street gangs by focusing upon patterns of criminal gang activity and upon the organized nature of street gangs, which together, are the chief source of terror created by street gangs.

Penal Code Section 186.22: Key Provisions

The Street Terrorism and Enforcement Act (STEP Act) makes "active participation" in a criminal street gang a separate criminal offense punishable independently of the underlying felony. Specifically, Penal Code Section 186.22(a) provides that

> Any person who actively participates in any criminal street gang with knowledge that its members engage in or have engaged in a pattern of criminal gang activity, and who willfully promotes, furthers, or assists in any felonious criminal conduct by members of that gang, shall be punished by imprisonment in a county jail for a period not to exceed one year, or by imprisonment in the state prison for 16 months, or two or three years.

The section defines "criminal street gang" broadly and vaguely as

> [an] ongoing organization, association, or group of three or more persons, whether formal or informal, having as one of its primary activities the commission of one or more of the [specified] criminal acts …, having a common name or common identifying sign or symbol, and whose members individually or collectively engage in or have engaged in a pattern of criminal gang activity.
>
> (Subd. (f))

The Act does not criminalize membership in a gang because that would be unconstitutional, punishing people for their status rather than their acts, but it does criminalize "active participation."

Although the statute fails to define "active participation," "actively participating" in a criminal street gang is itself punished by imprisonment either in county jail for up to one year, for a misdemeanor, or in state prison for up to three years, for a felony.

> *In addition and consecutive to the punishment prescribed for the felony or attempted felony* of which he or she has been convicted, a person convicted under the section shall be punished with an additional enhancement as follows: (A) [Except as provided in subparagraphs (B) and (C)], by an additional term of two, three, or four years at the court's discretion.
>
> (emphasis added)

And "serious" felonies are punishable by an additional term of five years, while "violent" felonies by an additional term of ten years. Under the Act, the court is ordered to impose the middle term of the sentence enhancement, unless there are circumstances in aggravation or mitigation, and during sentencing is required to state the reasons for its choice of sentencing enhancements on the record.

The Act also provides enhancements for specified serious and violent felonies, mandating variable "minimum to life" sentences. Any person who convicted of an enumerated felony committed for the benefit of, at the direction of, or in association with any criminal street gang, with the specific intent to promote, further, or assist in any criminal conduct by gang members, shall be sentenced to an indeterminate term of LIFE IMPRISONMENT with a minimum term of the indeterminate sentence calculated as the greater of:

> (A) The term determined by the court pursuant for the underlying conviction, including any enhancement … if the felony is any of the offenses enumerated in subparagraph (B) or (C) of this paragraph.

(B) Imprisonment in the state prison for 15 years, if the felony is a home invasion robbery, … (C) Imprisonment in the state prison for seven years, if the felony is extortion, … Finally, … except as provided in paragraph (4), any person sentenced to state prison for life under this subdivision shall not be paroled until a minimum of 15 calendar years have been served.

In addition, California's gun enhancement laws (Penal Code § 12022.53) will result in additional sentence for attempted murder involving a firearm of 25 years to life imprisonment if it caused great bodily injury. Attempted murder is also a violent felony and counts as a strike under California's Three-Strikes Law (§667.5), with a third strike carrying a 25 years to life prison sentence. Penal Code section 186.22, California's criminal street gang enhancement, subjects you to an additional 15 years-to-life in prison sentence, if the prosecutor shows that the attempted murder was in furtherance of gang activity. Finally, Penal Code §672 subjects you to a $10,000 fine for an attempted murder conviction.

Attempted Murder Charges Against the 4th Street Boys

In the primary case, the four defendants, the twins Marcos and Mario, their cousin Junior, and Mario's girlfriend, Tina Marina, were facing attempted murder charges and the prosecution sought to charge them as adults under Proposition 21 and California's Anti-gang Statute, Penal Code § 122.20. They were accused of being members of an organized criminal street gang and of attempted murder under the Act and faced possible 15-year-to-life sentences and a number of gang enhancements. The girlfriend of one of the twins, Tina Marina was also initially charged with the hope and expectation that she would be induced by the prosecution to accept a plea bargain and testify against the boys, which she eventually did.[3]

The boys were very close. Marcos and Mario were identical twins. Junior was a *primo hermano*, or first cousin and raised with the twins. In Mexican culture, a *primo hermano* is more like a brother or sister than a cousin. In addition, the boys all lived in the same household under their grandmother's roof. Junior's mom was a single parent and the grandmother was a successful career woman who worked for the County in a white-collar job. The household was very cohesive and included the three boys, Junior's mother, and the maternal grandmother, Mrs. Mercado, and her husband. I soon discovered that like 38th Street gang, the 4th Street gang, Calle Cuatro, was made up largely of the boys and their friends who lived in the neighborhood but they were not an organized and structured gang.

I first met my client at the Juvenile Court at a hearing to determine whether the boys would come under the jurisdiction of the juvenile court or be tried as adults. The juvenile court proceeding was more informal, like a sentencing hearing, because the judge had the power to determine whether the boys would come under the jurisdiction of the Juvenile Court or be tried as adults.

Per Welfare and Institutions Code § 707, when a juvenile is alleged to have committed a crime for which he or she could be tried as an adult, a hearing is held to determine whether the youth is amenable to the juvenile court. Following submission and consideration of a probation report and other relevant evidence, the judge determines whether the juvenile is amenable to the care, treatment, and training programs offered by the juvenile court. The court makes its determination based on any one and/or a combination of the following factors: (1) the criminal sophistication demonstrated by the minor; (2) whether the minor can be rehabilitated while under the juvenile court's jurisdiction; (3) the person's prior delinquency history; (4) the prior success of the juvenile court in rehabilitating the minor; and (5) the circumstances and gravity of the offenses alleged in the petition. The juvenile court proceeding was short and predictable. At the end of the hearing, the judge determined that the boys were in fact members of a criminal street gang and serious offenders who were not amenable to rehabilitation by the juvenile court.

The Preliminary Hearing

I should begin by saying a little bit about the preliminary hearing ("Prelim"), which is not a full-blown trial but an initial proceeding before the judge or grand jury. It is used in felony cases to determine whether there is sufficient evidence to establish probable cause to believe that a crime was committed and that the defendants should be held to answer for the charges at trial where the standard of proof is beyond a reasonable doubt. Also, subsequent to the Proposition 115, in California, hearsay evidence is now admissible at the Prelim.[4] Hearsay evidence is generally not admitted in a trial unless it falls within one of a number of generally accepted exceptions. As a result, evidence at the Prelim is usually presented through the arresting officer. The burden of proof is, therefore, very low and defendants are generally held to answer at the Prelim unless there is little or no evidence.

Additional Violent Felony: Discharging a Firearm (Penal Code 246.3)

Before discussing the major attempted murder charge, I will address an additional lesser, charge that was filed against the twins, their friend Mario Pérez, and Marcos' girlfriend Dora Martínez, for discharging a firearm under Penal Code §246.3. This charge was based on an incident, which was said to have occurred on January 19, about 10 days before the January 27 shooting. The first witness at the preliminary hearing was Dora Martínez, Marcos' girlfriend at the time who admitted that she was driving a white Honda Civic, license number 4POD431, on the evening in question in the vicinity of the 22nd Street neighborhood.

All of the initial questions by the prosecution at the Prelim were leading. Despite strenuous objections by the defense, the questions were allowed. The District Attorney asked, for example, "And so let's just pretend that I don't know anything about Twenty-Second. Can you tell me how you would know that a gang called 'Twenty-Second' controls that neighborhood?" There was a lack of foundation because no evidence had been introduced that a gang called Twenty-Second existed or that they controlled the neighborhood. The court sustained the objection only relative to the use of the word "control" and asked the DA to rephrase her question, as "How do you know that there is a Twenty-Second Street neighborhood? Can you tell me some details about that?" Dora responded that you knew because of "the streets, the people who live there. I mean, the graffiti on the wall and stuff."

Dora testified that on the evening in question she had driven the twins and another person by the name of Robert Pérez to the rival neighborhood. She had known Mario for several years from school but had only recently met Marcos. Dora said she could tell the twins apart and identified each of them in court. Attempting to label the boys as gang members, the District Attorney asked Dora about monikers and whether the boys used them. She responded that Marcos was known as "Dreamer," Mario as "Sneaky," and Robert was called "Sleepy." She said the boys responded to their respective names or monikers.

The witness admitted that Chico's Market was a place were members of 4th Street met and that she also hung out there and at other places in the strip mall. Dora said that she was not a gang member, although she hung out with members of the 4th Street and 22nd Street gangs. The DA tried hard to link the boys to the 4th Street "gang," suggesting they used graffiti to mark their turf. The witnesses testified that you could see graffiti throughout the neighborhood but that she had never seen the twins writing graffiti on walls or on anyone's else property. Significantly, Dora said that she had observed Marcos and Mario writing "4th Street" on paper when they hung out at home but not anywhere else and that they normally discarded the paper when they finished drawing the graffiti.

It should be noted that at the time the twins were 17 and their cousin 16. The boys generally rode their bicycles to the strip mall and they relied on the girls, who were older, to give them a ride to the rival neighborhood. Dora said that on that evening Mario had asked her to drive them to 22nd Street, which was near the freeway but she initially refused. Mario asked again and when she refused, he said that they would take their bikes. She finally agreed and they got into her car with Mario sitting in the front, next to Dora, with Marcos sitting in the back seat behind his brother. Robert sat in the back behind, Dora, the driver.

Mario gave Dora directions and it took about ten minutes to get to the rival neighborhood, when he abruptly asked her to stop and park the car at a designated destination. Dora testified that she saw four or five people standing together. Although she did not recognize them, Dora said that they looked like gang members from 22nd by their looks and attire. She went on to say they had big jackets, loose-fitting pants, and shaved heads.

Marcos and Robert got out of the car and started walking towards the group. Robert had a baggy Dickies-type jacket and Dora saw him pull out a gun. She tried watching the boys for a few minutes but could not see because it was dark and she didn't have her glasses, so she started listening to the radio to pass the time. After a few minutes she heard two or three gunshots and saw Robert and Marcos running toward the car. She saw two guns, with Robert carrying a shotgun, which he had hidden in his jacket and Marcos a handgun, although she did not see them fire the weapons. She heard someone saying something about "someone screaming like a bitch" but she could not recall who said it.

She testified that Mario directed her to leave and that they went back to Chico's Market. Dora said that Marcos and Robert got out of the car and started talking to other people from 4th Street but they did not reference the incident and they never talked about it again after that. When asked if she felt concerned about the incident, she responded that she did because she was obviously involved, "but I didn't want to know because the less you know the better."

Dora said Marcos had been her boyfriend and that she had corresponded with him after the boys were arrested. When the District Attorney asked whether Marcos had said anything about testifying, she indicated that he said "not to go against him," which she took to mean "for me not to say anything."

During cross-examination, the other defense attorneys and I tried to impeach the prosecution witness by showing that she was Marcos' disgruntled girlfriend and that she was testifying so that the charges against her would be essentially dropped in exchange for her testimony. I began by trying to show during cross-examination that she was as culpable for the incident, if not more culpable, than the boys. She was, after all, an adult at the time, at age 20, and the twins were 17-year-old juveniles. She also was the one who drove the car and took them to the rival neighborhood. Dora admitted that she was in control of her actions and the vehicle, and was not coerced to go to the 22nd Street neighborhood. I tried to show in my questioning, in other words, that she knowingly and willingly drove to the neighborhood, even though she expected that there would be "trouble" and that when she decided to give them a ride to the 22nd Street neighborhood that, in her words, she knew "nothing good could happen."

Finally, Dora admitted that she entered into an agreement with the District Attorney so that she would get credit for time served (58 days) and three years probation in exchange for her testimony, if she pled guilty to Discharging a Firearm, even though she had not actually discharged it. An additional condition was that she enter a recovery home for drug addiction. She was currently in a recovery home because she had been using speed for more than two years and was an abuser of methamphetamines. Dora admitted that she would have used meth the day of the incident or the day before, as she generally got loaded daily when she got home from work around 4:45 p.m. But she stopped hanging around with the people from 4th Street once she got out of jail.

Attempted Murder Charge: The Police Report

On or about January 27 at approximately 2:00 p.m. officers responded to a shooting that had just occurred in the vicinity of Melrose and Center. The shooting was believed to have been gang-related and witnesses identified the Mercado twins and their cousin, Junior Díaz, as suspects. The boys were said to be members of the 4th Street (Calle Cuatro) and the shooting occurred in the 22nd Street neighborhood, an area controlled by a rival gang. An arrest warrant was issued on February 18, and the three suspects were arrested. Mario's girlfriend, Tina Marina, was also charged.

When the police arrived, a large crowd had gathered. The victim, an admitted 22nd Street gang member, had suffered a gunshot wound to the leg and was on the street bleeding. He said he was standing outside of a friend's house drinking a 40-ounce beer, and that he had been attending a wake for a friend along with his girlfriend, family, and friends when he saw three Hispanic males spray-painting "Calle Cuatro" on the wall of an adjacent house. Although the victim had never seen the suspects before, he walked over to them and asked, "What the fuck are you doing? Why are you disrespecting us?" The boys argued with him, telling the victim to "Fuck off" and walked to a nearby car. As they drove away, the suspects allegedly shouted, "Calle Cuatro." The victim became angry and threw the 40-ounce beer, which hit the side of the car. This angered the occupants of the car. The victim said, "The piece of shit leaned out of the window and shot me." The shooter who had been riding shotgun on the front passenger seat, leaned out the window and fired about five rounds at him, shooting him in the leg. The victim was very cooperative with police but indicated he was unwilling to prosecute anyone involved in the crime and would not testify in court. The police observed a stucco wall on the south side of the street near where the shooting occurred with the letters "Calle Cuatro" spray-painted on it. Witnesses indicated that the suspects, driving a blue Honda Civic with tinted windows, had spray-painted the wall.

Further investigation revealed two additional suspects, Robert Pérez and Tina Marina, and that Tina was reportedly the girlfriend of Mario Mercado, and the driver of the car, a blue Honda Civic, which belonged to her mother. Witnesses identified the primary suspects as the twins, their cousin, and Robert Pérez, a known 4th Street gang member who was reportedly in the front passenger seat. The driver of the vehicle was identified as a female. Junior Díaz (AKA "Baby Bull") was identified as the occupant of the rear passenger seat of the vehicle.

Witnesses attending the wake reported that they approached the boys when they began spray-painting the wall and asked them to leave the area. They were also observed getting into the suspect vehicle that fled the scene. Witnesses identified either Díaz or Pérez as the shooter, while the Mercado twins were reported as being in the back seat of the vehicle.

Attempted Murder Charge: The Preliminary Hearing

Four persons were ultimately charged with attempted murder in the January 27 incident—the twins, their cousin Junior, and Tina Marina, Mario's girl-friend and the driver of the suspect vehicle. The two persons who testified at the Prelim were detectives Hyatt and Gordon, self-described gang experts. Neither the victim, the defendants, nor any other witnesses took the stand.

Detective Hyatt testified that he had responded to the January 27 inci-dent after several 911 calls were received by the local police department. The testimony was multiple hearsay. For example, Hyatt indicated that when he spoke to the victim on February 11, the victim said that he had spoken to a woman named Rosita Alvirez, who had reported that she wit-nessed the shooting and that two of the suspects were the twins from 4th Street. But Hyatt also testified that when he spoke to Alvirez, she denied witnessing the incident. However, Rosita's father had told Hyatt that his daughter had told him that "she had witnessed the shooting and two of the suspects were the twins from 4th Street, Mario and Marcos Mercado."

Hyatt also testified that when he went to the crime scene on January 27, people were generally uncooperative but that this was very common in gang shootings. He said that another gang member, Rick Ortiz, "walked past me at my side and he said something—'Look at the twins from 4th Street,' or something to that effect." The detective added that "it was a soft voice to where only I could hear," so it was clear that he feared retaliation. Under cross-examination from me as to the credibility of Ortiz, Hyatt reluctantly admitted that Ortiz was a gang member but described him as "an ex-gang member," rather than a current one, which supposedly made him more credible. He also admitted that Alvirez had initially identified a man named Ron Vera as being a suspect. Vera was initially charged but was no longer a defendant in the case.

The second witness to take the stand was Detective Gordon who was assisting Detective Hyatt on the case and was part of the Special Enforce-ment Gang Unit in the area. Gordon testified that he had interviewed Tina Marina. She initially denied any involvement or knowledge of the case until the detective told her that her vehicle had been placed at the scene of the shooting and that records from the video store at the shopping center showed that she had rented a video six minutes before the shooting.

Tina indicated that she was Mario's girlfriend and that on the night of the shooting, she and the boys drove to the video store at the strip mall to rent a movie, before going to 22nd Street. She told the detective that Mario was sitting in the front seat next to her, that Junior was sitting behind her, and that Marcos was sitting in the back seat behind his brother. She said they drove to the area controlled by 22nd Street until someone, she could not remember who, told her to stop the car.

Tina remained in the car with Mario, while Junior exited the vehicle. Junior went to a wall that was painted white and started spray-painting the wall. A male, apparently the victim, approached and confronted them. At that point, "a skinny female with dark hair started yelling at them to stop disrespecting the neighborhood or stop disrespecting the house." She said that Marcos had gotten out of the car and "She believes that one of them, I think she said it was Marcos, she believed apologized to the lady and said that they would leave."

Tina then said that they all got into the car, with Mario sitting next to her, Marcos sitting behind his brother, while Junior sat behind the driver. The male who approached them turned out to be the victim who was shot. "As she passed, she said she heard something hit the back of the passenger side of the car but she didn't know what it was." And then she heard gunshots. Gordon said that Tina started crying but that she eventually admitted that the gun was fired and that she heard two or three shots. She also admitted that the gun was fired by her boyfriend, Mario Mercado.

The Trial and Verdict: A Forgone Conclusion

With four defense attorneys, one prosecutor, and a busy court calendar, it was difficult to set a trial date, there were numerous continuances, and it took about four years before the case went to trial. Unfortunately, I had accepted a position to teach at a law school in another state but had hoped to do the trial before I departed. The trial was initially set for June, some 18 months after the shooting but was continued because one or more of the attorneys had a conflict. The trial was re-scheduled for that September. At the pre-trial conference in September, I informed the court that I was withdrawing from the case and the judge appointed a member of the defense panel to replace me as Marcos' attorney.

Two years later when I returned to California, I ran into a colleague who had represented the cousin, Junior Díaz, at the local County Law Library. The colleague told me that the boys had been convicted and, unfortunately, each received 45-years-to-life sentences. I was not surprised but felt bad that I had not finished the case and that the sentence was so severe but I would be lying if I did not admit that I was somewhat relieved to be spared having to go through the trial and witnessing the inevitable outcome. The conviction was obtained by dropping the charges against the girls, in exchange for their testimony. Dora had accepted the plea bargain prior to the Preliminary Hearing in exchange for time served, and Tina accepted a similar offer prior to the trial.

Reflections

Although I was not present for the trial, the outcome, like that of the 38th Street boys, was perhaps inevitable. The case obviously did not receive the publicity or press coverage of Sleepy Lagoon but there has been great focus and growing concern with criminal gang activity in Los Angeles and southern California. Like 38th Street, the boys were part of a neighborhood but they were not an organized criminal street gang. "Calle Cuatro" was simply used to identify kids in the neighborhood, including the twins, Junior, Robert Pérez, and other youth who hung out at the strip mall, Rosa's Mexican Restaurant, Chico's Market, and the local video store. The boys generally used their bicycles for transportation, and relied on the girls, who were older, to drive them over long distances, including excursions into the rival neighborhood. While the boys had been in trouble with police and had done time in juvenile hall before the incident, it was never established that one of their primary activities was the commission of one or more of the felonies specified in the statute or that members had engaged in a pattern of criminal activity. In fact, I recall that one of the serious felonies that was used to establish the fact the boys were part of a criminal street gang in the juvenile court proceedings was the allegation that, at age 14, they had stolen a wheelbarrow from an old lady in the neighborhood. In short, prior to the incident the boys had only been charged with petty crimes and misdemeanors. Ultimately, they were labeled as a gang by police like detectives Hyatt and Gordon who were part of a local Gang Unit, whose primary mission was to identify gangs in the area, to appear in court as gang experts, and to testify against the boys and verify that they were members of a criminal street gang. Since an early age the boys in the neighborhood were labeled and identified as members of the 4th Street gang by members of the local Gang Unit.

There was a further parallel to Sleepy Lagoon in that the 4th Street defendants sat in a special holding cell during the Preliminary Hearing and were not allowed to sit with or confer with their attorneys during the proceedings. While permitted to bathe and get hair-cuts, the fact that they were dressed in orange prison jumpsuits rather than street attire reinforced the image of them as violent criminals and gang members.

During the course of the case, I grew close to Marcos and his family. The grandmother, the daughter (Junior's mother and the twins' aunt), and other family members attended the proceedings regularly and bonded with the defense attorneys. In fact, while the grandmother sometimes could not attend because of work, Junior's mom was a regular and provided a great deal of support for the boys and their attorneys. The family was also a great source of information and a conduit for communicating with the boys. The family would send messages through us to the boys, like that they were going to be visiting them at the County Jail the following Sunday, or in providing news of the neighborhood. They also had their pulse on the community and conveyed information such as telling us that someone else in the neighborhood had taken credit for the shooting. The family told us, for example, that the victim in the shooting had been convicted of a gang shooting himself, that he was doing time in state prison up north, and that he had refused to testify against the boys.

I have to confess that I grew close to Marcos and his family and that it was difficult for me to see him as a gang-banger or a hardened criminal. In addition to court appearances, I would visit him regularly at the County Jail on Sundays. In fact, he reminded me a lot of my own son who was the same age. Marcos was a charming, charismatic, smart, and engaging youngster who was curious about a lot of things. He talked about his girlfriends, asked me questions about children, my background, college, and surprisingly, how one got to be a lawyer. Like my son, he was also very artistic and shared some of his artwork. His twin, Mario, seemed more serious and reserved, although, in fairness, I didn't know him well.

Although the boys were not part of a structured criminal organization, they shared certain values with gang-affiliated youth. Sociologist Robert Durán has identified four core ideals of barrio gangs that seem applicable to the boys and their associates. These ideals include: (1) Displaying Loyalty; (2) Responding Courageously to External Threats; (3) Promoting and Defending Gang Status; and (4) Maintaining a Stoic Attitude Toward Gang Life (Durán 2013, 151–171). The boys' escapades into the rival neighborhood can be seen as mechanisms for defending the status of their group and responding courageously to external threats. They also maintained a stoic attitude toward gang life and toward the serious charges they faced. In fact, at one point, they were offered a plea deal of 25-years-to-life and declined. But perhaps the ideal that was most evident during the case was how they displayed loyalty to the group.

There is a strong ethic among barrio youth that strongly discourages, frowns upon, and negatively sanctions snitching against fellow gang members, or *carnales*. The group demands loyalty because such faithfulness is key not only to its foundation but its survival (ibid., 151). Snitching, even among rival groups, is strongly frowned upon. Even the victim in this case refused to testify against the boys. Because of the code of silence, none of the boys, regardless of their individual culpability or lack of culpability, was willing to testify or to snitch on a member of the group. The prosecution strategy was to charge the girls, knowing that while they associated with members of 4th Street and were clearly as culpable as the boys, they were not loyal to the group and would eventually fold. They would ultimately testify against the boys in order to avoid long prison sentences, whereas the boys would not testify against each other.

I wanted to close by pointing to some important constitutional issues in the STEP Act. While the Act has withstood legal challenges, it continues to raise due process and First Amendment concerns because it essentially punishes people for who they are and who they associate with, rather than what they do. One concern is that the statute, particularly gang injunctions issued subject to Penal Code §186.22 may infringe on people's First Amendment right of association. A second concern is that the Act severely limits the court's discretion by providing fixed enhancements of five years for serious and 10 years for violent felonies, and mandates the judge to impose the intermediate penalty or state the reasons for not doing so on the record. A final concern is that rather than being required to prove that a person is a member of a gang, the prosecution simply has to demonstrate active participation in a gang, subjecting parents, family members, and friends to possible prosecution. Since the boys were constantly in association with one another, they were active participants of the gang by definition.

The STEP Act places an especially heavy burden on families, particularly close-knit Mexican families like the Mercados. Given that Mario and Marcos were twins and lived in the same household with their cousin, Junior, it would have been virtually impossible for them to comply with a gang injunction that prohibited them from associating in public with any member of the 4th Street gang.

In closing, like the Sleepy Lagoon defendants, their conviction was also a forgone conclusion. Ironically, under the STEP Act, it really didn't matter who had fired the shot, as long as the prosecution could show that there was a 4th Street gang, and that the boys actively participated in the gang with knowledge that its members engage in or have engaged in a pattern of criminal gang activity. While Marcos was said to have been in the back seat during the incident and did not actively participate in the shooting, he was held responsible for the actions of the shooter. Although he reportedly apologized to the victim and other bystanders from the rival gang, and agreed to leave the scene, he was held to be responsible for the shooting and attempted murder. And it is in this strange sense that he may ultimately have been his brother's keeper, as the scriptures commanded.

Notes

1   The names and all personal identifying information have been changed to protect the identity of the parties.
2   Ayres, Chief of the Foreign Relations Bureau of the Los Angeles Sheriff's Department, testified that Mexican criminality was biologically based. He presented a report that was an indictment not only of the 38th Street boys but all the Mexican people. While acknowledging discrimination, the Report concluded that in

explaining Mexican Delinquency "the biological basis is the main basis to work from" (Sleepy Lagoon Defense Committee 1942, 14). Ayres added that it is, therefore, just as important to incarcerate not only the leaders of a gang "but every member of a particular gang, whether there be 10 or 50" (ibid., 18).

3 The boys were charged with a secondary crime in a separate incident involving discharging a firearm. Dora Martínez, Marcos's girlfriend and driver of the vehicle, was similarly charged with the hope and expectation that she would eventually testify against the boys.

4 The Ninth Circuit recently resolved this issue holding that "the admission of hearsay statements at a preliminary hearing does not violate the Confrontation Clause." The challenged statements were admitted at a preliminary hearing under California Proposition 115. In *Peterson v. California* (604 F.3d 1166), the Ninth Circuit joined the Fifth and Seventh Circuits in concluding that "there is no right to confront witnesses at a preliminary hearing before being required to stand trial," in *Peterson v. California* (604 F.3d 1166).

References

Adler, Patricia R. 1974. "The 1943 Zoot-Suit Riots: Brief Episode in a Long Conflict." In *An Awakened Minority: The Mexican Americans*, ed. Manuel P. Servin, 2nd ed. Beverly Hills, CA: Glencoe Press, pp. 142–158.

Ballotpedia. 2017. "Treatment of Juvenile Offenders: Proposition 21." In *Encyclopedia of American Politics*. Available at: https://ballotpedia.org/California_Proposition_21,_Treatment_of_Juvenile_Offenders_(2000)

CA Legislative Analyst. 2000. "Proposition 21: Juvenile Crime. Legislative Analyst's Office." Available at: www.lao.ca.gov/ballot/2000/21_03_2000.html

Durán, Robert. 2013. *Gang Life in Two Cities: An Insider's Journey*. New York: Columbia University Press.

Endore, Guy. 1944. *The Sleepy Lagoon Mystery*. Los Angeles, CA: The Sleepy Lagoon Defense Committee.

Greenfield, Alice. 1986. "Interview with Alfredo Mirandé." December 8. Ventura, California.

Jones, Killian. 2011. "The STEP Act, Criminal Street Gangs and You." Available at: www.jdsupra.com/…step-act-criminal-street-gangs-and-26193

Jones, Solomon James. 1969. "The Government Riots of Los Angeles, June 1943." Master's thesis, University of California, Los Angeles.

McWilliams, Carey. 1968. *North from Mexico*. New York: Greenwood Press.

Mirandé, Alfredo. 1987. *Gringo Justice*. Notre Dame, IN: University of Notre Dame Press.

Sleepy Lagoon Defense Committee. 1942. *The Sleepy Lagoon Case*. Los Angeles, CA: Citizens' Committee for the Defense of Mexican-American Youth.

Tuck, Ruth D. 1946. *Not with the Fist: Mexican Americans in a Southwest City*. New York: Harcourt, Brace and Company.

Cases Cited

People v. Zammora, 1944, 66 Cal. App. 2d 176.
Peterson v. California, 604 F.3d 1166 (9th Cir. May 17, 2010).

Statutes Cited

CA Penal Code §186.20.
CA Penal Code §246.3.
CA Penal Code §667.5.
CA Penal Code §672.
CA Penal Code § 12022.53.
CA Proposition 15. 1990.
Welfare and Institutions Code § 707.

Chapter 6

Latino Street Gangs, La EME, and the Short Corridor Collective

Richard A. Alvarado

Introduction

In 2006, a seemingly uneventful decision was made at the California Department of Corrections (CDCR), Pelican Bay State Prison (PBSP), to move the recognized leaders of the major prison gangs to a more secure area of the prison. The leadership of the four main prison gangs, which included the Mexican Mafia (La Eme), the Black Guerilla Family (BGF), the Aryan Brotherhood (AB), and Nuestra Familia (NF), was moved to a smaller multi-occupancy corridor or POD, duly named the "short corridor" within the Security Housing Unit (SHU). The short corridor at the prison had fewer cells, less inmate movement, and no direct contact with other inmates in the SHU (Alvarado 2015, 230–232).

The cell housing change was intended to provide a more controlled environment, where communication links to their prison gang cadre would be substantially limited and investigative staff could more easily monitor and intercept potential criminal evidence. While the intent was to reduce nefarious prison gang activities statewide that were directed by the prison gang leaders within the SHU, the CDCR had unwittingly created the opportunity, albeit forced, for the leaders of the prison gangs to interact, coalesce, and advance mutually beneficial interests.

The four main leaders, all of whom had a history of directing "green light" assaults on inmates, including each other, now found themselves as cell neighbors. These were alpha males, seasoned convicts, whose criminal and prison histories denoted unwavering refusal to surrender to prison rules and regulations. Within five years, the CDCR would come to the painful realization that it had unwittingly created a hybrid *gang-of-convenience* among the four prison gang leaders (AB, La Eme, NF, and BGF) who appropriately called themselves the "Short Corridor Collective."

The emergence of the Short Corridor Collective would signal a new era in prison/street gang influence and prison administration, with a manipulation unprecedented in the history of penology in the United States. First, the Short Corridor Collective successfully orchestrated a statewide prison hunger strike in

2011, involving nearly 6,000 inmates locked up in Administrative Segregation and SHU units throughout the state's 33 prisons. When their demands were not met, they staged another strike in 2013 involving 30,000 inmates (Alvarado 2015).

The four reputed prison gang leaders achieved this remarkably successful hunger strike from the dungeon-like cell blocks of the SHU at Pelican Bay Prison. Incredibly, this was a cell block where prisoners were isolated from the general population, alone in a cell, 23 hours each day and in one of the most secure supermax prisons in the nation. Ultimately, because of the strike, California's departmental policies regarding prison gang documentation, isolation and segregated housing conditions would begin to change (McLeod 2017, 657–658).

It should be noted that the unprecedented influence of the Short Corridor Collective in California prisons did not happen overnight. In fact, the metamorphosis from former street gang member, prison gang involvement, and ultimately to Short Corridor Collective leadership, took decades to effect. Street and prison gang growth does not happen in a vacuum, nor do young men and women wake up one morning wanting to be delinquents and/or criminals. In fact, though often surrounded by gangs, most juveniles growing up in the inner cities do not see themselves as hard-core gang members (Esbensen et al., 2001; see also, Pyrooz, Sweeten and Piquero 2012). Those of us who grew up in the barrio have seen peers who readily identified with their neighborhood but when provided with positive alternatives, avoided becoming "hard-core" gang bangers. In fact, existing research supports the view that for most barrio youth, gang membership is the exception rather than the rule (Bolden 2013).

What leads to the emergence of a "gang banging" mentality is a combination of factors that begins with a person's feelings of belonging to something that is valued and meaningful. Juveniles who do not have a sense of belonging to family, school, or community are inclined to view gang involvement as a natural alternative for fitting-in. The more satisfaction derived from gang banging, the more entrenched the attachment. It's been my experience as an officer and prison administrator that most hard-core prison gang members live a circular journey of gang banging. These youth often come to feel like they are going nowhere fast but taking a young lifetime to get there, often failing to recognize that the prison gang lifestyle does not benefit them, costs them precious time and despair, and sometimes their lives. They may victimize strangers, friends, and family by their conduct, while unknowingly victimizing themselves. Understanding how California became a hotbed for gangs is important, if we want to develop strategies for combating their growing influence.

Let me be clear. Despite my law enforcement background, I am not suggesting that delinquent youth in the barrio are the ultimate cause of gangs. On the contrary, the development of street gangs goes beyond normal adolescent misbehavior like truancy, running away, unruliness, drinking alcohol, marijuana use, and curfew violations. Yet, today we have criminalized these behaviors by putting cops in schools and implementing zero-tolerance policies for nuisance type offenses (Vera Institute 2017). The growth of street gang participation can be linked to the school-to-prison pipeline and attributed to the nation's social, class, and racial inequality. Spurred by racism, discrimination, limited educational and career opportunities, and 40-plus years of draconian criminal justice polices (War on Crime, 3 Strikes, Determinate Sentencing) that have been brought to bear primarily on people of color (Acuña 1972; Gottschalk 2015; Mirandé 1987).

The United States has been described as a prison industrial complex and today incarcerates more people than any other nation in the world (Hernandez 2017). By 2010, Latinos were three times more likely to be incarcerated and Blacks five times more likely to be incarcerated than White youth (Pew Center 2017). This so-called "carceral state" that stimulates repeat offenders and reinforces carceral practices (Gottschalk 2015) begins with our youth. In short, as the incarcerated population of the United States has risen, so has the prevalence and influence of street and prison gang members.

Gang "Banging" History

Following the Mexican-American War, the Mexican government ceded a large portion of its northern territory to the United States. Under the Treaty of Guadalupe Hidalgo, Mexican citizens living in Texas, Arizona, Nevada, Utah, and California became US citizens unless they declared their intent to retain their Mexican citizenship. Mexicans living in the United States were physically and socially separated from Mexican society after the annexation. Although, they were in their "new" homeland, the United States, they were treated as second-class citizens (Griswold del Castillo 1990; Mirandé 1987; Montejano 1987).

Newly formed local government and economic entities viewed them as outsiders or foreigners. As a result, the isolation contributed to the marginalization of the Mexican community based on language, as well as cultural and socio-economic differences. This isolation further engrained existing prejudices in Anglo-American communities as immigration continued unabated following the Mexican Revolution (1910–1920). Railroad and agriculture labor needs saw nearly two million more Mexican immigrants enter the United States during a 20-year period. The older established Mexican neighborhoods or barrios became even more isolated, "colonized" by cultural, racial, and socio-economic barriers (Acuña 1972, 118).

Youth gangs have been prevalent in the United States since the growth of urban centers and the migration of minorities to this country. From the mid-1860s to 1920s, there were many Irish, Italian, Polish, Chinese, and Jewish minorities living in impoverished neighborhoods in Chicago, Detroit, New York, and other parts of the Northeast. These areas quickly became prominent breeding grounds for youth gangs. In New York, for example, gang members were the same age as most members of current street gangs, averaging about 16–24 years of age. The most notable being: The Five Pointers, the Monk Eastman, the Gophers, the Hudson Dusters, and the Chinese Tongs (Howell and Moore 2010).

During the 1940s, immigration and job opportunities spurred the introduction of Latinos to the Northeast region. By the 1960s, 60 percent of the New York street gangs were estimated to be Puerto Rican or Black. By 2008, the Northeast region had "approximately 640 gangs with more than 17,250 members" (ibid., 4). Currently, the most significant street gangs on the East Coast are the Crips, Latin Kings, MS-13, Neta, and United Blood Nation. Today, Latino gangs are estimated to outnumber Black gangs in the Northeast region of the United States.

In California and other parts of the southwest, the lowliest of the young marginalized immigrants, Cholos—a derivative of the Spanish *solo*, meaning "alone"—were young male youth who were neither Anglo nor Mexican by culture. But being a Cholo allowed them to proudly assert their unique Latino identity while simultaneously denying "being agabachado [Anglicized]" (Vigil 1998, 42). They dressed the same in jean or khaki pants with ironed pleated t-shirts, using local idiom dialects or *caló* to distinguish themselves from others. These street youths shaped their own Cholo subculture, and were the first of what later would be called "vato locos [crazy guys]" (Howell and Moore 2010, 4).

The Zoot-Suit Charade

It wasn't until the early 1940s that Mexican-American youth, called *pachucos*, a so-called "hip" version of Cholos in Los Angeles, was discovered by the media. Many Pachucos wore distinctive clothing called a zoot-suit, a colorful and brash style of clothing that was the social rage for urban youth. The "outfit" consisted of a flat-crowned, broad-brimmed hat, long draped coat, and high-waisted baggy-legged trousers with tight fitted pegged cuffs. The hair was long and combed into a ducktail. They also wore long, elaborate watch chains hanging from their pants to complete the look. The zoot-suit style was made popular in the movies of the time and was worn by White, Black, Mexican, and Filipino youth, especially those who followed the jitterbug dance craze.

The Sleepy Lagoon Case brought these young Mexican-American youth to national attention (see Chapter 5). A young alleged gang member, José Díaz, had been found unconscious on a rural road in the outskirts of Los Angeles. He later succumbed to his injuries. Twenty-two members of the 38th Street Gang, many of whom embraced the zoot-suit style of dress, were charged with his murder. The case was dubbed the "Sleepy Lagoon Murder." The prosecution rested much of its case on the boys' "distinctive appearance" and "love of jazz fashion was evidence of their social deviancy." During and after the trial, the *Los Angeles Times* and Hearst newspapers exploited the trial "with sensationalist journalism emphasizing alleged Mexicano criminal activity" (Meier and Ribera 1993).

This so-called "crime wave" put pressure on local law enforcement to round up Mexican teenagers based on racial profiling and the vaguest suspicions, most of which centered on their distinctive appearance and zoot-suit attire (Acuña 1972, 203–206). Seventeen members of 38th St. were convicted of the murder of José Díaz and received sentences ranging from life in prison to a year in county jail. The Mexican community, several progressive groups, and celebrities such as Orson Welles, Rita Hayward, and Anthony Quinn formed the Sleepy Lagoon Defense Committee, which united behind the boys and protested what was perceived as a racially motivated trial. With the aid of community activists, the conviction was reversed on appeal in 1944.

Although, zoot-suiters were characterized by the media in Los Angeles as marauding Mexican thugs or gangs, only a small percentage were from local barrios and even those Pachucos had no structure. On the contrary, "they were just boys who hung around street corners and formed shifting, informal allegiances …" (Mirandé 1987, 185). The nineteenth-century image of Latinos as "bandidos" was now closely associated with Chicano street gangs. And, by extension, a negative image of Latino youth was linked directly to the media presentation and law enforcement bias that remains unchanged today.

Southern California street gangs were distinctive from the East Coast gangs. First, they were tighter-knit than other street gangs, partly, owing to "Colonia" history and family ties (Howell and Moore 2010, 11). Young Mexican males, raised in the barrio communities, gave rise to street gangs loyal to their neighborhoods. This historical social context created an allegiance to the neighborhood that was nearly equal to family, albeit because many family and extended family members lived in the same neighborhoods. Likewise, the ancestral history extended more than one generation and was being infused with a constant surplus of new, but familiar, immigrants (primarily Mexicans) each year. This cultural infusion kept the language and customs of Mexicans intact. It also served to keep them isolated, and without the larger Anglo political arena support for education, jobs, and social services.

The rise of pachuco or cholo street gangs in California would grow during the 1950s and 1960s. South and North migration of Blacks to Los Angeles similarly fueled the growth of Black street gangs.[1] Much of the gang growth stemmed from the continued isolation and marginalized ghetto and barrio experience and partly from the normal youthful zeal to be different from the older generation. For example, young Blacks fell into two camps, Crips or Bloods, and began to emulate the territory-marking practices that had been established by the early Latino gangs. Crips controlled housing projects in Watts during the 1950s, such as Jordan Downs, Nickerson Gardens, and Imperial Courts. Bloods became strong in South Central Los Angeles cities, such as Compton, Pacoima, Pasadena, and Pomona.

The Los Angeles Police Department (LAPD) has described Los Angeles County as the "gang capital" of the nation, although the veracity of the title remains questionable. The LAPD reported, "more than 450 active gangs in the City of Los Angeles. Many of these gangs have been in existence for over fifty years. The gangs of Los Angeles have a combined membership of over 45,000 individuals" (Los Angeles Police Department Official Website, 2017). But the Mexican Mafia "La Eme," became a new and more powerful influence among street gangs in the 1950s and continues unabated to impact Southern California Latino street gangs in one form or another today.

La Eme Infusion

There remains an embryonic connection between the Mexican Mafia (La Eme) and street gangs in Southern California. La Eme had its beginnings during the 1950s at the Deuel Vocational Institution (DVI), a prison located in Tracy, California. Conditions were so severe at DVI that it was described as a "Gladiator School," since the most incorrigible minors incarcerated in youth authority would be transferred to DVI for a presumably more secure celled environment. Youthful offenders who were former street gang leaders now doing time at DVI decided to form a group, which ultimately began to prey on other inmates. Most, if not all, of the members came from street gangs in Southern California.

The fledging group members called themselves the Mexican Mafia and later, "La Eme" (for the letter "M" in Spanish). Former street gang and Eme dropout, Ramon "Mundo" Mendoza described the new prison gang as "an idea that would unite the street gangs once and for all ... one in which leaders of the street gangs represented inside could join hands as allies and 'carnales'—brothers." Mendoza maintains that it was a "more appealing alternative to perpetuating their bloody gang warfare into the prison system ... a purely democratic system in which everyone was equal, and no single member could give orders to another." This new prison gang sought to control narcotic trafficking within the prisons and organize the street gangs outside the prison system to reduce tensions among them once they entered the prison (Mendoza 2005, 16).

By 1959, the Eme, with less than 30 original members, very quickly established itself as merciless and cunning in the willingness of members to assault anyone who might pose a threat to their power. The Eme readily used violence to instill fear among general population inmates. In fact, because of their ruthlessness with other inmates, a group of inmates (mostly from Northern California) decided to organize their own prison gang, calling themselves *La Nuestra Familia* (NF). They had their origins among street gangs residing in northern California.

The 1960s and 1970s saw bloodshed rise to its highest levels at Soledad, DVI, San Quentin, Chino, and Folsom State Prison as the Eme and the NF sought to gain control over drug and extortion activities in all the mainline prisons. Other prison gangs (the Aryan Brotherhood, the Black Guerilla Family, and the Texas Syndicate) took sides or remained neutral to protect their own interests, as well as protect themselves from being preyed upon. By the 1980s, the Eme had created a cultural morass of respect through intimidation, fear, and hatred, that extended well beyond the walls of the California prisons and into the low-income urban communities from which the Eme members had originated.

Neighborly Protection

The Eme's connection to street gangs was a predictable extension of why young men joined street gangs in the first place. The loyalty and kinship of young, defiant youth, whose developed bonds from growing up together, sharing similar experiences and identifying with their neighborhoods, are important traits attributed to street gang membership. The sense of family and love, which may have been lacking in the home, was replaced by the companionship and support gang membership offers many adolescents. Like a supportive family, the gang becomes part of their individual identity and is both protector and protected. Mendoza describes the street gang mentality:

> The street gang is a common force that draws love-hungry brown-skinned kids into the protective umbrella that hides them from what they perceive to be an insensitive society—the same society that thumbed its nose at them in school, during job interviews, at shopping malls, on the bus, and wherever Chicanos and Gavachos [Whites] crossed paths. On the other hand, it encouraged a complete disregard for authority, especially for those who choose crime as a way of expressing their defiant and rebellious attitudes. It is a way of receiving the recognition and acceptance they desperately crave and an avenue in which the guys could demonstrate their macho [manliness]. The gang offered complete independence.
>
> (Mendoza 2005, 79)

For the same reasons, the creation of the Eme by hard-core leaders of various street gang members doing "hard-time" had fashioned a safe haven in prison. For other inmates, however, who were not aligned with their agenda, it created a living hell, since they were routinely subjected to "paying rent," in the form of canteen, money, or favors to the Eme, including isolation from the general inmate population for their own safety. Those inmates who did succumb found the Eme protective shield the same nurturing source young men of color found in the ghettos and barrios of Southern California, but only to the limited extent allowed by a hostile prison environment.

In southern California, Varrio Nuevo Estrada Courts, White Fence, The Avenues, 18th Street, La Rana, Varrio Trece, Maravilla, Hazard, Artesa 13, Florencia 13, Wilmas, Monte Flores, Puente Trece, SanFer, Logan Heights, Canta Ranas, Varrio Jardin and other less celebrated street gangs became the *raw meat* from which La Eme drew its membership and gained its muscle. The older street gangs had established an informal local hierarchy called "Cliquas" based primarily on age (ibid., 72).

The unspoken, and in most cases, the unconscious goals for dedicated or hard-core street gang members start as they become more involved with La Eme. They soon find themselves arrested and placed in youth authority camps, juvenile hall, jail and prison. There, they are indoctrinated by the institutional inmate sub-culture dominated by the prison gangs. From an outsider's perspective, this may appear as a dysfunctional aspiration to be sure and only limited to those "vato locos" (crazy guys) particularly suited for violence and destruction. However, it has been my experience that most street gang members "doing time" did not have any interest in ascending the ladder of the proverbial career-criminal success. Unfortunately, many were swept away by the supposedly romantic notion that "la vida loca" (the crazy life) was somehow the only way to live. Most street gang members simply cooperated willingly to avoid conflict with La Eme.

Within the prison, La Eme had established its own hierarchy by the late 1970s. The Eme "Carnales" (literally "meat," meaning blood brothers, as in the concept of "carnalismo") sit at the top of the prison gang pyramid. Associates or "Camaradas" are loyal followers. Associates were usually hard-core street gang members. They did much of the work connected with directives issued by Eme Carnales.

The use of Eme associates became the norm after the California Department of Corrections and Rehabilitation (CDCR) began to isolate Eme members from the general population in management control units—administrative segregation (Ad-Seg). By the 1980s, "validated" Eme members were being placed in the newly created Security Housing Units (SHU).[2] The term validated refers to the documentation used to verify the prison gang status of inmates. In the past, three separate forms of proof were needed to support validation. For example, self-admission, gang tattoos, pictures, letters, associations on the street with other validated members, etc. After the 2011 and 2013 hunger strike, the gang validation process was changed as a direct result of inmate hunger strikes. CDCR replaced the old policy for identifying prison-based gang members with a new model that identifies, targets and manages Security Threat Groups.[3]

The "Buzz" Experience

The SHU environments assured limited contact among Eme members and other general population inmates. As a result, Eme associates, by default, became "shot callers" in the general population. They gave the orders, "hits" (assaults), and became the eyes and ears for drug trafficking, and other nefarious business in the general population mainline on behalf of the Eme. I had the opportunity to interview a young man, whom I will call "Buzz" to protect his identity. Buzz had served 15 years in the California prison system and became an Eme associate.[4]

Buzz had committed a carjacking with a gun (unloaded) in Riverside County. He had no felony priors and only misdemeanor offenses for curfew, possession, fighting, and truancy. Buzz was 18 years old when he was convicted. His family lived in the Westside in the Casa Blanca barrio of Riverside, but his father and extended family were from the Eastside of the city and he was accepted by the street gangs in both barrios.

Buzz's family had a history of alcohol and drug addiction and he had been placed in various foster homes prior to his conviction. His two half-brothers either had served or were serving time in prison and were associated with La Eme. Buzz could best be described as an athletic, alpha-male with a high IQ for numbers who had already made a name for himself in the barrios of Riverside as a hustler of marijuana, cocaine, and methamphetamine trafficking.

Buzz readily admitted to doing favors for the Eme once he was placed in the Presley Detention Center in Riverside, California. "I already knew people there from the Eastside and Casa Blanca. They knew my brothers, so I was taken care of." When asked, why he got involved with the Eme, Buzz said, "I wanted to be somebody. My brothers got respect and always had money and drugs. They walked around like they owned everything and everybody and I wanted the same thing." He went and described an incident when he was first incarcerated:

> I was involved in a yard fight the first day with some white dudes who attacked us. I didn't know why they attacked all the raza but I just fought back until the tower officer fired some shots and everyone got down except me. I was stabbed in my shoulder, back and chest. I realized I was in the middle of all these white dudes around me. All the Mexicans (Chicanos) were across from me. I refused to lay next to the white boys. The officer kept yelling for me to "get down" but I just stood there yelling at him to get one of the Chicanos off the yard who was seriously bleeding-out across from me. They eventually took him and everyone else off the yard before removing me.

Buzz shared, that the word quickly got out about his exploits and he received a kite (hand written message) from the Eme shot-caller in the unit. Buzz was not happy and told the shot-caller that he should have been warned about the conflict with the whites when he first arrived in the prison. When I asked about the response from the shot-caller, Buzz said that the shot-caller apologized and asked him to take the lead on the tier. Buzz said it didn't take long before he was running his own housing unit. His entrance into the Mexican Mafia circle was solidified owing to his fearlessness and willingness to take charge.

Buzz described running Eme business in prison as if it was a corporation and he was a valued member of the organization. He revealed that on any given day, he was responsible for the trafficking of narcotics into his unit. He would ensure portions of the narcotics (methamphetamine, cocaine, marijuana, or heroin) would be evenly distributed among the Eme associates with a portion sent directly to the Eme carnales housed in Administrative Segregation or the SHUs, depending on where they were located. Buzz would also always ensure inmate-manufactured weapons were readily available and accountable to selected carriers each day. All the Sureños in the unit were required to share their canteen or contribute in the purchase or movement of contraband. Finally, he oversaw any disputes or issues. This was his life for 15 years.

Buzz admitted that after the first two years he became addicted to heroin and only cleaned up after his first parole violation. When asked what changed for him and why he turned his life around, his response was simply:

> The guys I knew when I first went to prison were either dead or in the SHU or in trouble with the Eme. I didn't want to end up like that. I realized that they [La Eme] would turn on each other for stupid reasons that didn't make any sense. It was always personal or some power-play and I didn't want to end up like my father.

Buzz's father had died of a heroin overdose. Buzz is no longer addicted to drugs, has discharged from parole status, and is making an honest living as a big-rig driver in southern California. He is engaged to be married and hopes to buy a home in the immediate future. He is an exception-to-the-rule for young men who get caught up in "la vida loca" with La Eme.

Sureños

The term "Sureños" originated in the California prison system and refers generally to Southern California street gang members. The 1970s prison war between the Nuestra Familia (NF) and La Eme forged recognition of street gang members' loyalty based on a geographic regional identity of a

"North vs. South" street gang mentality (Schoville 2008). Bakersfield was the demarcation line for regional identification but only loosely enforced. Allegiance, in most cases, was defined by actions and individual choice.

It became the norm for newly arriving Latino offenders in California prisons and jails to recognize and acknowledge the regional identification tag. Just like a street gang member would ask, "¿de donde? (where are you from?)" to a youthful stranger in his barrio or territory on the street, the same question would be asked in jails and prisons to verify allegiance to the north or south. Latino street gang members had to pick a side; they had no choice. The expected response was "Puro Sur/Norte" depending on what the Latino street gang member claimed. Latinos not claiming any gang status or from another country still would be asked. Latinos born in Mexico, referred to as "Border Brothers," and unaffiliated Latinos from other regions of Latin America, would have to find their own place in the prison pecking order. The "Sureño" or "Norteño" (northern street gang member) label, readily used in prison, became the connecting thread that regionalized the street gang mentality in the community. At the same time, the prison system itself inadvertently helped to intensify gang affiliation and membership.

What was once only used in prison to denote allegiance, became a much broader street gang label honoring or acknowledging the Eme or NF. The prison gangs had become part of "the norm" in street gang nomenclature. The 13th and 14th letter of the alphabet (M & N) used in southern and northern California by taggers, in tattoos, and part of the street gang name to signify allegiance to the prison gangs Mexican Mafia (M) and Nuestra Familia (N).

CDCR law enforcement personnel use, what is arguably a broad brush, by employing various means to identify these alleged NF and Eme sympathizers. Inmate cell partners, tattoos, letters, yard assignments, pictures, drawings, social associations (who they hung around with), and self-admission were some of the primary means by which correctional staff identified them. But this did not occur without some institutional prodding and encouragement. Housing assignments, yard assignments, and placement in Administrative Segregation or SHU, required identification of inmates' allegiance as a Norteño, Sureño or "non-affiliated" status. This discussion will focus on the Sureño tag, although the same process applies to Norteños.

The identification of an inmate's gang status was a critical prison management function, ostensibly used to both safeguard the inmate in question and to protect others. Some inmates would admit being "Sureño" while others would not. Some inmates reported during housing reviews to custody staff or committees, "it doesn't matter, put me where you want." This left supervisory and counseling staff to determine the best cell and yard placement based on the other factors (county of commitment, body tattoos, personal letters, Probation Reports, etc.). One assumption generally made was evidence of any previous gang ties in the community. If they were recognized as a Southern California street gang member, they were considered, by default, Sureños, regardless of how long ago that association may have occurred. Once identified by staff as a Sureño, the label would be documented as fact and would forever follow that prisoner's incarceration trail. Ironically, then, the CDCR itself has played a critical role in identifying and perpetuating prison gangs.

The status of the inmate then would be formally noted by a prison classification committee in the inmates' Central File. The Central File was the main harbinger of an inmate's history. It included:

- legal documents;
- medical history;
- prison classification documents and Chronos;
- custody level score sheets;
- court documents;
- parole documents;
- criminal and in-prison disciplinary history.

These voluminous files have only recently been converted to digital form. They remain the primary source for determining the gang status of an inmate.

The fluid nature of prison politics among the various inmate groups and within the Eme itself led to a constant need for oversight of associates and sympathizing Sureños by the Eme leadership. Although not all Sureños were loyal or even interested in supporting the Eme cause, they had to remain silent and avoid being shunned by other Sureños. However, when tension rose between inmates of another race, all the inmates would be obliged to "back up" their own people or face the consequences for not supporting their race.

The author spent five years as a "rank-and-file" employee with CDCR: As an officer in various assignments in a Level II facility at the California Rehabilitation Center, Norco, and as a Correctional Counselor assigned to the facility 4B SHU and the Max Level IV Facility at the California Correctional Institution in Tehachapi. On many occasions, inmates would express their indifference about "politicking" but acknowledged that if something happened they'd have no choice but to participate. Their best effort to "lay low" was futile if a riot or racial incident in a cell block, dorm or yard were to "kick off." This was recognized by staff as a matter of "prison business" among the inmate population.

Prison race-profiling *by inmates among inmates* was similarly mandatory to ensure some measure of protection. This is a sub-culture nuance familiar to most jails and prisons. Thus, the races (Black, Brown, White, and Asian) generally sat separately, walked among their own race, ate and exercised separately, too. If an assault or fight were to ensue, the inmates would already be among their own for protection. At the same time, over the years it was expected that inmates only congregate with their own race. To do otherwise would create tension and an inmate not adhering to the practice would have to answer to *his* people.

If an issue developed between inmates of a different race, the shot callers for that race would decide the best resolution for their own people. Paying the debt with a beating or death (by their own race) was usually the outcome to avoid a larger racial conflict. If no resolution could be worked out by the prison gang "shot callers," then a prison race riot was virtually inevitable. Moreover, it didn't matter whether an inmate had a pending release date, family visit, or court appearance, if a racially motivated incident occurred, all inmates were expected to participate or face negative consequences for not backing up their people.

The "Corridor-4" Conundrum

Criminal activity has changed dramatically over the past 20 years with the advent of advanced technology, and that technology has not gone unnoticed by street gang members involved in drug trafficking and prison gang control from within institutions. In fact, the expanded use of smartphones, drones, and internet communications has created more intrusive and sophisticated ways of handling prison gang business. The Short Corridor Collective was particularly attuned to taking full advantage of modern communication networks using family and friends to establish a prisoners' advocacy website, *Prisoner Human Rights Movement*, to campaign for their struggle against CDCR policies and procedures.

No one could have predicted, for example, the extent to which social media would play a part in orchestrating the hunger strikes by the Short Corridor Collective (Corridor-4). The major prison gangs—the Aryan Brotherhood (AB), the Mexican Mafia, the Black Guerilla Family (BGF), and Nuestra Familia (NF)—united because all had a vested interest in seeing changes in SHU policy. It is doubtful they believed change would result in freedom from prison, but they would certainly want to be freed from the SHU cellblocks and get back to the general population mainline. The critical question to be posed is not for prisoners' advocates, scholars or CDCR officials to ask and answer. It is for other inmates not aligned with the Corridor-4 to ask. What would happen if these prison gang members were released from the SHU? Answering that question requires examining what the four principal prison gang leaders involved in the Corridor-4 have done in prison.

Todd Ashker, the 50-year-old AB leader and principal lawsuit writer for the Corridor-4 was 19 years old when he first arrived in prison. He had a history of assaultive behavior against staff and other inmates before he was convicted of the 1987 stabbing assault against another AB member. Over the years, Ashker became a "prison lawyer" who was adept at filing lawsuits and winning in court. *Sacramento Bee* journalist Dan Morain reported that when Ashker first arrived at Pelican Bay in September of 1990:

> He kicked open his cell door—a defect costing $8 million to fix—and tried to kill another inmate. A guard broke up the fight shooting Ashker in his wrist. Though he was the aggressor, Ashker filed a suit ... and won. A federal jury in Oakland awarded him $225,000.
>
> (Morain, 2013)

The other three prison gang leaders in the short corridor of Pelican Bay SHU took notice and realized that, with his legal research skills, they could forge a formidable argument against what would soon be viewed as the archaic and suppressive SHU policies. Ashker can hardly be viewed as a victim. And the same can be said of the other Corridor-4 members.

"Chuco" Guillen, for example, a high-ranking leader in the NF, was convicted of narcotic sales and assault with a deadly weapon in 1990. He was released from prison in 1999 and was out less than a year before being arrested for a murder, believed to be an NF-sanctioned "hit."

Ronald Dewberry is similarly serving a life sentence for a murder committed in 1981 and has been living in SHU since 1987. He is believed to hold the rank of Lieutenant in the BGF and was alleged to be an enforcer. He was serving time at the California Correctional Institution, at Tehachapi during my tour-of-duty there and was an active participant in BGF business on the SHU yard during that time.

Arturo "Tablas" Castellano, a validated EME member, was convicted of murder in 1979 and sentenced to 26-years-to-life. His prison record included six documented stabbing assaults. Gang investigators consider him to be the "undisputed" leader of Florencia 13, one of Los Angeles County's oldest gangs. A recent federal indictment alleges that the Eme used Florencia street gang members to traffic narcotics. The indictment also alleges that Florencia 13 was allied with La Familia Michoacán, a drug cartel based in Michoacán, Mexico, which paid the Mexican Mafia $150,000 to be able to sell drugs in the area. During my tour-of-duty at the California Correctional Institution, Facility IVB SHU, Castellano was suspected of fashioning the weapon used by his cellmate, Gabriel "Sleepy" Huerta (also a member of the Short Corridor Collective Representative Body) to murder Eme member, Niko Velasquez in the Tehachapi SHU.

None of these Corridor-4 leaders have ever acknowledged membership in any prison gang. Likewise, the last ten years or more of their incarceration has not revealed any disciplinary action for nefarious activities in prison. Prisoner advocates point to this fact as a viable reason to release them from the SHU. But seasoned law enforcement personnel have a different understanding based on experience. The prison gangs don't have to do anything but send the message out to their cadre of followers to get nefarious business done, including murder. They have proved themselves to be cunning and treacherous in holding power and control over other prison gang members and loyal street gang members. Jeffery Beard, Secretary of CDCR, in an Op-ed piece for the *Los Angeles Times* regarding the hunger strike orchestrated by the Corridor-4, said this about their motives:

> Some prisoners claim this strike is about living conditions in the Security Housing Unit, commonly called SHUs, which house some of the most dangerous inmates in California. Don't be fooled. Many of those participating in the hunger strike are under extreme pressure to do so from violent prison gangs, which called the strike in an attempt to terrorize fellow prisoners, prison staff, and communities throughout California … the corrections department created SHUs to safely house gang members and their associates while minimizing their influence on other prisoners. Restricting the gangs' communication has limited their ability to engage in organized criminal activity and has saved lives both inside and outside prison walls … So what is this really about? Some of the men who participated in the last hunger strike and have since dropped out of the gangs … said it best … "We knew we could tap big time support through this tactic, but we weren't trying to improve the conditions in the SHU; we were trying to get out of the SHU to further our gang agenda on the mainline."
>
> (Beard 2013)

The notion that four inmates and a small cadre of other SHU inmates could somehow influence 30,000 inmates statewide to heed their call for "justice" but not wield the power CDCR claims they have, has little merit. They do have power and they have proved it.

California prisons have had a history of federal court incursion and oversight to remedy the very issues (due process and conditions of confinement) that continue to spark debate.[5] However, it was more probable that the hunger strike protest was manufactured by the Corridor-4 to support the hidden agenda goals of the prison gangs. Author, Chris Blatchford describes EME dropout Rene "Boxer" Enriquez's view on prison gang "goals" from previous hunger strike protests when the EME used inmate Steve "Smiley" Castillo, another known jailhouse lawyer. Castillo filed lawsuits on behalf of SHU inmates and eventually won reforms regarding the SHU program, claiming it to be "capricious and cruel." His intent was to have prison gang members released back into the general population and out of isolated housing. Castillo's lawsuit, contended that " 'hundreds of prisoners' were misidentified as gang affiliates with 'flimsy and trivial' information and held in the SHU unjustly for indeterminate amounts of time." The lawsuit was eventually dropped (Blatchford 2008, 275). However, it did draw considerable legislative interest.

On September 15, 2003, Senator Gloria Romero, for example, convened a hearing of the Senate Select Committee on the CDCR's SHU policies and practices. Nothing of substance came from that hearing since the federal court had already addressed the living condition issues in the SHUs.

Ten years later, the July/August 2013 hunger strikes had spurred the Senate to conduct more hearings. This time there was substance given to the "living conditions" complaints. On October 9, 2013, a Joint Legislative Hearing on "Segregation Policies in California Prisons: Current Conditions & Implications on Prison Management and Human Rights" was conducted. Loni Hancock, Senate Public Safety Committee Chair, and her counterpart, California Assembly member Tom Ammiano, Chair of the Assembly Public Safety Committee, both raised concerns regarding the hunger strike and conditions in California's supermax (SHU) prisons (White 2013). The Corridor-4 had pursued the same strategy that inmate Castillo had pursued ten years previously.

The hunger strike strategy appeared more indicative of the "Just Us" goals driving the Corridor-4 than "justice" regarding living conditions of the SHUs. The advent of public opinion had sparked a political regurgitation on prison reform and genuine public interest regarding prison policies, including opposition to apparent draconian forms of punishment. The Corridor-4 had effectively put the solitary confinement and prison gang due process debate in the court of public opinion. Isolation, access to meaningful programs, and a legitimate process to escape "Indeterminate" SHU status were legitimate human rights issues brought forward by the Corridor-4.[6]

CDCR had already revamped the procedures related to documenting gang involvement and providing a shorter timeline and a less invasive (no snitching required) means to walk away from gang activity following the 2013 hunger strike. The new gang policy created a behavior-based "step-down" program for validated affiliates, which allowed a process by which gang affiliates had an opportunity to work their way out of restricted housing (like the SHUs) to the general population. During the joint legislative hearing of October 2013, the California Inspector General, Robert Barton testified that over 4,000 inmates reside in the SHUs statewide, with over 500 having lived in the SHU environment beyond five years. As many as 60 percent are serving "open-ended terms" or "indeterminate" SHU status based on their alleged gang associations. This is the crux of the SHU placement issue—why gang association and not specific behavior—for determining the reason for separation from other inmates? More importantly, how long must gang members remain in continued isolation?

To be sure, the demands made by the Corridor-4 about living conditions are relevant. The "torture," characterized by them and their supporters as: long periods of non-contact with other inmates, limited movement outside the cell, and restricted program opportunities, are valid issues that have not been adequately addressed. Research has determined that prisoners who are subjected to long periods of sense-deprivation: lack of touch, sound, and movement, are more prone to mental illness. The author spent three years working in the Tehachapi SHU in the late 1980s and saw, first hand, the depression and spatial disconnect that occurred due to long-term isolation by some inmates.

Mental health clinicians, for all their efforts, could not counter the security-based policy effect of segregated housing on the mental health of inmates which became part of the focus for the Coleman federal court injunction. In *Plata v. Schwarzenegger*, a three-judge court sitting for the Eastern District of California ultimately held that a reduction in the California prison population was necessary to provide constitutionally acceptable levels of medical and mental health care.[7]

The United Nations has similarly decreed that long periods of non-human contact and isolation are torture. In fact, testimony at the 2013 Joint Legislative Hearing revealed that in 2011, the United Nations Special Rapporteur on Torture and Terror called for a ban on solitary confinement lasting longer than 15 days and an absolute ban on solitary confinement for youth and the mentally ill. During the same 2013 Joint Legislative Hearing on Segregation Policies, it was also revealed that the federal government and many states are re-evaluating the continued use and benefit of long-term solitary confinement.[8] Today, many organizations and most state correctional agencies oppose prolonged segregation for inmates with mental illness. Ironically, it took a hybrid *gang-of-convenience*, the Corridor-4, to bring the issue of solitary confinement back to the public dialogue.

The Twenty-first-Century Morphing of Street Gangs

The unique circumstances that led to the morphing of leadership of the major California prison gangs into the Short Corridor Collective is a first in the nation. To be sure, there have been many instances where street gangs and/or prison gangs have voluntarily joined forces (be it temporarily) to meet a collective agenda, including tactics like work or program strikes and sometimes riots. Usually, their interests have to do with control of drug or contraband trafficking in the institutions or streets. However, no prior prisoner strike in this nation has had the unique policy agenda, social media-driven focus, and multiple prison interchange as its backdrop. The Corridor-4 had, in fact, achieved the largest offender-instigated protest in the nation's history. The transformation of hybrid gang cooperation should not go unnoticed because the same trend can be seen happening in the community.

The "Money Gang" of San Jose, California, is an example of morphing street gang activities. Sometime in 2013, it came to the attention of San Jose Police Department (PD) that something different was going on with the street gangs in San Jose. San Jose is home to some 4,000 street gang members, most of whom are Latino. Norteño gangs dominate the landscape based on their location north of Bakersfield. San Jose PD, during a stake-out of a funeral for a known gang member killed by his rival, noticed that many of the attendees drove new sporty cars. Likewise, during subsequent arrests, many of the young gang members were in possession of large amounts of cash, numbering in the thousands of dollars. Much of the contraband (watches, jewelry, etc.) found was stolen property identified in burglaries around San Jose's exclusive residential neighborhoods (Anthony 2016).

What surprised the San Jose PD Gang Investigators was that the suspects were not from the same gang but members of different rival gangs, who were sworn enemies of each other, yet cooperating together. Some of the suspects who eventually were convicted for burglary-related crimes were interviewed by the Gang Investigators. The investigation revealed that the perpetrators called themselves the "Money Gang," and worked independently from their own street gang. They paid no "Tax" to the NF or Northern Structure prison gang because they viewed their acts as separate from street gang business. Therefore, they reasoned, all the spoils from the burglaries belonged to them.

The Money Gang *modus operandi* was unique: The gang members purposely used new cars during burglaries, so they would "fit in" the neighborhood. They cruised the good neighborhoods to watch and see which cars would leave for work in the morning. Once satisfied they had an empty house, one person would enter by breaking a backyard patio door, and disable the alarm by pouring water on the alarm system. His partner-in-crime would quickly search for money, jewelry or cash only, staying no longer than a few minutes before leaving the home. The "Money Gang" crews would use amphetamine-laced drugs during commission of the crime because they believed it maximized their focus. They were eventually tracked and convicted by their use of social media. San Jose PD monitored the Facebook and Twitter pages of known street gang members, which eventually revealed key evidence. The false bravado of young street gang members wanting to extoll their criminal successes to their friends quickly put them in the cross-hairs of law enforcement.

Although some street gang members commit crimes, it is not the principal reason young men or women get involved with gangs. What is unusual in the case of the "Money Gang" is the fact that multiple gang members from different barrios were colluding in an organized fashion for a long period of time. Second, they consciously recognized the "Tax" owed to the NF prison gang but justified their actions as outside the purview of their street gang allegiances, characterizing their burglary stings as a "side-job." The same example of cooperating "rival" gang members has been seen in other communities as well.

Kings of the Asphalt Jungle

The collusion of street and prison gang business, using loyal hard-core street gang members in partnership with drug trafficking organizations (DTOs) appears to be on the rise. In California, the influence of the Mexican Mafia is not limited to the state prisons or community barrios where they tax local drug dealers or extort local businesses. They have ventured into other states and crossed the Mexican border as well.

Investigative journalist, Anabel Hernández, in her (2010) landmark book, *Narcoland*, revealed one aspect of the Mexican drug cartels outreach was the use of the Mexican Mafia to aide their endeavors in the United States and Mexico. The threat DTOs hold for Mexican society looks like the threat the Eme poses for many American Latino youth today. Hernández describes the attraction of membership in the cartels as "the droves of Mexican youth without a future are fertile ground for them and other criminal organizations—mere boys and girls, robbed of all chance for a meaningful life" (ibid., 204). Clearly, security on both sides of the border has not been a deterrent to criminal activity between the Eme and drug cartels.

Today the bulk of cocaine, heroin, methamphetamine, and marijuana sales and distribution in the United States is controlled by Mexican cartels. They have moved ahead of Columbian, Chinese, and Russian mafias to control the illegal drug market into the United States maintaining Mexican DTOs in every single region of the United States. Mexican DTOs have increased their cooperation with street and prison gangs in the states, representing approximately 20,000 street gangs in more than 2,500 cities (ibid., 296).

The Eme has assumed a major role in drug trafficking outside of the prison and jails, especially in Southern California. For example, in June of 2016, a multi-agency gang bust occurred in Corona, California, resulting in the arrest of 52 people. The investigation, dubbed "Operation CVL Gun Shop," followed a string of violent attacks carried out by members of the Corona Varrio Locos gang. It is believed by law enforcement that the gang is affiliated with the Mexican Mafia (*The Press-Enterprise*, June 10, 2016). Over $1.6 million dollars' worth of methamphetamine, cocaine, and marijuana was seized, including, 67 firearms and over $95,000 in cash.

Similarly, in November 2016, federal prosecutors and local police arrested 18 members of Wilmas Street Gang in Wilmington, California. The investigation dubbed "Operation Tidal Wave," targeted 29 members and associates of the Mexican Mafia. The indictment accused them of murder, attempted murder, drug trafficking, robbery, and witness intimidation, stretching back to 2008. Prosecutors said the Wilmas gang had operated in the Wilmington area of Los Angeles since the 1950s and is affiliated with the Mexican Mafia, whose members issue orders to kill rivals and members of law enforcement.

The indictment stated, in part, that the Wilmas gang is "a racist organization and has been historically antagonistic to the presence of African-Americans in Wilmas gang territory ... Wilmas gang members have frequently targeted African-Americans who enter or attempt to reside within the area claimed by the Wilmas gang" (*Los Angeles Times* 2018). The 111-page federal indictment filed in Los Angeles outlines a criminal enterprise that controls the drug trade in Wilmington, collects "taxes" from drug dealers for the benefit of Mexican Mafia members, maintains a supply of often-illegal firearms, and takes retribution against people who may be cooperating with law enforcement.

In June of 2017, the San Bernardino County Sheriff's Department, in conjunction with County Probation, the District Attorney's Office, the Bureau of Alcohol, Tobacco, Firearms, and Explosives, the FBI, and the California Department of Justice, similarly completed "Operation Green Hand," resulting in 86 arrests, the seizure of 43 firearms and 4,800 rounds of ammunition, as well as the seizure of cocaine, black tar heroin, marijuana, methamphetamines, and nearly $30,000 in cash, according to a Sheriff's Department news release (*The Press-Enterprise*, June 30, 2017). The investigation also targeted the Eme gang hierarchy running the illegal operations from prison and gathered intelligence beneficial to the operation.

More recently, Federal Authorities carried out coordinated raids on May 23, 2018, in Los Angeles, based on an investigation dubbed, "Operation Dirty Thirds." Thirty-two people were charged in two federal indictments, with three dozen others who were charged in the cases currently serving time in state prison or county jails. In all, 83 people were named in the two cases. The indictment details how members of the Mexican Mafia and their associates carried out drug trafficking, orchestrated assaults on people who failed to obey allegiance to the Eme and "maintained a steady flow of cash through an intricate system of taxes and fines" (*Los Angeles Times*, May 23, 2018).

The prosecutors detailed the inner workings of the Mexican Mafia in making their case, describing the Eme as "a gang of gangs." It is alleged, Jose Landa-Rodriquez, age 55, ran the tiers in the Los Angeles County Jail system for over three years on behalf of the Eme. According to the indictment, narcotics smuggled into the jails were sold to other inmates. Other groups or inmates wanting to sell drugs were told to wait until the Eme supply had been sold and had to give up a third of their stash to the Eme. Those who disobeyed were assaulted.

Landa-Rodriquez's attorney is accused of abusing attorney-client privilege by conveying messages and orders from Landa-Rodriquez to other Mexican Mafia members. He traveled to state and federal prisons for meetings with other Eme members. He allegedly passed on names of people potentially cooperating with law enforcement and facilitated a plot to extort $100,000 from another gang.

The Eme today is the "Gang of Gangs" especially in the southwest United States. Despite the criminal justice arena's best efforts to eradicate their power, not much except the local jail/prison leadership names has changed. Nicola T. Hanna, U.S. Attorney for California's central district, commented following the raids that, "We have made a very substantial blow against this gang." Hanna revealed that those accused in the indictments had been placed in local federal facilities. The truth of the matter is that those same accused Eme members will continue to do business regardless of where they are placed. In fact, some of the original federal RICO cases brought against the Mexican Mafia (*United States v. Shryock*, 1976) were the precursors of establishing the Eme in federal penitentiaries.

Steve Slaten, former Special Service Unit Agent for the Department of Corrections and Rehabilitation and expert consultant with the FBI and local law enforcement agencies on California prison gangs, has characterized the Mexican Mafia as akin to the TV program, "The Sopranos. You got to think like Tony Soprano and the Italian Mafia ... the Eme has become more sophisticated, more deadly, more treacherous ..." (Alvarado 2015, 276). When I inquired recently about the latest indictments in Los Angeles, Slaten acknowledged that maybe a few were Eme members, but most were just associates being used by the Eme. "Things change quickly behind prison and jail walls. In an eight-month span, everything you thought you knew becomes old news and you have to start over."

For the Mexican Mafia, it's a simple case of economics and power. There is easy money to be made by those with the guile and grit to control nefarious activities. The Eme has both, which in our prisons, jails, and urban locales, makes them look like kings of the asphalt jungles to a younger generation of gullible and disenfranchised youth who aspire to be gangsters.

Following the October 2011, implementation of AB 109, the Public Safety Realignment Act in California (AB 109), nearly 40,000 low-level offenders were placed back under the jurisdiction of the local counties from which they were convicted. Probation departments and county jails felt the brunt of more offenders in the community. One of the immediate outcomes of AB 109 were longer stays in county jails pending trial or serving time. This is where the Mexican Mafia finds its next generation of members, camaradas and ample Sureños to do their bidding.

The reality is that California prisons and jails are housing a higher percentage of violent offenders than ever before. These inmates are younger and serving longer sentences. They are also primarily offenders of Color. Blacks and Latinos, mostly from Southern California, representing nearly 70 percent of the prison population. This new generation of offenders has limited access to therapeutic programs, education/vocational training. Tragically, California's Realignment sought to bring more opportunities to reduce recidivism by bringing low-level offenders closer to home. Instead, it seems we only brought them closer to the deceptive exploitation of the Mexican Mafia.

The Anti-Discrimination Principle and the Short Corridor Collective

The California Department of Corrections and Rehabilitation's (CDCR) informal policy of segregating the recognized leaders of the major prison gangs in a more secure area of the Pelican Bay Prison in solitary confinement was intended to reduce prison violence and illicit gang activities statewide that were directed by prison gang leaders. Ironically, the enhanced segregation housing action enabled the leaders of the gangs to coalesce in order to advance mutually beneficial prison gang interests and achieve a modicum of badly needed prison reforms. Not only does placing gang leaders (or any inmate for that matter) in solitary confinement constitute cruel and unusual punishment, but the policy and practice of classifying prisoners by race is clearly a violation of the equal protection clause of the 14th Amendment, which states that no state shall deprive any person within its jurisdiction of the equal protection of the law because of their race.

This issue was addressed but not resolved by the U.S. Supreme Court in *Johnson v. California* (2005). The Johnson case dealt with the constitutionality of the CDCR unwritten policy of segregating all male prisoners by race in double cell reception centers, during which time inmates are assessed to determine their ultimate placement. The rationale offered for this practice by the CDCR is to prevent violence caused by racial gangs, citing numerous incidents of racial violence. The CDCR further subdivides prisoners within each racial group when possible; so that Japanese inmates are housed separately from Chinese inmates, Northern California Hispanics are separated from those from Southern California, and Black Crip or Bloods are celled separately from non-affiliated Blacks. Based on the evidence reviewed in this chapter, segregation of inmates by race as a housing policy has not reduced racial violence, but may in fact be the basis for the continued racial violence in California prisons.

Garrison Johnson, an African-American inmate, filed suit alleging that the CDCR had established and enforced an unconstitutional policy of housing inmates based on their race in violation of the equal protection clause. The District Court granted summary judgment to the defendants—CDCR—on the grounds that the state was entitled to qualified immunity because its conduct was not clearly unconstitutional. The Court of Appeals for the Ninth Circuit upheld the ruling (321 F. 3d 791, 2003), arguing that the CDCR policy should be reviewed under a more deferential standard than strict scrutiny and that the burden was on the plaintiff to refute the defendant's "common-sense connection" between the policy and prison violence (321 F.3d, 802, 2003). The Supreme Court held that the Ninth Circuit had erred in using a less stringent standard than strict scrutiny because the CDCR's policy is based on expressed racial classifications and remanded the case to the Ninth Circuit Court of Appeals to require the CDCR to demonstrate that its policy is narrowly tailored to advance a compelling state interest.

The CDCR countered that its policy should be exempt from strict scrutiny review because it is "neutral," in that all prisoners are equally segregated and the policy "neither benefits nor burdens one group or individual more than any other group or individual." But the Supreme Court answered that the CDCR's argument ignores the Court's repeated position that "racial classifications receive close scrutiny even when they may be said to burden or benefit the races equally" (*Shaw v. Reno 1993*, at 651). The Court added that by insisting that inmates be housed only with other inmates of the same race, prison officials may be breeding further hostility among prisoners and reinforcing racial and ethnic divisions. In fact, by perpetuating the idea that race matters most, the racial segregation of inmates "may exacerbate the very patterns of [violence that it is] said to counteract" (*Shaw v. Reno 1993*, at 648).

In retrospect, it is clear not only that the CDCR policy is in violation of the Equal Protection anti-discrimination principle but that its contention that the policy neither benefits nor burdens one group or individual more than any other group is dubious. Not only was the policy ineffective in reducing prison racial violence, the segregation of the leaders of the major prison gangs at the Pelican Bay "short corridor" within the SHU clearly benefitted and helped to advance the interest of the major prison gangs.

On the other hand, the CDCR did have a compelling penological interest in shielding inmates from racially motivated violence. The Johnson case may have imposed an explicit strict scrutiny standard for state-mandated racial segregation policies like housing. But proof of a compelling interest by CDCR may be too high a bar that is "Strict in theory, fatal in fact."[9] No one knows which came first, racial cell segregation policies or prison sub-culture behavior of "sticking with your own race." The truth is more than likely somewhere in the middle. I have had the experience of placing two Eme lifers together in a cell who willingly agreed to the double cell. And that night one murdered the other. I have also seen a first-term lifer, White inmate over 50 years of age, placed in a reception center cell with a 47-year-old, non-affiliated, Latino with less than a year to serve. The Latino was murdered the same night. Anecdotal examples, notwithstanding, there are no simple non-segregation doctrines that can easily be imposed in a prison context. History reminds us that human behavior is rarely that accommodating to constitutional canons.

Likewise, the current informal policy and practice by the CDCR of housing inmates based on race as a primary determinate should be considered in the context of the demographics of the California prison population. Prisoner profiles reflect that 43.3 percent of the total male prison population is Hispanic, 28.4 percent is African American, 21.5 percent is White, and 6.8 percent is classified as other (Asian, Islanders, and Native American). Given that nearly 70 percent of the California prison population is either Black or Hispanic, I argue that the so-called "neutral" policy and "equal" treatment of various racial groups by the CDCR in prison is merely an extension of a structure that has historically served to advance and perpetuate systemic racial discrimination resulting in higher incarceration rates of Blacks and Latinos. The criminal justice system "end game" should be about reform and transformation. Instead, it continues to embrace punishment and incarceration that largely impacts people of Color.

The "school to prison pipeline" begins with zero tolerance in schools, criminalization of nuisance offenses (Taggers, truancy, fighting, vulgarity, etc.) and ends in juvenile court proceedings (Nelson and Lind 2015). This starts the trajectory for many marginalized poor and people of color in the criminal justice arena. Similarly, the placement of inmates in management control housing, like California's Security Housing Units—segregated and isolation housing—via established policies that argue for "safety and security" justifications only serve to promote the continuation of prison gangs without realistic alternative programming remedies to change behavior.

Finally, the Short Corridor Collective (Corridor-4) has been successful in launching a prison reform movement that has led to several successful hunger strikes, including one that involved 30,000 inmates throughout California's prisons and has led to favorable court rulings that have resulted in improved medical services and prison conditions for thousands of inmates. The success of this movement is consistent with Derrick Bell's Interest Convergence Theory (ICT), which holds that the dominant society will move to advance the interests of Blacks, as it did in *Brown v. Board of Education* (1954), when the interests of Whites and Blacks converge so that such action is also seen as advancing the interests of Whites. Corridor-4—all recognized prison gang leaders—may have had nefarious reasons for changing CDCR policies, but their actions forced the CDCR to re-evaluate and ultimately change policies on indeterminate placement status for prison gang members and living conditions in segregated housing. For the dominant White culture, it can be argued that prison reform met a limited interest in that it presented to the world, and to an ever-changing American society that is multi-ethnic and socially mixed, a United States that supports civil and human rights.

Notes

1 For a discussion of Chicano gangs, see Durán (2013), E. Flores (2014); J. Flores (2016); Rios (2011); and Vigil (1988; 2002).
2 Title 15, California Code of Regulations, Section 3341.5(c)(2)(A)(2), specifies an *indeterminate* SHU term for validated prison gang members and associates, who are deemed "a severe threat to the safety of others or the security of the institution."
3 The term "security threat group" has generally replaced the term "prison gang," "disruptive group," or "street gang" within CDCR. Similarly, affiliates are inmates who are identified as "members," "associates," or "monitored" by staff as interacting with a certified Security Threat Group.
4 The subject of the interview has family members serving time in prison and chose to remain anonymous to protect them and himself from possible retaliation from the Mexican Mafia. This in-depth interview was conducted over a period of two months and completed in the Fall of 2017.

5 For a more definitive discussion on the primary court case: *Plata*, see: www.pris onlaw.com/cases.php#health_care. Other significant cases included; Dental Care (*Perez v. Tilton*, 2006), Developmental Disabilities (*Clark v. California*, 1996), and Licensed Health Care Facilities within Prisons (*Budd v. Cambra*).

6 Title 15, California Code of Regulations, Section 3341.5(c), provides for "an inmate whose conduct endangers the safety of others or the security of the institution" to be housed in a security housing unit (SHU). Inmates may be placed in a SHU for either a *determinate* or an *indeterminate* term. Inmates sentenced to *determinate* terms in SHUs are those who have been found guilty through a formal disciplinary process of having committed one or more specified serious offenses, ranging from murder to threatening institution security. Prison gang members remained on indeterminate status.

7 The court's order is part of a two-decades-long battle over medical and mental health care conditions in California prisons. *Plata v. Schwarzenegger* was filed in the U.S. District Court for the Northern District of California in 2001 and alleged "constitutional violations in the delivery of medical care" in California prisons. *Coleman* was filed in 1990 in the U.S. District Court for the Eastern District of California and alleged "inadequacies in the delivery of mental health care to inmates." While neither plaintiff initially alleged that overcrowding caused the constitutional violations, the problems presented by prison overcrowding had increased as the prison population in California had expanded 750 percent since the mid-1970s. Given the lack of improvement in medical and mental health care conditions in California prisons, the plaintiffs from *Plata* and *Coleman* combined to request a prison population reduction which was ultimately upheld by the United States Supreme Court.

8 During testimony at the October 2013 Joint Legislative Hearing, Margaret Winter, Associate Director of the ACLU National Prison Project advised the panel regarding several agencies, associations and states who have revamped their solitary confinement policies. In some cases, like Mississippi, the state chose to close them down. Retrieved on October 11, 2018 from http://sfbayview.com/2013/10/margaret-winter-aclu-california-can-be-in-the-vanguard-of-the-movem ent-to-limit-solitary-confinement/

9 Robinson (2006), quoting *Johnson v. California*, 514 U.S. 499, 505 (2005), and quoting *Adarand Constructors Inc. v. Pena*, 515 U.S. 200, 237 (1995).

References

Acuña, Rodolfo. 1972. *Occupied America: The Chicanos' Struggle Toward Liberation.* New York: Harper & Row.

Alvarado, Richard. 2015. *10–33 On the West Yard: A True Crime Story About Politics, Policies and Prison Gangs.* West Conshohocken, PA:Infinity Publishing.

Anthony, K. 2016 "#3790, Crime Stoppers Presentation." March 6, 2016, Monterey, California.

Beard, Jeffery. 2013. "Hungry for Control." *Los Angeles Times.* Op-Ed, August 6.

BellJr., Derrick A. 1980. "Brown v. Board of Education and the Interest-convergence Dilemma." *Harvard Law Review*, 93: 518–533.

Blatchford, Chris. 2008. *The Black Hand; the Bloody Rise and Redemption of "Boxer" Enriquez. A Mexican Mafia Mob Killer.* New York: HarperCollins.

Bolden, Christian. 2013. "Tales from the Hood: An Emic Perspective on Gang Joining and Gang Desistance." *Criminal Justice Review*, 38(4): 473–490.

Bureau of Justice Assistance. 2013. "Compstat: Its Origins, Evolution, and Future in Law Enforcement." Washington, DC:Police Executive Research Forum, U.S. Department of Justice.

California Department of Corrections and Rehabilitation. 2013. *Gang Life in Two Cities: An Insider's Journey*. New York: Columbia University Press.

California Department of Corrections and Rehabilitation. 2017. *Offender Information Reports*. Sacramento, CA: California Justice Department.

Durán, Robert J. 2013. *Gang Life in Two Cities: An Insider's Journey*. New York: Columbia University Press.

Esbensen, Finn-Aage, L. Thomas Winfree, Jr., Ni He, and Terrance J. Taylor. 2001. "Youth Gangs and Definitional Issues: When Is a Gang a Gang, and Why Does It Matter?" *Crime & Delinquency*, 47(1): 105–130.

Flores, Edward Orozco. 2014. *God's Gangs: Barrio Ministry, Masculinity, and Gang Recovery*. New York: New York University Press.

Flores, Jerry D. 2016. *Caught Up: Girls, Surveillance, and Wraparound Incarceration*. Oakland, CA: University of California Press.

Gottschalk, Marie 2015. *Caught: The Prison State and the Lockdown of American Politics*. Princeton, NJ: Princeton University Press.

Griswold Del Castillo, Richard. 1990. *The Treaty of Guadalupe Hidalgo*. Norman, OK: University of Oklahoma Press.

Hernández, Anabel. 2010. *Narcoland: The Mexican Drug Lords and Their Godfathers*. London: Verso.

Hernandez, Kelly. 2017. *City of Inmates; Conquest, Rebellion, and the Rise of Human Caging in Los Angeles 1771–1965*. Chapel Hill, NC: The University of North Carolina Press.

Howell, James C. and Moore, John P. 2010. "History of Street Gangs in the United States." *National Gang Center Bulletin*, 4, May.

Los Angeles Police Department. 2017. Official website of the Los Angeles Police Department. Retrieved, October 28, 2017 from www.lapdonline.org/get_inform ed/content_basic_view/1396

Los Angeles Times, May 23, 2018.

McLeod, Allegra. 2017. "Review Essay: Beyond the Carceral State." *Texas Law Review*, 95: 651–706.

Meier, Matt S. and Feliciano Ribera. 1993. *Mexican Americans/American Mexican: From Conquistadors to Chicanos*. New York. Hill and Wang.

Mendoza, Ramon. 2005. *Mexican Mafia: From Altar Boy to Hitman*. Spartanburg, SC: Police and Fire Publishing.

Mirandé, Alfredo. 1987. *Gringo Justice*. Notre Dame, IN: University of Notre Dame Press.

Montejano, David. 1987. *Anglos and Mexicans in the Making of Texas, 1836–1986*. Austin, TX: University of Texas Press.

Morain, Dan. 2013. "The Real Story Behind Hunger Strike." *Sacramento Bee*, August 11, 2013. Retrieved August 14, 2013 from www.sacbee..com

Nelson, Libby and Lind, Dara. 2015. *The School to Prison Pipeline, Explained*. Washington, DC: Justice Policy Institute.

Pew Center. 2008. "One in One Hundred: Behind Bars in America." The Public Safety Performance Project. Washington, DC: Pew Center.

Pew Center. 2017. "Social and Demographic Trends Retrieved, October, 2017 fromwww.pewsocialtrends.org/2013/08/22/chapter-3-demographic-econom ic-data-by-race/#incarceration

Pyrooz, David C., Gary Sweeten, and Alex R. Piquero. 2012. "Continuity and Change in Gang Membership and Gang Embeddedness." *Journal of Research in Crime and Delinquency*, 50(2): 239–271.

Rios, Victor M. 2011. *Punished: Policing the Lives of Black and Latino Boys*. New York: New York University Press.

Robinson, Brandon N. 2006. "Johnson v. California: A Grayer Shade of Brown." *Duke Law Journal*, 56: 343.

Schoville, C. 2008. "Surenos 2008 One Rule, One Law, One Order: A Special Report from the Rocky Mountain Information Network." Retrieved on July 30, 2013 from http://info.publicintelligence.net/surenosreport.pdf

The Press-Enterprise, June 10, 2016.

The Press-Enterprise, June 30, 2017.

Vera Institute. 2017. "Just Kids: When Misbehaving Is a Crime." Retrieved August 2017 from www.vera.org/when-misbehaving-is-a-crime#understanding-adolescen ce-acting-out-and-calls-for-help

Vigil, James D. 1988. *Barrio Gangs: Street Life and Identity in Southern California*. Austin, TX: University of Texas Press.

Vigil, James D. 1998. *From Indians to Chicanos: The Dynamics of Mexican-American Culture*. 2nd edn. Prospect Heights, IL: Waveland Press.

Vigil, James D. 2002. *Rainbow of Gangs: Street Cultures in the Mega-City*. Austin, TX: University of Texas Press.

White, Jeremy B. 2013. "California's Solitary-Confinement Policies Scrutinized at Hearing." *Sacramento Bee*, October 9, 2013. Retrieved on January 1, 2014 from http://blogs.sacbee.com/

Winter, Margaret. 2013. "Joint Legislative Hearing Testimony by Margaret Winter, Associate Director of the ACLU National Prison Project." Retrieved on January 2, 2014 from http://sfbayview.com

Cases Cited

Adarand Constructors Inc. v. Pena 515 U.S. 200, 237 (1995).

Budd v. Cambra San Francisco County Superior Court, 319578 (2002).

Clark v. California (1996).

Johnson v. California 321 F. 3d 791 (2003).

Johnson v. California 543 U.S. 499 (2005).

Perez v. Tilton, Not Reported in F.Supp.2d (2006). 2006 WL 2433240. Only the Westlaw citation is currently available. United States District Court, N.D. California. 2006.

Plata v. Davis. www.clearinghouse.net/chDocs/public/PC-CA-0018-0001.pdf

Plata v. Schwarzenegger No. C01-1351-THE (N.D. Cal. 2001)

Shaw v. Reno 509 U.S. 630, 650 (1993).

United States v. Shryock 537 F.2d 207 (1976).

Chapter 7

"Captives while Free"

Surveillance of Chicana/o Youth in a San Diego Barrio

José S. Plascencia-Castillo

As a child, I witnessed numerous incidents of police abuse as well as stigmatization of the community. I was a young Chicano growing up in Los Angeles, with a teenage father who was part of a neighborhood gang. One morning, while washing clothes in the barrio's Laundromat, and after experiencing the watchful and criminalizing eye of the *lavandería*'s owner, my father, a youngster known for his thick *brocha* (moustache), and I were approached by a sheriff's deputy who had been called "at random." The officer demanded we step outside and ordered us to sit on the curve. My father was searched, as I helplessly observed his interaction with the deputy. The officer emptied my father's pockets, only to find a few dollars in quarters and a black comb. Concerned with what was happening and becoming increasingly alarmed, I asked—what is happening to my father? The officer looked at me and did not respond. While the officer remained silent, the laundromat owner paced back and forth, verbally commanding him to check my father thoroughly as he considered him to be a dangerous criminal. Upon checking my father for weapons, drugs, or any other sources of criminalization, the deputy ordered us to leave, but added a warning, "you can go, but don't come back here, the owner doesn't want any problems." Approximately two weeks later, my father and I walked to the same laundromat only to be told that all the washing machines were "out of order."

Some two decades later, while conducting ethnographic field research and participant observations in Barrio Pico,[1] a working-class neighborhood in San Diego County, I witnessed many events similar to the one described above with individuals who faced "a dual system of justice." Under this dual system, low-income urban Chicanas and Chicanos are targeted and receive harsh punishment for things that are unremarkable outside of stigmatized neighborhoods and the criminalized status of gang membership (Muñiz 2015). This chapter is based on these observations.[2]

After coming to the painful realization that little had changed since my childhood, the ghosts of the past came back to haunt me but instead of ignoring these incidents, I remained critical and followed Avery Gordon's (1997) sage advice, "if you let them, the ghosts will lead you to what has been missing, which is sometimes everything." During this process of reflection, I learned about Jewelz,[3] Rana, Pelón and seven other young Chicanas and Chicanos and made the theoretical connection between the central mechanisms of panoptic surveillance, hyper-criminalization in communities of Color, and my own experience of seeing my father labeled a deviant criminal. Ultimately, in what has become my life's vocation, I've learned that the negative experiences with the state and community members that my father and I endured were not rare or atypical occurrences but normative experiences for young Chicanas and Chicanos coming of age in the streets of Barrio Pico.

In highlighting the effects of panoptic surveillance on the Chicana and Chicano youngsters of the Barrio, I engaged in direct observations, which often included the "shadowing" of youth, and employed a conversational semi-structured interview schema. My direct observations in the barrio included but were not limited to, playing basketball with youth in the local park, grocery shopping in the community market, and even getting my hair cut in the local barbershop. In these settings, I encountered a variety of people—law enforcement agents, some gang-affiliated youngsters, and older Chicanas and Chicanos, street vendors, mothers, grandmothers, community members, who had no problem with young people, and some who avoided them at all cost. This level of immersion allowed me to begin to see the world from the inside and to assess how youth managed their lives, how they carried out their daily rounds of activities, what they found meaningful, and how the process of hyper-criminalization and panoptic surveillance was omnipresent in their day-to-day interactions with law enforcement agents and community members.

Criminologist Robert Durán (2013) has corroborated findings that suggest that once a certain group of people have been socially constructed and labeled as different, the markers of class, culture, and skin color help to easily point out those labeled as criminal and underserving. In Pico, gang-affiliated youth who adopted a cholo or chola culture—a shaved head, baggy clothes, and visible tattoos—to get away, for leisure, or to feel empowered, experienced the creation of difference from institutions that are consumed with what Jonathan Simon (2007) has termed "governance through crime." This process refers to the everyday impact that citizens experience from encounters with a society obsessed with punitive penal practices. Interestingly, while some of the older Pico residents embraced the idea of "chola or cholo" as a larger subculture not necessarily associated with crime and violence but rather with a youthful, temporary identity, law enforcement agents, ignorant or disdainful of barrio life, labeled youth who wore implacably clean white tennis shoes, shaved their heads, or wore long socks, as deviant. Once police officials managed to convince community members about their potential criminality, barrio youth also often experience shame from their neighbors, which transformed the community into an instrument of hyper-criminalization and surveillance (Rios 2011). The criminalization of the youngsters' style of dress is reminiscent of the criminalization of Chicana and Chicano youth during the Zoot-Suit era in the 1940s.

Pachucas, Pachucos, and el Zoot-Suit

The heightened criminalization deployed by state and non-governmental institutions and experienced by Pico youth is not a new phenomenon. In the 1930s and 1940s, young Angelenos who took part in pachuquismo, a youth subculture whose most salient identifying feature was the zoot-suit, were also treated as "impudent adolescents and juvenile delinquents," particularly by those in law enforcement. For young Chicanas coming of age in World War II-era Los Angeles, the zootsuit generally consisted of a cardigan or V-neck sweater and a long, broad shouldered "finger-tip" coat; a knee-length pleated skirt; fishnet stockings or bobby socks; and platform heels, saddle shoes, or *huarache* sandals (Ramirez 2009) (Figure 7.1). Her male counterpart, the pachuco, wore a suit known as "drapes" or *el tacuche*, an outfit consisting of a finger-tip coat, which sometimes extended to the knee, and a pair of billowing "Punjab" pants that tapered to the ankle.

For some, pachuquismo symbolized youthful insouciance and nothing more. For others, it symbolized rebellion, difference, and even un-Americanism. The latter position represents a critical violent moment in the history of the zoot-suit subculture. In June of 1943, for at least ten

Figure 7.1 38th Street women in police line-up. Herald Examiner Collection/Los Angeles Public Library.

days, White servicemen violently attacked young zooters. In some instances, they stopped and boarded streetcars, burst into businesses and private homes, and set upon people of Color, especially youth, irrespective of their attire. When they apprehended zooters, they frequently sheared their hair and stripped them of their distinctive clothing. In brief, the events that took place in 1943 expressed anxiety over Chicana and Chicano bodies and their place in a rapidly changing social order (ibid.). Undoubtedly, the Chicana and Chicano body has been under surveillance not only in the post-war era but also in succeeding decades. Clearly, an examination of the zoot-suit epoch and the contemporary youngsters of Barrio Pico reveals the existence of fragmented and conflictual relationships not only with law enforcement but also with community members who employ panoptic methods of surveillance to control not only the body of young Chicanas and Chicanos but also their minds.

The Panopticon in the Barrio

I should note that my personal narrative and background provide a context for my theoretical engagement with Foucault's panopticon of hyper-criminalization. According to Foucault, the panopticon model achieves hyper-surveillance in two distinct ways. First, the panopticon surveils members of society, whether or not a human monitor is actually watching them. Second, the surveillance mechanisms of power produced by this design are reiterative in the sense that individuals never know whether they are being observed and thus must always assume and act as if they are being monitored. As a result, control is achieved as much by the physical constraints of architectural space as it is by the internalization and self-regulation of the self. In Pico, for example, Chicana/o youth experienced the effects of the panopticon in two ways. First, youngsters were scrutinized by officers and often told to "stay in their side of town," which signaled law enforcement control not only of the body, but also of space. Second, young people often experienced stigmatization when they attempted to use the community park. In fact, I frequently overheard people stating they would call the police to have the youngsters removed from the premises, an extreme irony given that parks are ostensibly designed for youth.

Although this chapter employs Foucauldian theory to understand hyper-criminalization, it sharply diverges in its intent from Foucault. As a postmodern theoretician, Foucault was far less concerned with causes and subjects than in the process itself. In other words, he was not so much invested in the "who" portion of the problematics of hyper-criminalization as much as in the "how." In contrast, I contend that the examination of "who" is vital to understanding the "how" in the hyper-criminalization process of Chicana/o youth. In *Discipline and Punish*, Foucault (1977) observed that control does not exclusively necessitate physical domination over the body but can be achieved through isolation and the constant possibility of observation. Whereas in a true panopticon, prisoners are isolated by the architectural construction of the cells, in Pico, the process of hyper-criminalization and isolation entails surveillance beyond an architectural design. That is, youth who live in Pico experience surveillance not only from the criminal justice system, but also from institutions that are traditionally intended to nurture and support community members.

Panopticism and Its Effects

To better understand the effects of the panopticon, the question of *what exactly the panopticon is* must first be addressed. The panopticon is a social control mechanism first introduced by Jeremy Bentham. The basic architectural construction entails a circular prison complex with a tower in the center of the building. The idea of the panopticon is that its structure would allow for the perpetual monitoring of the behavior and movements of the incarcerated people. Surveillance in a panoptic state becomes so permanent in the minds of the surveilled, it instills the psychological trepidation of constantly being watched, thereby ensuring the behavior demanded by authority, even in its absence (Glover 2007). In fact, "the perfection of power should tend to render its actual exercise unnecessary." According to Foucault, "the inmates should be caught up in a power situation of which they are themselves the bearers." The process is, thus, so insidious that the subject enforces its own obedience out of fear of being watched. Hence, the actual mechanism of power need no longer be tangible. Instead, it becomes an idea weaved into one's social existence and fueled by fear (ibid.).

The panopticon as a criminological tool of control that, Glover has suggested, helps to understand the transition in society from one concerned with the body to one concerned with surveillance and power that, to some extent, binds the mind through coercion. Foucault explains,

> The major effect of the panopticon: to induce in the inmate a sense of conscious and permanent visibility that assures the automatic functioning of power ... the surveillance is permanent in its effects, even if it is discontinuous in its action; that the perfection of power should tend to render its actual exercise unnecessary.
>
> (Foucault 1977: 201)

In deconstructing this statement, the connection between the "permanent visibility" of Chicana/o youth in the barrio as a marker of criminality (evidenced by the hyper-criminalization processes) and the permanent visibility induced by the panopticon effect becomes evident. Foucault remarked that the main purpose of the panopticon is to make the individual conscious and aware of their status. By doing so, an "automatic" functioning of power ensues as the individual—here, Chicana/o youth—are reminded of the power relationship they are in with the state and community members. Once permanent monitoring, surveillance, and formal and informal patrolling are initiated and instilled in individual experiences, its actual consistent occurrence need not be present for the sense of permanent visibility to operate. The individual is thereafter mindful of power dynamics. Clearly, the panopticon is the ultimate mechanism of social control because it becomes self-sustaining and enduring.

In the following excerpt, Foucault describes how the state deploys disciplinary power through panoptic surveillance:

> Disciplinary power ... is exercised through its invisibility; at the same time, it imposes on those whom it subjects a principle of compulsory visibility. In discipline, it is the subjects who have to be seen. Their visibility assures the hold of the power that is exercised over them. It is the fact of being constantly seen, of being able always to be seen, that maintains the disciplined individual in his subjection. And the examination is the technique by which power, instead of emitting the signs of its potency, instead of imposing its mark on its subjects, holds them in a mechanism of objectification.
>
> (ibid., 187)

My engagement with panopticism provides a theoretical nexus for the examination of hyper-criminalization and its effects on the barrio experiences of Chicana and Chicano youth. My concern is not only with the resistance strategies that emerge from youth but also the conscious peer-to-peer socialization that arises from such social control practices. Surveillance is about identity. The processes of the panopticon, as with the processes of hyper-criminalization, impose an identity that suggests, among other issues, guilt and wrong-doing (Glover, 2007). The following narratives illustrate not only the deep sense of panoptic governance that youth experience in the streets of Barrio Pico but also how they mobilize mechanisms of resistance against the pervasiveness of an increasingly intrusive hyper-criminalization complex.

"I Am Still Here, I Am Still Alive": Jewelz's Story

Jewelz, a petite Chicana whose glimmering blue eyes have earned her the nickname she so proudly accepts, opens the door to her small two-bedroom home and welcomes me in. She politely offers a glass of freshly-squeezed orange juice, "Hey, want some?" I respond, "Sure" and we proceed to the backyard. Her mother, a 40-something single mom who migrated to the United States in the late 1980s greets me, "Hola, muchacho" and continues to irrigate *hierba buena*.

I should note, that in my search for stories, I have sought to ask questions that would help me experience the world of my participants through their eyes, rather than either producing a minstrel-like caricature of their social reality or pathologizing their experiences. I have taken the position that participants who opt to share experiences will provide powerful insights that may address barrio concerns and offer new perspectives on how life experiences sustain and influence social dynamics. Viewing their experience from the inside out in this way has increased my already heightened "insider view" and, hence, provided a deeper, more nuanced understanding of barrio life.

Jewelz's personal life is exceptional in at least one way. At a time when government spending for schools has been slashed, and schooling is increasingly based on inflexible curriculum (Pearl 2002), she has successfully completed high school and has enrolled in college. She has also worked hard to learn how to navigate college bureaucracy and to pass all of her first semester coursework. During the interview, she relates:

> I have a lot of friends who, you know, are down, and we have been cool since high school, we've done a lot of crazy ass stuff together, but I think about how, you know, I just don't want to end up a nobody. It's depressing living here. I really want to get my mom and I out of the neighborhood. It's not normal here, I can't sleep at nights. Sometimes I think someone is going to break in and do something to us. So, I think, if I at least do something in school, maybe get my college degree, well, that will help us.

Despite her involvement with her homies, Jewelz's high school years were exceptional in the sense that she always passed her classes with high grades and was praised by teachers and school administrators. Her admirable persistence has now translated to college, a setting where despite many obstacle, Jewelz is thriving. Interestingly, Jewelz's exceptional academic standing does not protect her from the constant thought of danger and apprehension that inhabits her mind. During our conversation, Jewelz spent much of the time talking about "making a move" and leaving the neighborhood. Her heightened awareness of danger evidenced the effects of the panopticon. Regarding surveillance, Jewelz stated,

> I am doing good in school and all that. The only problem and the thing that I really don't like is having no damn car. Honestly, it's depressing. I hate waking up early and walking to the bus stop or the station. I just don't like how my day has to start with seeing cops parked right in the front of my house, or right next to the park. I just don't know why they do that. People are still sleeping. They don't even give us a chance to wake up. You know, if I had my own car, I

would just be able to leave without having to walk right past them all
the time. Sometimes, I hate that I have to feel like I did something bad,
but I know I have not, that's depressing too.

Beneath the picture of stability and scholastic success, there were real problems. Because Jewels did not have a vehicle at the time of our interview,
she felt irritated that she had to ride the bus to local community college.
According to Jewelz, a simple walk to the bus stop was problematic and
enough to ruin her day. Jewelz and 80 percent of the gang-affiliated Chi-
cana/o youth I interviewed reported that seeing police in their community
made them feel uncomfortable, depressed, and apprehensive. Foucault's
observation that the move in governance from one concerned with control
of the body to one concerned with the mind is evident in Jewelz's remarks.
Foucault suggested that while both the mind and the body were bound in
early times, the effect of the panopticon ushered in

> [a] shift in the point of application of this power: it is no longer the
> body, with the ritual play of excessive pains, spectacular brandings in
> the ritual of the public execution; it is the mind or rather a play of
> representations and signs circulating discreetly but necessarily and evi-
> dently in the minds of all. It is no longer the body, but the soul.
>
> (1977: 101)

When Jewelz was not studying, her after-school leisure activities included
staying home and practicing the application of her make-up, as a way of
coping with the constant surveillance and harassment she experienced from
police. In Pico, police officers often viewed the behavior of gang-affiliated
Chicanas with mistrust, derision, and suspicion (Diaz-Cotto 2006; Schaffner
2006). It is not surprising then that Jewelz preferred isolation to exposure to
constant police surveillance. She explained,

> Oh, I don't like dealing with the shit that goes on around here …
>
> A lot of things help me deal with stress and make me feel less
> depressed, I guess, you know. I like to draw. I like to practice my
> make-up skills, like how to apply my make-up. I want to for sure finish
> school but also become a make-up artist, maybe get a nice job, like
> maybe at a make-up store, or something in the mall. Maybe become
> the manager, that would be nice. I would be a good manager.

Like other young people who come of age in hyper-policed neighborhoods,
Jewelz had a deep desire for acceptance, recognition, and incorporation into
conventional society (Rios 2017). She imagined herself in a nine-to-five job,
with a college degree, taking care of her family. Her statement lays bare the
intractable links between hyper-policing, surveillance, and depression. Clearly,

depression and despair—via her interactions with police—have become enmeshed in the everyday life of Jewelz, often interfering with her dreams for the future. Jewelz sadly recalled the most damaging consequence of policing and surveillance on her physical health.

> It's not cool to have these fools always thinking you are doing something bad. You know, always watching you. Sometimes, I just don't know how to deal with it. I don't want to say it, but sometimes I hate my own life, just everything about it, if you grow up here, you know that you are not ever going to be a normal kid. Like, I go to school and try really hard and I want to do good things and some-times it doesn't feel like I am going to be successful. Sometimes I don't know where I'm heading. I've even cut myself, to remember, I am still here, you know, to remember that I am going somewhere, like it's OK. I'm going to be better, and things will get better.

For Jewelz and many of the Chicana/o youth in Pico, the experience of being watched, managed, and treated as criminals affected not only their outlook on the future, but also their physical health. In a study of community attitudes toward police, Mirandé (1987, 153) similarly observed in a study of Casa Blanca, a hyper-criminalized barrio in Southern California, that "perhaps the most persistent overriding concern expressed by Chicanas/os is that police treat them with less respect and courtesy, and with less regard for their rights." For young adults like Jewelz, the disregarding of their rights by police officers significantly impacted their mental and physical health, for Jewelz enough to potentially derail her pursuit of a college degree. Like other Chicana and Chicano youth in Pico, Jewelz is faced with a dilemma. She can either comply with the demands of authority figures, and become obedient and compliant, and suffer the accompanying loss of identity and self-esteem, or, adopt a resis-tant stance and contest social invisibility to command respect in the public sphere (Miranda 2003; Rios and Lopez-Aguado 2012). Jewelz's dilemma prominently illustrates not only how she comes to view herself but also the world in which she finds herself trapped.

"The Homegirl Lets Me Push the Stroller": Rana's Story

I look at my watch and it is 4:30 in the afternoon, I am 30 minutes early for my interview with Rana, a young Chicano whose shiny black hair emits the smell of Tres Flores, a popular hair product that my father and many other Chicano men, used on their hair. Rana has agreed to meet with me on a bench just outside the local community park and speak about his experiences with law enforcement. I am patiently waiting for him when suddenly a loud whistle and high-pitch voice breaks the silence. "Hey, it's me," Rana exclaims as he crosses the street. Rana grew up in the same community as Jewelz in the heart of a barrio that hosts one of San Diego's most criminalized Chicana youth. Rana, like other youngsters in Pico has experienced criminalization in various forms, such as gang injunctions, civil lawsuits against neighborhoods that prohibit young people from engaging in activities such as congregating in groups of two or more, standing in public for more than five minutes, wearing certain clothing, and making gang gestures or signs (Muñiz 2015).

Gary Stewart (1998) draws a parallel between modern gang injunctions and the Black Codes. Like the vagrancy ordinances that targeted Blacks after the Civil War, gang injunctions criminalize anyone who fits the profile of a gang member, thus creating a state of criminalization for youth who live in such communities that resonates with the history of slavery. As an added measure of control, police in the streets of Pico use the language of "The Street Terrorism and Enforcement Act" (the STEP Act) to incapacitate Chicana and Chicano youth who associate with persons believed to be members of Pico's gang or dress in distinctive "gang attire" (see Chapter 5). While legally sanctioned, the STEP Act, like the barrio's gang injunction, promotes what Menjívar and Abrego (2012) conceptualize as legal violence, or "the suffering that results from the implementation of laws that delimit and shape individuals' lives on a routine basis" (ibid., 1387). For Chicana and Chicano youth in Pico, such legally sanctioned forms of violence ensure the perpetuation of fear, isolation, and policing of the self.

While Stewart's comparison of gang injunctions and the Black Codes is critical to an understanding of racialized criminalization, it does not fully capture the idiosyncrasies of Rana's Chicano experience; an experience of coming of age amidst legally sanctioned violence, criminalizing labels, and social control. C. Wright Mills (1959) detailed, "Neither the life of an individual nor the history of a society can be understood without understanding both." Following Mills, in what follows, I attempt to make sense of Rana's experience with law enforcement and surveillance by bringing to the forefront and interrogating the larger-than-life historical pressures and externally imposed structural forces that override individual characteristics and influence not only his family life but also community dynamics (Vigil, 2002). Like Jewelz, whose family owns a modest home, Rana's family has lived in his grandmother's home for as long as he can remember.

> We have lived in the same place for a while already. I am never going to move. This was my grandma's house and my mom and me and if I have a baby, you know, one day, this will be their place. We clean it up all the time, no trash. It is nice here. You know, I don't think I should feel like I need to leave just because they got us all wrong. I am in my place, these fools, they come from who knows where, they are out of place, you get me?

Rana loves his barrio, he is very proud of living in his grandmother's home. For him, it is extremely important to keep the property clean. He mentions, however, that too often, police officer disrespect his grand-mother's property,

> I was sleeping the other night, doing nothing wrong, and heard like someone was screaming, an officer was saying, you know, like, stop, and all that. I looked outside to see what was up and I saw an officer walking around our property, I guess looking for whoever they were looking for. But you know, I was a little mad, I guess a little scared too, like, they know me by name, what if they think, "hey, he doesn't live here" and force me out of my home, or what if they start shooting because they think I'm breaking in.

Rana's account reveals how the panopticon effect produces a sense of hyper-awareness and panic even when "you are doing nothing wrong." Under the effects of the panopticon, this operates as a function of power. When I asked Rana how he felt when he was not at home, and whether he was just as scared or nervous to encounter police officers on the streets, he responded:

> When I am not home, it's the same. I feel a little nervous, if I hear, "Hey, stop right there," I know why, it has to be because of my looks, you know. But the thing that I like is that my neighbor, the homegirl has a baby, so it's funny, I ask her, "Hey, can I push your baby's stroller?" I know it sounds crazy but if I am walking with her and the baby, I don't get harassed as much, you know, so every time I kick it with her I ask, or she will tell me, "Hey, push the stroller." I think that cops probably think, "Hey, that fool has a family," and they leave me alone. But I stay in a lot, a couple of years ago I was always out, but now I don't.

Rana, like Jewelz, highlighted a familiar theme among the Chicanas and Chicanos I spoke with. For Rana, "staying indoors" and not seeing his friends were depressing. But the effects of the panopticon were not expunged by staying indoors. The constant feeling of being observed and judged was always present. While the home should be a place of refuge, safety, and relaxation, Rana compared the solitude he experienced at home to his days in a juvenile detention center. In other words, Rana's carceral experience did not vanish once he walked out of the juvenile detention center.

> Yeah, it's sad, man, you know when I was in Juvi, I felt like, when I am free I'm going to be out and I'm going to go all over the place and eat whatever I want and it will be cool. But, nope, nothing changes, it's the

same. I don't know about other people, but if cops know you by name like they know me, they see me out and about and already think, "he must be up to no good." Then there is no difference when you are out or in.

Rosenbaum (1981) argued that the preferred mechanism of colonization for the majority of Mexicanas/os from 1846 to 1916 included spatial and social separation from the Anglo community (Durán 2013, 59). In Pico, young Chicanos like Rana experience what can only be described as a "forced spatial segregation," a regulatory mechanism that enhances panoptic surveillance while controlling the movement of young Chicanas/os, even when they are not directly dealing with law enforcement or engaging in criminal activities. In the midst of panoptic surveillance, criminalization, and depression, a unique method of resistance develops. Forrest Stuart (2016) found that residents in hyper-policed neighborhoods develop the technique of displaying "innocence signals," a way for residents to carefully manage their outward appearances and demeanor in order to reduce their relative suspicion in the eyes of officers, to more conspicuously differentiate themselves from officers' "privileged targets."

In Pico, Rana engages in conscious efforts to avoid police scrutiny. In a community where the threat of unwanted police contact and enforcement is constant and looms large, Rana has developed and sophisticated a particular "cop wisdom." As Stuart (2016) explains, Cop wisdom allows people to render seemingly random police activity more legible, predictable, and manipulatable. Like the "kites"—a unique method of communication used by people who are captives of the state—which allows incarcerated people to subvert the intrusive nature of correctional officers and to socialize with one another, pushing his homegirl's stroller is one mechanism, for example, that has allowed Rana not only to engage in a creative tactic for deflecting, and destabilizing criminal justice contact but also to socialize with people outside of his residence, and to minimize the isolation that is afforded to him via panoptic surveillance.

"I Am Being Watched": Pelón's Story

"Pelón," like Jewelz and Rana, has spent his youth navigating the streets of Barrio Pico. He is a sturdy and stocky 5'5" Chicano, 19 years old. When I first met him in the basketball courts, he wore black Vans, navy-blue shorts, a navy-blue short sleeve shirt, and a San Diego Padres baseball cap. I approached him and told him I was interested in learning about his experiences in the neighborhood. Pelón agreed to meet, but I would first have to walk with him to the barbershop. "We can talk, I'll see you tomorrow at my pad," Pelón murmured before he walked into the night. The next morning, I drove to his home and casually knocked on his door three times, "Pelón I am here," I said in a friendly tone. "I am coming, bro," Pelón said. After a few minutes of waiting he came out of his home and said, "We can't go to Lupe's for a haircut, the owner knows me, she thinks she saw me doing some shit one night but it wasn't me, now she is scared so I'm not allowed in. We are going to have to walk to the other side of town."

In Barrio Pico, we can see how racialization, especially signified through skin tone, certain clothing, hair, tattoos, signals not only to the police, but also to some community members, that these young men deserve scrutiny, even—and perhaps specially—when they are doing nothing illegal (Rios 2017). I asked Pelón to tell me more about his barbershop experience:

> One day, I just went in there, you know, I keep my hair short but I still like to look good. It was packed, you know, I waited for forty minutes and finally they called me up and at the same time they said, "You're next," the owner was walking in. She is like, "We can't cut your hair here, I don't want people to think that I am fine with what you and your friends are doing." I told her, like, well, I haven't done shit, you got the wrong person. She didn't care. She said she doesn't want to see me around. So, I guess she doesn't want my money, but, yeah, that shit was embarrassing.

Sociologist Robert Garot (2010) has argued that preemptive harsh sanctions imposed by school officials on gang-associated students actually work to reinforce "tough identities." When schools center on managing and controlling students, the youth disengage from learning, which facilitates their adoption of a tough role, a process Garot labels, "the contradiction of control." I extend Garot's theorization by arguing that this process also takes place outside of educational settings. I argue that when community members who come into contact with gang-associated youth center on criminalizing and controlling young men and women, the youth become resistant and frustrated, as was the case with Pelón. I asked Pelón if he ever confronted the barbershop owner.

> Nah, not with words. I mean, she lives here so I see her all the time. Every time I see her, I get fucking mad. I don't like people accusing me of shit I didn't do. I tell her, fuck you, you know, and I keep doing my thing. At this point whatever, but the way I see it is, like, you are not going to tell me what the fuck to do. I think she just thinks we all look the same or maybe dress the same or something, but she is tripping.

In his classic work, Goffman (1990) discussed unique forms of stigma, some more visibly obvious than others. Those hapless enough to bear a stigma immediately apparent to others—what Goffman called a "stigma symbol"—garner troubling reactions from other members of society. Clearly, Pelón believes that his attire is such a stigma symbol. Goffman noted that the public reacts with emotions ranging from terror to hatred of those who wear a stigma symbol. People may feel pity for the stigmatized, resort to abusive commentary, or organize to quarantine the stigmatized individuals away from society as if they festered with contagion (Rios 2017).

Like other Chicana and Chicano youth who come of age in Barrio Pico, Pelón's life trajectory has been impacted by criminalization, stigma, and policing of the self. Though not a fan of his once a week, 20-minute walk to the barbershop, given how he is treated, he has no other option:

> You know, I kind of don't like the walk and I do at the same time, you know. I don't like dealing with the bullshit here, so it's cool, I go get my cut somewhere else … Here, people are always watching everything you do … everyone here is nosey … there no one cares that's why I kind of like the other barbershop. Because it's cool, I don't know anyone there. I leave here and it's, like, it's relaxing.

Pelón's comment about leaving the neighborhood is suggestive of the panopticon and the consistency of its effects. For Pelón, there is an emphasis on behaving in a manner that will lessen not only feelings of being hyper-surveilled, but also the constant policing of the self. Pelón's narrative also illustrates Foucault's concern with how constant surveillance and the panopticon effect impact the mind. In this instance, it is particularly striking because Pelón leaves the neighborhood for a haircut, not because he prefers a particular barber but because he feels like he can ease the perils of confrontation with the owner of Lupe's barbershop. By removing himself from the barrio, Pelón feels that the ways in which he is scrutinized and harassed will be lessened.

Barrio Pico and the Panoptic Effect

Young Chicanas and Chicanos who live in Barrio Pico struggle to navigate the community. They constantly feel the force of hyper-criminalization employed by both representatives of the state and from non-criminal justice structures and agents. Although the participants whose stories I shared in this chapter highlighted how navigating the community is difficult and at times depressing, it was interesting to listen to them and to learn about techniques they have developed in order to overcome some of the central causes affecting the navigation of their barrio. After listening to my participants talk about hyper-criminalization, surveillance, and the effects of the panopticon, it is clear that the lines between the state and non-criminal justice structures are becoming increasingly blurred. Perhaps Pelón said it best when he observed, "La Doña de la tienda just needs a badge, fuck, and she is way strict, I don't even feel comfortable in her store." Jewelz, Rana, and Pelón indicated that they constantly experience punishment from community members and that past experiences tend to mark their paths, creating tension between them and the community.

Although I have identified how community members employ tactics paralleling those used by the criminal justice system to police young Chicanas and Chicanos, I want to also argue that the community at large is equally affected by the measures deployed by the criminal justice system, and while community members who live in the barrio exercise power to punish and control young people, many of them knowingly or unknowingly are under the same apparatus of governmental surveillance experienced by the youth.

Conclusion

In this chapter, I have sought to demonstrate how Chicana and Chicano youth who come of age in the streets of San Diego County today, like their Pachuca and Pachuco counterparts in the 1940s, experience a criminalization that is concerned not only with the physical surveillance of their bodies but also with covert forms of social control, such as coercion of the mind, which, as Foucault suggested, may induce more harm than traditional mechanisms of social control. Despite efforts to control and incapacitate the youth of Barrio Pico, cholo and chola styles, like Pachuquismo, function as "a spectacular reminder that the social order fails to contain their energy" (Cosgrove 1984, 78). For Pachucas/os and contemporary Pico youth, adopting alternative styles becomes somewhat of an informal social movement in which marginalized youth portray their culture through dress and appearance (Rios 2017, 81).

Two things should be noted about hyper-criminalization in the barrio. First, young people who experienced hyper-criminalization and heightened surveillance learn to develop unique techniques to avoid not only formal, but also informal punishment. Jewelz explained how she has come to find ways to stay "under the radar." She mentioned, "I like staying in, I don't have to deal with anyone who doesn't want to deal with me." This type of response to hyper-criminalization is a problem for young people who live in the barrio. While isolation may create a protective barrier to help youngsters stay "under the radar," it also blocks youth's chances to socialize with people who might facilitate meaningful connections with mentors and support systems. Second, community members often exhibited learned techniques from representatives of the state regarding control and punishment. My observations revealed, for example, how liquor store owners systematically displayed signs that read, "no backpacks allowed" in their stores. Ironically, these signs only appeared as young people traveled to school. I learned that store owners characterized a school backpack as a criminal tool, intended to hide stolen goods. Young people often internalized the message that their backpacks were a marker not of academic performance and success but of criminality. Rana once told me, "Teachers used to get mad because I only carried my binder around, but I hated taking all my things to school, you know, it looked like I was hiding shit when I had my bag." While the young Chicanas/os I interviewed were currently "free" and not experiencing the panopticon effect within the confines of prison or jail cells, their experiences revealed that freedom is not a reflection of statistics but rather, a dynamic, ongoing accomplishment that occurs within a particular structure, culture, and historical context. Freedom is not static. "It is work" (Rios 2011, 164). The concept of "freedom as an ongoing accomplishment" reminds me of my father's greatest piece of advice. In September of 2007, after my father had been deported to México, we spoke on the phone, he said, "I am sorry that I cannot make it okay, but I want you to know that I feel good and that even when the Border Patrol and Immigration and Customs Enforcements (ICE) constantly had an eye on us, I always had an eye on them." That day my father taught me that "power is everywhere," that it "comes from everywhere" and hopefully perhaps, that where there is power, there is also resistance (Foucault 1998: 63).

Notes

1 The names of identifiable neighborhoods and persons have been changed to protect the identity of all parties.
2 This chapter is a revision and expanded version of an earlier, shorter draft essay which was published in a special dossier issue of *Aztlán: A Journal of Chicano Studies,* 43(2), 2018.
3 Nicknames are of particular importance for gang-affiliated Chicana and Chicano youth. Nicknaming provides avenues for proving commitment and unwavering group loyalty. In some ways, a nickname also allows a person to take on a unique identity created in the barrio (Vigil 1988). Nicknames are often reflective of a particular physical or personality trait. For example, "Pelón" as a nickname for a person with a shaved head, "El Midnight" for someone who is dark, or "Mickey Mouse" for someone with large ears.

References

Cosgrove, Denis. 1984. *Social Formation and Symbolic Landscape.* London: Croom Helm.
Diaz-Cotto, Juanita. 2006. *Chicana Lives and Criminal Justice: Voices from El Barrio.* Austin, TX: University of Texas Press.
Durán, Robert J. 2013. *Gang Life in Two Cities: An Insider's Journey.* New York: Columbia University Press.
Foucault, Michel. 1977. *Discipline and Punish: The Birth of the Prison* (trans. Alan Sheridan). New York: Random House.

Foucault, Michel. 1998. *The History of Sexuality: The Will to Knowledge*. London: Penguin.

Garot, Robert. 2010. *Who You Claim: Performing Gang Identity in School and on the Streets*. New York: New York University Press.

Glover, Karen. 2007. "'Racing' Racial Profiling Research: Complicating the 'Trust of Rights and Powers' Through an Analysis of Racial Profiling Narratives." PhD thesis. Texas A&M University.

Goffman, Erving. 1990. *The Presentation of Self in Everyday Life*. London: Penguin, original 1959.

Gordon, Avery. 1997. *Ghostly Matters: Haunting and the Sociological Imagination*. Minneapolis, MN: University of Minnesota Press.

Menjívar, C. and L. J. Abrego. 2012. "Legal Violence: Immigration Law and the Lives of Central American Immigrants." *American Journal of Sociology*, 117: 1380–1421.

Mills, C. Wright. 1959. *The Sociological Imagination*. New York: Oxford University Press.

Miranda, Marie. 2003. *Homegirls in the Public Sphere*. Austin, TX: University of Texas Press.

Mirandé, Alfredo. 1987. *Gringo Justice*. Notre Dame, IN: University of Notre Dame Press.

Muñiz, Ana. 2015. *Police, Power, and the Production of Racial Boundaries*. New Brunsweick, NJ: Rutgers University Press.

Pearl, Arthur. 2002. "The Big Picture: Systemic and Institutional Factors in Chicano School Failure and Success." In Richard R. Valencia (Ed.), *Chicano School Failure and Success: Past, Present and Future*, 2nd ed. New York: Routledge, pp. 335–364.

Ramirez, C. S. 2009. *The Woman in the Zoot Suit: Gender, Nationalism, and the Cultural Politics of Memory*. Durham, NC: Duke University Press.

Rios, Victor M. 2011. *Punished: Policing the Lives of Black and Latino Boys*. New York: New York University Press.

Rios, Victor M. 2017. *Human Targets: Schools, Police, and the Criminalization of Latino Youth*. Chicago: University of Chicago Press.

Rios, Victor and Patrick Lopez-Aguado. 2012. "Pelones y matones: Chicano Cholos Perform for a Punitive Audience." In A. J. Aldama, C. Sandoval, and P. Garcia (Eds.), *Performing the U.S. Latina and Latino Borderlands*. Bloomington, IN: Indiana University Press.

Rosenbaum, Robert J. 1981. *Méxicano Resistance in the Southwest*. Dallas, TX: Southern Methodist University Press.

Schaffner, Laurie. 2006. *Girls in Trouble with the Law*. New Brunswick, NJ: Rutgers University Press.

Simon, Jonathan. 2007. *Governing Through Crime: How the War on Crime Transformed American Democracy and Created a Culture of Fear*. New York: Oxford University Press.

Stewart, Gary. 1998. "Black Codes and Broken Windows: The Legacy of Racial Hegemony in Anti-Gang Civil Injunctions." *Yale Law Journal*, 107(7): 2249–2279.

Stuart, Forrest. 2016. *Down, Out, and under Arrest: Policing and Everyday Life in Skid Row*. Chicago: University of Chicago Press.

Vigil, James D. 1988. *Barrio Gangs: Street Life and Identity in Southern California*. Austin, TX: University of Texas Press.

Vigil, James D. 2002. *A Rainbow of Gangs: Street Cultures in the Mega-City*. Austin, TX: University of Texas Press.

Chapter 8

Hyper-Criminalization

Gang-Affiliated Chicana Teen Mothers Navigating Third Spaces

Katherine L. Maldonado

Introduction

> I was 5 years old the first time I sat in the back seat of a police car. I have a blurred memory of this moment in my childhood, but I clearly remember my mother holding my hand tight. In recalling this memory, adrenaline begins to rush through my body, and I write because I go back to the fear I felt as a child when Child Protective Services (CPS) got involved in our lives. My mother's words were soothing, "Mija, todo va a estar bien," but the laughter of the police officers past the steel barrier or cage in the back seat of the police car, and my mother's worried face did not make sense to me as a child who was raised to fear police officers due to my parents' undocumented status. When we arrived at our destination, I held my mother's hand tighter, and as they separated us, I recall crying and being taken to a separate room. My mother asked me in Spanish if I could translate for her and to ask the officers if there was any way that we could get interviewed together, but they said it was part of their standard procedures. After the interview, they took us back into the police car and my mother reassured me again that we would be okay. Thankfully, after two more visits in our home from officers and social workers, CPS never got involved with us again.

Fifteen years later, my two sons sat in the back seat of a police car for their first time, but without me. My oldest was aged 5 and the youngest was aged 1. When I received a call from a police officer and was informed that my children were being taken out of UCLA University child care for proceedings with a child welfare case, I could not help but become overwhelmed with flashbacks of the one time I too sat in a police car as a young child. I asked, begged them, to allow me to drive them to the hospital where they would be checked out but the urgency to make sure my kids were not physically and mentally harmed by me was more important. I wish they would have believed me when I said that it would be traumatizing for them to experience this "simple ride" without me. I knew the fear of being taken inside a police car with my mother, but I could not communicate to the officers that it was important for my children to at least hold my hand in the ride through the heavy traffic from West Los Angeles to East Los Angeles.

Upon their arrival, they conducted a full inspection of their bodies, with x-rays, and conducted a mental health assessment. Everyone agreed that the children were healthy and that my 1-year-old's burn on his leg was accidental. The officers told me, "You'll be good. The kids look all happy and good. We've seen really worse cases." I remember feeling relief, telling myself that this was just protocol. When it was over, I said, "Okay, kids, we're getting ready to go." But the social worker said, "Ms. Maldonado, the kids are being placed under foster care. My boss and I have ordered an emergency removal."

My heart dropped. I could not believe what I was hearing. For weeks, I believed that all of these procedures were simply part of the protocol so that they could confirm that my children were safe with me. I cried, telling the social worker, "How could you do this to them? They are not safe with anyone besides me." I wanted to get on my knees to beg her not to take my children. I was pleading, "They have never been away from me. They have never been under a stranger's care." She took my children as they were crying. I tried to keep a straight face and told my 5-year-old son to please take care of himself and his brother and never to separate from each other. They both looked scared, but I had to show strength so they could walk away feeling okay.

My ride home felt like an eternity that night, and the question that consumed me was "Where did I fail as a mother?" I got home and curled up in a corner, grabbing my knees tight into a fetal position. I cried again. I pulled my hair. I wanted to die, but I thought about my kids the entire night. How could they be sleeping in a foster home when their beds were at home for them? How could the social worker and others rip away my parental rights when I gave birth to those children and did all the things required of a mother? My educational achievements, and the fact that I was a UCLA student, also meant nothing. My soul felt dead. I was angry at the system because its power hurt my children and me. The system had failed us yet again. And this time, it felt undefeatable.

While growing up I had many incidents in which the state intruded into my personal life. However, because this time it involved my children, it was especially traumatic and painful. The hyper-criminalization I experienced from culturally insensitive staff at hospitals, police officers, and social workers was immense. Here are some examples:

UCPD OFFICER: "It's not that you're Hispanic but this is protocol …"
LAPD OFFICER: "Tell me about your history with gangs …"
SOCIAL WORKER: "How do you parent two kids, being that you're so young?"

As a teenager, I would have challenged their authority, but now I just asked them probing questions. I really wanted to understand their position so that I could comply and regain custody of my children. These questions and words became more inscribed in my soul than before. More so than when police officers pulled me by the hair in middle school since I engaged in physical fights and they screamed racist things. More than when teachers told me I wouldn't get far in life. More than when a police officer screamed at me "you're just a little bitch and that's why you won't be shit in life so keep your hands where I can see them," as she tightened the handcuffs as much as she could.

This incident surpassed those experiences. While being criminalized and having my civil rights violated; this was the right I needed most, my right to parent. Hyper-criminalization was exacerbated beyond my neighborhood of South Central at UCLA child care and hospital facilities when it became clear to me that despite my educational trajectory, I was outside the mainstream role of motherhood. Cultural biases and stereotypes about teen mothers and gang members were the point of departure the minute my case began.

After becoming pregnant with my first child at 15, I began to experience a two-fold criminalization process that stemmed from the intersections of my three most salient identities: gang affiliate, Chicana, and teenage mother. It is precisely these types of interactions that make me question the heightened harassment orchestrated by the state that labels me as dangerous and neglectful. From being told to sit on the curb to being arrested and having my children temporarily removed by the child welfare system, the control and surveillance I experienced as a youth continue to impact the way I navigate my everyday life as an educated Chicana.

Years later, while collecting data for a research project as an undergraduate at UCLA, I realized that what I thought were isolated instances were in fact common occurrences for women like me who were coming of age on the streets of South Central, Los Angeles. I learned, in other words, that these were systemic and recurrent experiences with state violence and control that were also experienced by many of my close friends and barrio associates and acquaintances.

I also began to observe how students at the university had unstated privileges, which in turn affected their interactions with the state. The use of alcohol and drugs in the college setting, for example, were not pathologized as they were in the barrio. I soon came to the realization that my research agenda was influenced by the realities of those close to me and their daily battles against multiple forms of social control and oppression. I also discovered that the forms of control experienced by young gang-affiliated women, who are also teenage mothers, have not been adequately explored. I began to rely on my own intuition, experience, and cultural capital to formulate a Chicana methodological schema which drew upon personal, academic, professional, and analytical processes.

This chapter draws on the *testimonios* of Chicana mothers I began researching as an undergraduate student to learn about their negotiation as young mothers and gang affiliates.[1] The women were members, sisters, girlfriends, and *home girls* from the local barrio gang (Vigil 2008). They identified as teenage mothers, which often meant having a child before the age of 20. Their *testimonios*, or personal narratives, helped me capture their stories of struggle, survival, and resistance (Huber 2009). To capture more personal and holistic experiences, they provided photographs. Photo elicitation is a research method that positions the participant as an active agent—a method that not only empowered the mothers by giving them a choice in which data (visual images) was collected, but also offers a voice in reflecting on and interpreting the meaning of the images as they related to the research topics (Clark-Ibañez 2007).

I also provide an analytical framework that hopefully deepens our understanding of a group of Chicanas who are highly stigmatized and must navigate their public and private worlds in places of constant retribution. I seek here, in other words, to provide the appropriate theoretical nexus to investigate the structural position of young Chicana mothers, and show how the state constantly shapes their subordinate status. I begin with a feminist intersectional theory which takes into account the structural position of women of Color, and specifically the relationship of the public and private spheres that are often explored separately but which are inextricably linked for women of Color. In order to gain an understanding of the daily lives of gang-affiliated Chicana mothers' relation to the state, I wanted to develop a theoretical framework that did justice to the complexity of their lived experience. I, therefore, examined their lives not only in relation to subordination and "spirals of violence" but also relative to their gendered agency and survival skills (Menjívar 2011: 5). The following section describes how these young women challenge the dominant discourse on gender and crime by successfully navigating the public and private spaces they inhabit.[2]

Chicana Feminism: (*Third Space*) Where the Public and Private Meet

Considerable feminist energy has been directed at deconstructing and challenging the public/private divide (Boyd 1997; Collins 2000). Since the private sphere has been constructed as a non-political realm, many re-examinations of the public/private split have criticized previous analyses of the institutions of the family, the state, and the economy. Where this myth of separate spheres exists, the relationship between the private sphere and patriarchy is often assumed, and consequently leaves its political nature unexamined (Miranda 2005: 79). For gang-affiliated Chicana mothers, public and private may not be useful categories, since this dichotomy is based on the "archetypal white, middle-class nuclear family" (Collins 2000). Feminists argue that "The public and private spheres, when they can be identified as such, exist not so much in opposition to one another, but rather in *reciprocal connection with one another*" (see also Olsen 1982; Boyd 1997). The state has played a fundamental role in the formation and functioning of families, and thus the concept of non-intervention has been called a myth (Olsen 1982). In fact, the state has always played a role in regulating and intruding into the private sphere of Women of Color (Crenshaw 1991) and the extent of this regulation is dependent on factors such as race, class, and sexual orientation (Koshan 1997, 90).

In this study, I examine factors of race, class, and gender and move beyond them, to understand how other factors in subcultural, highly stig-matized groups among Chicanas—gang affiliates and teen mothers—are constantly being regulated. I use, in other words, the concept of a *third space;* a Chicana feminist lens to turn away from the public/private binary and propose a more complex theoretical approach to examine the lives of gang-affiliated Chicana mothers.

Using a Chicana feminist lens reveals omissions of subcultures and stigma-tized groups that expand race, class, and gender analyses. Gloria Anzaldúa (1987), for example, challenged us to show how duality is transcended. The Chicanas in this study illustrate navigation of in-between spaces that are created at intersections—whether material, metaphoric, or discursive. In recognizing these in-between spaces, I also recognize the *third space* within intersecting structures of power in which Chicana mothers construct claims to human agency (Arredondo 2003). Third space can be understood as a location and/or practice. As a practice, it captures the day-to-day interactions that join different networks of consciousness, and as a location it can be a space of meaning-making (Sandoval 2000; Licona 2005). For the Chicanas in this study, geo-graphic location is not in the borders, yet borders work much like dichotomies (i.e. public/private) to force false and subordinating oppositions. As Adela Licona (2005) says, "Resisting binary spaces is, for me, a third-space tactic that allows for the exploration of multiple and, at times, contradictory sub-jectivities." Third space, as practiced in my work, similarly provides the theo-retical tool to understand how gang-affiliated Chicanas must navigate spaces that intersect their private and public lives.

Hurtado has noted that a private sphere for Women of Color does not exist except that which "they manage to create and protect in an otherwise hostile environment" (1989, 849). For the young mothers I interviewed, it is this "otherwise" space—a *third space*—that they navigate and resist which often goes unseen, unheard, and unacknowledged. While these women are pathologized by the larger society, I found them to be incredibly resourceful in developing and using extant survival skills as "urban guerillas" in battles with the apparatus of the state, and that these tactics are not only not recorded but often mis-understood (ibid., 853). Frequent interactions foster and reinforce these mothers' "socialization to docility, passivity, and allegiance" to the state, where multiple forms of social control are often exerted in direct and indirect ways.

Due to highly stigmatized identities as gang affiliates and teenage mothers, their treatment is related to distance and marginalization from the central power of the state. When there are interfaces between their private and public spheres, they face criminalization that becomes invisible. The structural position of young Latina mothers is a reflection of the public intruding into the private, given that the state constantly shapes their subordinate positions, thereby affecting their day-to-day interactions. What is unique about these women is that their identities are hyper-visible, yet the violence they experience remains invisible in this negotiation of a third space. Structural violence is exerted systematically but is often not visible in specific events (Farmer 2004, 307; Kent 2006, 55).

In applying Menjívar's work on Central American immigrant women, to my study, I put aside their hyper-visibility to focus instead on the structures they encounter, "while at the same time examining the relationship of social position to their response to the conditions they face" (Menjívar 2011, 9). I seek, in other words, to dissect how the intersection of the public and the private inevitably results in violence and criminalization for Chicana gang-affiliated teen mothers.

My work itself becomes a third space that enables me to interrogate and understand the hyper-criminalization of barrio teen mothers. It centers the Chicana experience, and is the standpoint from which I engage in dialogue with different audiences and participants (Arredondo 2003). In doing so, I recognize the active association and interface of the public and private spheres, as well as my feminist role and responsibility to "restructure the theory of difference without hopefully reviving binarisms of public and private that reify male authority and female dependence while closing off the interconnections of work, family, and the state" (Miranda 2003, 80). Having said this, my role, like other feminist criticism, involves the specification that dual-spheres paradigm is about power. Following Foucault's (1977) analysis of power, Chicanas exercise it from various points in the interplay of the injustices they experience, and these power relations are the immediate effects on the divisions and inequalities that occur within relationships—this power that comes from below points to a plurality of resistances. My aim is to make visible and explicit these sites, and make a case for third space, where the women not only physically navigate spaces where their public and private lives intersect, but also craft resourceful third space tactics to resist state power. Collectively, these stories point to the spaces that signal women's resistance to constant and systemic subordination. In the course of the research, I came to know and understand these women and their unique stories of pain, of survival, and I now present the three notable cases of three remarkable young women: Estefania, Monica, and Mayra.

"A Homegirl's Nightmare": Estefania

When I met Estefania, she was only 13 years old and living in one of the most dangerous streets that surround South Central, Los Angeles. Estefania is one of the few young women I know who remains strongly tied to her Chicana culture and follows the traditional Pachuca style. She wears khaki Dickies, black tucked-in shirts, dyes her hair black, wears dark lipstick and has a collection of large hoop earrings. She has tattoos on her chest and arms, and takes pride in her culture which is shown in her room, which is richly decorated with many lowrider and other Chicano-style Brown Pride images. She also often refers to her life in relation to Chicano rap music; once she even took the time to send me a music video from a famous Chicana rapper, Mz. Krazie, entitled "Mommy's Little Girl" and told me to "add that music video to the stuff you're doing, it describes my first pregnancy." Her life is one that is painful to write about because it reminds me of the pain and struggles I have been through, yet given the tragic events she has experienced, it is one filled with incredible resistance.

Estefania, a 20-year-old mother of three children, shared the difficulties she had challenging dominant ideas about what it is like to be a young mother with strong ties to the neighborhood. She became involved with gangs at the age of 13, through an older brother and close friends in gangs, beginning a relationship with her boyfriend and becoming pregnant for the first time at the age of 15. Before her daughter turned a year, her partner was shot and killed outside of their home as a result of gang rival violence, and she began a new relationship and had two more children. The cumulative effect of these experiences renders Estefania and other gang-affiliated women's engagement with the child welfare system very predictable and problematic, if not inevitable. Estefania said that her children became entrapped in the child welfare system after a family member called Child Protective Services (CPS) accusing her and her partner of neglect and substance abuse.

Unfortunately, research on the criminalization of Latina youth has focused on the effects within and out of the juvenile and criminal justice system, paying little attention to the criminalization that occurs for young Latina mothers in the child welfare system. Estefania shares that when her children were removed, she was struggling financially to pay for court-mandated parenting, substance-abuse, and anger management classes. Although research has shown a direct link with child welfare system targeting poor families, and unfortunately now "we spend more money to support children living away from their parents than we do on the essential services that would help families improve the material conditions of their lives and enable them to raise their children safely" (Lee 2016, 37). Estefania's personal financial issues highlight the public concern from social workers, attorneys, and judges.

Once her children got involved with CPS, they were rapidly removed from her custody; within days of the report of neglect. This is most likely because people of Color experience parental termination of rights more often than their white counterparts (Olsen 1982) and Latina/o children are disproportionately represented and highly victimized by the systemic discriminatory practices of public service agencies like the child welfare system and Child Protective Services (Church et al. 2005). Not surprisingly, the mothers in my study described their fear of having some form of contact with CPS. These mothers' exposure to surveillance by different institutions often caused them great discomfort and they feared removal, as their private lives were being investigated.

Mirandé (2011), in his observations of a young Chicana mother's dealings with CPS, which he describes as a "mother's worst nightmare," notes that there is no presumption of innocence for suspected child abusers and the parents, who are charged, are presumed guilty whether they are in fact guilty or not. They are thus "despised and treated with disdain not only by the public at large but also by various players in the legal and judicial system" (ibid., 70), including judges, attorneys, bailiffs, clerks, and child welfare workers. Estefania similarly stated that:

> Having both kids in the system, now it's more difficult to do this process because of all the allegations against me and my partner, from family and the system. So I have no family support but I had to start motivating myself again instead of being depressed, I have to do it for them.

Estefania highlights the stigma associated with gang involvement. Both her family and the system targeted her as a neglectful mother because motherhood and gang membership combine moral concerns of risky lifestyles (Moloney et al. 2011). The lifestyle of girl gang members, which often includes violence, drug and alcohol use, drug sales, and other criminal activities, is seen by gang researchers as an environment harmful for raising a healthy child and conducive to the generational transmission of delinquency (Fleisher 1998). When they come into contact with the juvenile or criminal justice system, young Latinas are not only criminalized but also "medicalized with the underlying assumption being that there is something wrong with them as individuals: they are either 'bad' or 'sick'" (López 2017: 144). The stigmatization of young Latinas has a great impact on how they are perceived by the child welfare system. Like Millbank's work on the parental fitness of lesbian mothers and child custody, I found that similar attitudes applied in Estefania's case.

> In this context, courts can and must scrutinize the gang-affiliated young mother to the fullest extent: there is no part of her life that can be held

as private … Lastly, a claim to rights or to privacy in this context is disastrous, and not only because of welfare discourses and the 'child centered' focus of family law—although these factors are operative. Rather it is because gang-affiliates are not viewed as rights-bearing subjects or as having entitlement because of the extent to which they have been pre-configured as dangerous, criminal, or pathological. Because of this, gang affiliated mothers also cannot claim privacy because there is no permissible private space for them in such a legal framework.

(Millbank 2008)

Estefania mentioned that authorities blamed her irresponsible behaviors on the activities she engaged in as a gang-affiliate (i.e. substance use and violence). What she saw as her private troubles now became public sanctions. She shared her experience at the dependency hearing where Officer Carter stated:

she interviewed mother in regards to the allegations of general neglect and caretaker absence. Per officer, mother stated that she had been admitted for four days at the hospital due to an overdose of methamphetamine. Officer Carter stating although mother appears to be sober, her present demeanor indicates of someone who might be coming down from a high and therefore there were safety concerns.

The statement above shows that authorities make assumptions and draw conclusions not only about the individual in question but also about the entire family unit. Despite Estefania's desire to regain the custody of her children, her oldest daughter was placed into adoption. She stated that, "there is no room for mistakes when you're a chola and have kids, because everyone goes against you." She added that she tried everything to get her daughter back, from discontinuing drug use and disconnecting from her partner to taking public transportation across the city to try and make it to court-mandated classes. Estefania agrees that she has had a rough life which led her to what she rationalized as "bad" decisions, but she also believes that she deserves a chance to raise her children.

The significance of her struggles lies in her ability to use humor to resist a very painful heartbreak caused by the state. She had a photograph and while she talked about how her rights as a mother were ripped away, she revealed strength by hiding her pain with a smile and jokingly, saying,

They just think I'm a kid (laughs) because I go on the playground slides over and over during visitation, and I see the social worker taking notes and I keep acting like a kid because I'm having fun like that and my kids love it.

Despite the trauma of the removal of her daughter, she clearly believes the experience of separation will be a tool for her to become a better mother for her other children. She also believes that this tool of pain will allow her to work hard so her daughter, who now lives with adopted parents, knows she has always been there for her, and hopes that when she turns 18 years of age, she can run back into her arms. The resistance that emerged from the regulation she experienced and the constant surveillance she must continue to experience are third spaces she continues to negotiate, by finding and using survival tactics to navigate her daily life.

"You're Not Gonna Make It": Monica

Monica, a 22-year-old mother of two, comes from a long line of survivors, as her parents were also gang-affiliated teenagers. Her father and husband are also gang members; the latter is serving a short prison sentence. "I was born into gang," she said, her beautiful smile, long black hair, and light brown eyes a reflection of her sympathetic character and stunning demeanor. Every time I interviewed Monica, she was bumping loud music—oldies' artists like Smokey Robinson or *norteñas* by Ramon Ayala. When meeting Monica, one would be unaware of the trails of obstacles she has had to overcome and the level of inspiration that drives her to continue in spite of her struggles. It would take more than an interview to understand her life, but I share the portion she shared with me. Her story points to the complexity of gang-affiliated mothers' lives that to date social science research has failed to explore or comprehend.

For the past few years, Monica has spent the majority of her time in school and work, trying to become a healthcare professional in the field of pharmacy, obtaining a license as a pharmacy technician and working as one for two years now. She spends her weekends making visitations to the prison to see her husband but she recently stopped when she gave birth to her daughter because the physical procedures that allowed her newborn daughter to see her father were too burdensome and intrusive. She said that her daughter would have to be physically examined by guards and her clothes and diaper would be removed in this standard procedure. She and her husband decided that it would be best to abstain from visitations until he was released from prison. Although Monica's life has not been an easy one, she refers to some of the most painful moments as the happiest and biggest lessons of her life. Throughout our conversations, she discussed dealing with stereotypes that have been central to negotiating her private life in public domains.

Monica, like the other study participants, described how her gang-associated identity led to a feeling of endangerment for themselves and their children. Navigating their gang-affiliated identity often meant transcending space in their own community. For example, they had to decide if they could go to particular locations in their neighborhood, if they could go out at certain times of the day, and whether or not they felt safe taking their children with them. For young mothers, like those in this study, an attempt to construct themselves as "good mothers" comes with challenges because, as gang affiliates, they also faced controls and criticism for not being good girls. Now they are also blamed for not being good mothers (Moloney et al. 2011).

Monica commented:

> He [her husband] almost got shot ... and it's been more than once, but it's unexplainable, to my mind, it's normality, something I've grown up with. I'm used to it. I'm numb to it but not wanting to put my son at risk, of course, this is where I realize that I cannot be anywhere with my son and him because if people see him from before because of the gang banging life, my son is at risk, my husband, and me, and this is what I don't like.

Monica has been navigating exposure to gang culture from a very young age. She explains how having a father in a gang made her middle school experience unpleasant. In fact, she questioned why she followed the gang identity in order to respect her father's status as a gang member. She had to negotiate her identity as a daughter, gang-affiliate, and a student. Later, she married a gang member and had to navigate how to be a gang member's wife and a mother of a son she wanted to protect. Monica, and the other women in the study, identified having to "watch their back" and learning how to maneuver in a community that forced them to live in this constant struggle, as a major problem. For these women, the streets and public locations rather than the home become places for analysis of gender dynamics. Monica's gendered experience shows that her attempt to construct herself as a protective mother comes with challenges because motherhood or leaving the neighborhood does not necessarily mean that they alter ties to the gang (Hunt et al. 2011). This is a dilemma for Monica because she is married to a gang member and is also a gang member's daughter.

In a conversation after the interview, she described a moment when she gained an understanding of the constant awareness of her private life in the public spheres. Awareness of stereotypes pushed her to tint all her car windows because she was tired of being stopped by police officers when her husband or father were in the car. This caused her to receive a ticket a few weeks after because it is against the law to have front windows tinted. While she argues that it was a good way for police stops to decrease, she was forced to remove the tint so she would not get in trouble with authorities again. Her constant contacts with law enforcement have not been pleasant, and in multiple instances the "bad mother" label comes from her direct relationship with gang members.

When a mother does not disconnect herself from a gang, she is grouped under the "bad mother" umbrella that includes teenage mothers, welfare mothers, drug-using mothers, and gang-involved mothers (Hunt et al. 2005; Moloney et al. 2011). For Latinas, these stereotypes are exacerbated when a woman falls into more than one category, a gendered form of multiple marginality (Vigil 2008), such as when she is at once a gang affiliate, teen mother, and the wife and/or daughter of a gang member. These stereotypes become so prominent for Latinas because they are rooted in structures like the media and politics that target the entire public.

> These stereotypes have real-world implications for Latinas because assumptions about cultural/racial groups often serve as the linchpin for institutional racism. This is especially true in youth settings such as schools and juvenile correctional facilities when people who work with Latinas over-rely on stereotypes to inform their practice.
>
> (López and Chesney-Lind 2014, 530)

Despite the prominent stereotypes that exist for the women in this study, I found counter-arguments and ways in which they resist these stereotypes. All of the women, for example, were either enrolled in school or aspiring to enroll at the time of the interview. Vigil (2008) similarly found that some girls in gangs have babies to find a purpose in their lives after overcoming multiple "marginalizations" at the hands of family, lovers, friends, as well as society in general. They find a baby to be the cure for the loneliness and hopelessness they lived through in their young lives (ibid., 67). For young women in an impoverished community, mothering can be a life-affirming choice, one that causes them to re-dedicate attention to various aspects of their lives, such as their education (Jacobs 1994). Many girls who have left school return to school during pregnancy or become more engaged with school after giving birth (Smithbattle 2006). In Monica's case, she remained in school to challenge the definitions of how society depicts the "scholarship girl" and "high achieving" person (Malagon and Alvarez 2010). Monica described a photograph of herself at 9 months pregnant where she is graduating high school as follows:

> I remember that day. I was the only girl walking up there pregnant. I graduated the year I was supposed to, tried my best and it was hard but I did it. I was very emotional that day and it means a lot because a lot of people thought I wasn't gonna make it and it's crazy because they would tell you "you're not gonna make it, there's no point in you keep trying because you're not gonna make it," but I made it. At the time I felt disappointed because I felt like I disappointed a lot of people, but looking back at it, I feel proud of myself because out of everybody that told me I wasn't gonna make it, or that I wasn't gonna be a good

mom or that I couldn't get into school or do school, or a kid is always gonna stop you from doing your goals. It's not true and I'm happy that people told me that because, if not, I wouldn't be proud of who I am now.

Monica shared that many people in her community did not believe she could make anything of her life, from friends and family to teachers and staff. For Monica and the other women, in contrast to men's capital, the value of women's symbolic capital must be evaluated in relation to community norms for their behavior and these norms require regular monitoring (Vlan Vleet 2003, 505). Yet, rather than internalize this view, she resisted it and fought to disprove it. Although she agrees to feeling disappointment during the time of her graduation, her reflection suggested the internal conflict she previously had about her status as a teen mother. As López and Chesney-Lind (2014, 535) observed, "Although the girls acknowledged that many Latinas are naturally good mothers, they adamantly denied wanting to be teen mothers. Notably, even the pregnant and parenting girls also expressed regret about getting pregnant." Despite her previous feelings of disappointment, Monica reflected on resisting these stereotypes; specifically, the idea that teen mothers were lost causes. For her challenging the dominant stereotypes of gang-affiliated teen mothers occurred through educational achievement. Her story is a testament to her cleverness, courage, and navigational capital in not succumbing to dominant stereotypes and imposed restrictions in public spaces.

"Invading My Space"

From the beginning, as I began to become familiar with Mayra's life, I was frequently struck by how she did not fit many of the categories or frameworks I had studied in the social sciences. She lives in a small humble one-bedroom house where she cares for her five children and often babysits other children. Yet, she takes great pride in decorating with elephant ornaments and other portraits she buys in local yard sales. Her home is filled with pictures of her children, toys, and books that they often receive from school. She gets her hair dyed often and goes to get her nails done with her two daughters at the local nail shop. Being a "welfare mother" does not dictate an unembellished existence or a depressing one where there is no attention to aesthetic values. Her humor, conversation, and critical engagement with the public world is not what we read about in the social science literature that describes poor, immigrant, gang affiliated, teenage mothers, especially those on welfare. Like Estefania's and Monica's stories, Mayra's story is filled with traumatic events. Her tears during the interview indicated strong reflections of painful times, but also demonstrated her tenacity and resilience.

Mayra, a 30-year-old single mother of five children has been through many incidents of violence. She was brought from Mexico at the age of 2 and raised to see what she described as, "things a child shouldn't see." When she was about 6 years-old, for example, the SWAT team broke into her house and her older (adopted) sister was taken to prison for life. The moment when her sister was taken from her was a moment of change because she described her sister as the one person who showed her love. She was recruited into a gang at the age of 8 and jumped into a gang at the age of 11. She describes these as times of abandonment when she turned to the streets and gangs and found a connection and love through this extended family. While it has been 15 years since Mayra last "rolled" with the gang, it has remained a salient part of her identity, an identity in which she continually navigates to protect herself from punishment, incarceration, or deportation. What she was describing is the way in which institutions build "mechanisms of observation ... that penetrate into men's [people's] behavior" (Foucault 1977, 204). Because of the mechanisms of observation, she learned to discipline and monitor herself. She describes how having a 15-year-old teenage daughter makes it difficult to engage in that surveillance because her daughter is growing up to navigate and face her own issues in a con-tinuation school. Young women like Mayra's daughter who are enrolled in continuation schools face increased surveillance and police contact that accelerates their path to incarceration (Farmer 2004). When her teenage daughter got in trouble for smoking in school and was placed on probation, she felt helpless.

> I got there and I cried. I cried because the officers were right there, and she's inside the office and they told me: "if I wanted to, I could have taken her," and me as an undocumented mother, and not having an ID, is, like, okay, if he would of taken her, how am I gonna take my baby out? That's one thing that concerns me with her is that she doesn't understand if she gets in more trouble, I'm not gonna be able to take her out, especially if you don't have an ID, and how stuff is right now, it even makes it harder, but at the moment when that happened, it broke me, it broke me a lot because when they released her to me, I cried.

Mayra further describes how her status impacted the way she negotiated this situation. Being present with the police officers when her daughter was being handcuffed was a moment when she felt helpless and fearful because of her undocumented status as well as fearing that she could not help her daughter if she was taken to juvenile hall. Not having an ID in this situation shows the structural limitation imposed by immigration laws that directly and indirectly punish undocumented immigrants for being in the United States without authorization. The spillover effects of immigration status have been described through the impacts that come from undocumented parents to children. In this case, multigenerational punishment occurs as social ties and daily interactions with the target population lead untargeted witnesses to share punishments and risk-management strategies produced by these laws. The punishment worked both ways. On the one hand, Mayra's life was under surveillance and threatened by the lack of an ID. On the other hand, Mayra's daughter, who was in direct surveillance, was afraid of being prevented from having her mother's support. The laws meant to shape and constrain undocumented immigrants' everyday lives also generate limitations across immigration status (Enriquez 2015). They produce broader consequences, as further explained.

> When we had that meeting before she started school, they asked me if I was a gang member when they already knew I was an ex-gang member … you already have it on record, why are you asking me? I don't like that, it irritated me, but I did tell them, if it wasn't for me getting pregnant with her, I would have been out there doing stuff, but since I had her, I changed my life, and they also knew I was an immigrant but they wanted to hear it from me.

Mayra's constant interaction with the officers was difficult because she continued to be questioned about her previous gang-affiliation and citizenship status. Not only were her interactions in public places, such as the school and the police station, uncomfortable, but being questioned in her home was even more intrusive because she was subject to random searches due to her daughter's probation.

> For me, it was really hard because I don't like people coming into my house. I don't like people showing up. I don't like the cops, I never messed with the cops when I was younger and neither [am I going to] do it now, you know. For them to be coming to my house unexpected, it's like invading my space as a mother with my children, and knowing that they already knew my background and they wanna ask that stuff again. I don't need someone on me because of her mistakes, cuz that could have led to something else and they [her children] could have all been taken away because of that.

It is not uncommon for involvement with the criminal justice system to become what Jerry Flores (2016) calls "wraparound incarceration"—a multidimensional surveillance of young women's behavior that works outside of formal institutions of confinement with the constant presence of police officers. In this case, the wraparound effect directly affected Mayra's daughter and indirectly affected Mayra by being investigated and questioned in her own home.

She also felt an invasion of her privacy in applying for and receiving welfare benefits. She compared this process as "almost going to jail."

> When they were taking fingerprints, pictures all that, I felt so low, and it took a couple years I felt like that, because me as a woman that I was so used to doing on myself, knowing how to hustle and get a job but once I had my other kids I had to … you can't do something stupid or they'll lock you up … it could be, like, if you're going to jail because, like, you do something stupid and its gonna pop up in the system cuz they know who you are. Like, when I got arrested once, they took a picture of my tattoos, so if I get in trouble and they're gonna look me up, they're gonna see the tattoos. So it's something, like, I feel, like, you gotta watch your back, cuz you do something stupid and with stuff like that, with the welfare stuff, they even say it, if you do something foul, we're taking this away from you, so let's say they found out you sell your food stamps, they'll take that away from you and you won't be able to apply ever again and its scary because you gotta survive.

Mayra talked about fear, surveillance, and how she felt being under the state's eyes by receiving aid. Having children put Mayra directly under state surveillance if her children happened to get in trouble, like her oldest daughter, because she was receiving public aid to sustain her family. Research has examined the way that racial attitudes influence public preferences regarding welfare policy, and have found "stereotype consistent markers" that strengthen the link between race and policy. Mayra illustrated awareness of this research through her personal experiences, since she understood that race and other characteristics of racial minorities influence welfare administrators' decisions to sanction clients.

Through descriptions of these mothers' stories, the complexity of the interactions of the state, race, and stereotypes, my study has presented the intersection that Estefania, Monica, and Mayra have had to negotiate in the third spaces they constantly navigate.

Conclusion

This chapter has attempted to illustrate the lack of any tangible or conceptual private arena for gang-affiliated Chicana mothers. Gang affiliation and teen motherhood have been the subject of demonization which form the substance of fears, risks, and dangers projected onto vulnerable children, whom the state has a duty to protect. As I listened to the mothers' stories, I became keenly aware of the heavy burden they carried, embedded not only in their tears but also their laughter. I was also able to capture very intimate moments, stories, and see photographs while being flattered when told that "they wouldn't be talking about this to anyone else."

While the overwhelming control over physical movement constrained them, curtailed their social interactions, and became a palpable source of distress in their lives (Menjívar 2011, 91), the women's stories revealed how relationships with the state are impacted in both subtle and obvious ways. On the one hand, all of the women's structural positions demonstrated subordination perpetuated by the state, such as with the removal of Estefania's children, the symbolic violence of dominant stereotypes that Monica was forced to endure, and the constant surveillance Mayra describes. In each case, violent encounters with the state became public and extended to the criminalization of their families. Nonetheless, their agency and survival strategies demonstrated the rejection of passivity and challenged prevailing conceptions of what it means to be a gang-affiliated mother. For Estefania, it was using the pain of separation as a tool to become a better mother for her two children, who remained in her custody. For Monica, it was using education to challenge expectations while she navigated public spaces that pointed fingers at her. Finally, for Mayra, it was continual growth and awareness of immigration status injustices she went through in order to pass that knowledge on to her five children.

Interactions with the public sphere helped these women develop a public identity and the necessary skills to fend off state intervention (Hurtado 1989). While some of their attempts failed, they helped to demonstrate that resistance does not erase public invasion into their private lives, because not only do their class, race, and gender shape their subordination but their identities as gang-affiliates and young mothers further marginalize them. Their strategies of resistance exemplify what is called "underground feminisms," which constitute those that remain unlabeled, undocumented, and beyond the reach of feminist theorizing (Arredondo 2003; Saldivar-Hull 2000).

Chicana/o families are products of intergenerational marginalization; of the intersections of racism, patriarchy, and poverty, and as reflected in these women's stories, three generations were often impacted by the violence of criminalization: parents, the mothers and their children. The actions and attitudes of gang affiliated mothers represent a pushback against state-sponsored violence. This level of theorizing, evidenced by the *testimonios*, acknowledge that young women, unlike men, faced a two-fold criminalization process. During this process, women are more likely to navigate not only the criminal and juvenile justice system, but also the child welfare system. For this reason, I argue that the experiences of the women who are criminalized while raising children in *third spaces* cannot be disconnected from the experiences of their children, parents, and families, who too are victims of state violence and hyper-criminalization.

In closing, I call for recognition and theoretical understanding of the multiplicity of the lived experiences of gang-affiliated Chicana mothers, and the fundamental ways women's lives are constrained and prescribed by racial, economic, gendered, and sexualized boundaries. "Foregrounding these boundaries would also clarify those spaces in which these women create opening for themselves that disrupt the borders of norms, prescriptions, and expectations" (Arredondo 2003: 292). Given the crucial role parents play, specifically mothers in the lives of criminalized children and youth, it is essential to "consider how we can better work with parents as opposed to blaming them for their wrongdoings while doing little to address the larger social forces and structures that contribute to family problems" (López 2017: 165). As my mother told me the first time I sat in the back seat of a police car, and as I told my children too, as they walked toward the LA County foster center "everything will be okay." It was, in fact, this agency that drove me to interrogate and address the larger structures that are meant to "serve and protect" but rather use their power to criminalize Chicana mothers.

Notes

1   An shorter draft of this chapter appeared in a special dossier issue of *Aztlán: A Journal of Chicano Studies* (43(2), Fall 2018). While that draft focused on the Youth Control Complex, this chapter utilizes new data and uses a more elaborate theoretical, feminist lens to develop the concept of a Chicana third space.
2   I have attempted as much as possible to present the narratives of the participants using their own words, syntax, and vernacular expressions in order to preserve and express their unique voice.

References

Aldridge, J., J. Shute, R. Ralphs, and J. Medina. 2011. "Blame the Parents? Challenges for Parent-Focused Programmes for Families of Gang Involved Young People." *Children and Society*, 25(5): 371–381.

Anzaldúa, Gloria. 1987. *Borderlands/La Frontera: The New Mestiza*. San Francisco: Aunt Lute.

Arredondo, Gabriela. 2003. "Grounding Feminisms through La Vida de Inocencia." In P. Zavellaet al. (Eds.), *Chicana Feminisms: A Critical Reader*. Durham, NC: Duke University Press.

Boyd, Susan B. 1997. *Challenging the Public/Private Divide: Feminism, Law, and Public Policy*. Toronto: University of Toronto Press.

Church, W. T., E. R. Gross, and J. Baldwin. 2005. "Maybe Ignorance Is Not Always Bliss: The Disparate Treatment of Hispanics within the Child Welfare System." *Children and Youth Services Review*, 27(12): 1279–1292.

Crenshaw, Kimberley. 1991. "Mapping the Margins: Intersectionality, Identity Politics, and Violence Against Women of Color." *Stanford Law Review*, 43(6): 1241.

Durán, Robert J. 2013. *Gang Life in Two Cities: An Insider's Journey*. New York: Columbia University Press.

Enriquez, L. 2015. "Multigenerational Punishment: Shared Experiences of Undocumented Immigration Status Within Mixed-Status Families" *Journal of Marriage and Family* 77: 939–953.

Farmer, Paul. 2004. "An Anthropology of Structural Violence." *Current Anthropology*, 45(3): 305–325.

Fleisher, M. 1998. *Dead End Kids: Gang Girls and the Boys They Know.* Madison, WI: University of Wisconsin Press.

Flores, Jerry. 2016. *Caught Up: Girls, Surveillance, and the Wraparound Incarceration.* Berkeley, CA: University of California Press.

Huber, L. P. 2009. "Disrupting Apartheid of Knowledge: Testimonio as Methodology in Latina/O Critical Race Research in Education." *International Journal of Qualitative Studies in Education*, 22(6): 639–654.

Hunt, G., K. Joe-Laidler, and K. MacKenzie. 2005. "Moving into Motherhood: Gang Girls and Controlled Risk." *Youth & Society*, 36(3)L 333–373.

Hurtado, Aida. 1989. Relating to White Privilege: Seduction and Rejection in the Subordination of White Women and Women of Color." *Signs*, 14(4), 833–855.

Jacobs, J. L. (1994). "Gender, Race, Class, and the Trend Toward Early Motherhood: A Feminist Analysis of Teen Mothers in Contemporary Society." *Journal of Contemporary Ethnography*, 22(4), 442–462.

Kent, George. 2006. "Children as Victims of Structural Violence." *Societies without Borders* I, 53–67.

Koshan, Jennifer. 1997. "Sounds of Silence: The Public/Private Dichotomy, Violence, and Aboriginal Women." In Susan B. Boyd (Ed.), *Challenging the Public/Private Divide: Feminism, Law, and Public Policy.* Toronto: University of Toronto Press, pp. 87–109.

Lee, Tina. 2016. *Catching a Case: Inequality and Fear in the New York's City's Child Welfare System.* New Brunswick, NJ: Rutgers University Press.

Licona, Adela C. 2005. "(B)orderlands' Rhetorics and Representations: The-Transformative Potential of Feminist Third-Space Scholarship and Zines." *NWSA Journal*, Summer, 104–129.

López, Vera. 2017. *Complicated Lives: Girls, Parents, Drugs, and Juvenile Justice.* New Brunswick, NJ: Rutgers University Press.

López, Vera, and M. Chesney-Lind. 2014. "Latina Girls Speak Out: Stereotypes, Gender and Relationship Dynamics." *Latino Studies Journal*, 12(4): 527–549.

Malagon, Maria and Cynthia Alvarez. 2010. "Scholarship Girls Aren't the Only Chicanas Who Go to College: Former Chicana Continuation High School Students Disrupting the Educational Achievement Binary." *Harvard Educational Review*, 80(2): 149–174.

Menjívar, Cecilia. 2011. *Enduring Violence.* Berkeley, CA: University of California Press.

Millbank, Jenny. 2008. "The Limits of Functional Family: Lesbian Mother Litigation in the Era of the Eternal Biological Family." *International Journal of Law, Policy and the Family*, 22: 149–177.

Miranda, Marie. 2011. *Homegirls in the Public Sphere.* Austin, TX: University of Austin Texas Press.

Mirandé, Alfredo. 2011. *Rascuache Lawyer: Toward a Theory of Ordinary Litigation.* Tucson, AZ: The University of Arizona Press.

Moloney, M., K. Joe-Laidler, K. Mackenzie, and G. Hunt. 2011. "Young Mother (in the) Hood: Gang Girls' Negotiation of New Identities." *Journal of Youth Studies*, 14 (1): 1–19.

Olsen, L. I. 1982. "Predicting Permanency Status of Children in Foster Care." *Social Work Research and Abstracts*, 18(1): 9–20.

Sandoval, Chela. 2000. *Methodology of the Oppressed*. Minneapolis, MN: University of Minnesota Press.

Smithbattle, L. 2006. "Helping Teen Mothers Succeed." *The Journal of School Nursing*, 22(3): 130–135.

Van Vleet, Krista. 2003. "Partial Theories: On Gossip, Envy and Ethnography in the Andes." *Ethnography*, 4(4): 491–519.

Vigil, J. Diego. 2008. "Female Gang Members from East Los Angeles." *International Journal of Social Inquiry*, 1(1): 47–74.

Part III

Race, Citizenship, and the Law

Chapter 9

"A Class Apart"
The Exclusion of Latinas/os from Grand and Petit Juries

Alfredo Mirandé

Hernandez v. Texas, 347 U.S. 475 (1954)

In 1951, Pete Hernandez, a 21-year-old, single, Mexican-American cotton picker,[1] was drinking with a friend at a bar in Edna, a small town in Jackson County, Texas, when he became disruptive and was removed from the bar. Pete went home, obtained a gun, returned, and shot Joe Espinosa.[2] In September 1951, he was indicted for murder.

Prior to trial, Hernandez's lawyers moved to quash the indictment and the jury panel. They argued that persons of Mexican descent had been systematically excluded from serving as jury commissioners, grand jurors, and petit jurors even though there were such persons living in Jackson County who were fully qualified to serve ... The state of Texas stipulated that "for the last 25 years there is no record of any person with a Mexican or Latin American surname having served on a jury commission, grand jury, or petit jury in Jackson County."

("Hernandez v. Texas"—State Bar of Texas.www.texasbar.com/civics/
HighSchoolcases. Case Summary)

The wholesale exclusion of Mexicans from juries in 1954 is shocking, given that the Fourteenth Amendment, ratified in 1868, prohibited any state from denying any person within its jurisdiction the equal protection of the law. The Fourteenth Amendment also granted citizenship to "all persons born or naturalized in the United States," including former slaves who had just been freed after the Civil War. The Treaty of Guadalupe Hidalgo similarly granted citizenship to Mexican citizens who opted to remain in the newly occupied territory and failed to declare their intent to retain their Mexican citizenship. In 1880, the Supreme Court used the Fourteenth Amendment to overturn the murder conviction of a Black man under a West Virginia statute that limited jury service to White men who were at least 21 years old (*Strauder v. West Virginia* 1880). Nonetheless, it was not until 1954 in *Hernandez v. Texas* that Mexicans were legally recognized as a separate and distinct class protected by the Fourteenth Amendment.

Relying on *Strauder*, Pete Hernandez's lawyers argued that exclusion of persons of Mexican or Latin American descent from the jury pool deprived him, as a member of this class, equal protection of the laws guaranteed by the Fourteenth Amendment to the U.S. Constitution. A unanimous Supreme Court agreed and Hernandez's murder conviction was reversed on appeal.[3] Ironically, the case was decided two weeks before the historic *Brown v. Board of Education* case and in the same term.

Just as *Brown* was critical for African Americans, so has *Hernandez v. Texas* emerged as a threshold case for Chicanos and Latinos (Olivas 2006; Perea 2006). The case was the first time that Chicano attorneys appeared before the Supreme Court and the first time the Court recognized that Mexicans had been denied equal protection of the law under the Fourteenth Amendment. Most importantly, the case challenged the racial binary, for the first time recognizing Mexicans as a legally cognizable category, separate and apart from Whites or Blacks.

The decision was also an essential step in the Latina/o struggle for civil rights and social justice, paving the way for further challenges of discrimination in various areas of American law including employment, education, housing, public accommodations, and voting rights. Despite the significance of *Hernandez*, Mexicans and other Latinos continued to be subjected to both *de facto* and *de jure* legally sanctioned discrimination.

This chapter focuses on the implications of *Hernandez* and the continual underrepresentation and systematic exclusion of Mexicans and Latinas/os from grand and petite juries in the United States. But before addressing *Hernandez* and jury exclusion in more depth, it is necessary to place the case in historical perspective by providing a brief overview of the evolution of the Fourteenth Amendment and equal protection doctrine and jurisprudence.

"Personhood" and Equal Protection in Historical Perspective

Dred Scott v. Sandford: Are Former Slaves Persons Under the Constitution?

At the time when the United States Constitution was ratified in 1788, Blacks and other racial minorities had no legal standing and were not considered persons subject to the jurisdiction of the United States or the protection of the Constitution. In the infamous *Dred Scott v. Sandford* case,[4] for example, the Supreme Court considered whether Blacks were persons under the Constitution.

Dred Scott, a former slave in Missouri, resided in Illinois, a free state between 1833 and 1843; an area within the Louisiana Territory where slavery was prohibited per the Missouri Compromise of 1820. Returning to Missouri, Scott sued unsuccessfully for his freedom, arguing that having resided in a free territory made him a free man. Once Scott brought suit in federal court, his master countered, claiming that a pure-blooded Negro, a descendant of slaves could not be a citizen of the United States or bring suit in Federal Court under Article III of the Constitution, which states that the judicial Power shall extend to all controversies between citizens of different states.

Treating Scott as property rather than as a person, in a 7–2 decision authored by Justice Roger B. Taney, the Supreme Court held portions of the Missouri Compromise unconstitutional and in violation of the Fifth Amendment due process clause that protects life, liberty, and property. Under Articles III and IV of the Constitution, argued Taney, no one but a citizen of the United States could be a citizen of a state and only Congress could confer national citizenship (*Oyez* 2017).

Taney concluded that Dred Scott, a descendant of slaves, was a slave and not a citizen or one of the "people:"

> The words "people of the United States" and "citizens" are synonymous terms, and mean the same thing ... They are what we familiarly call the "sovereign people," and every citizen is one of this people, and a constituent member of this sovereignty. The question before us is whether the class of persons described in the plea in abatement compose a portion of this people, and are constituent members of this sovereignty? We think they are not, and that they are not included, and were not intended to be included, under the word "citizens" in the Constitution, and can therefore claim none of the rights and privileges which that instrument provides for and secures to citizens of the United States. On the contrary, they were at that time considered as a subordinate and inferior class of beings who had been subjugated by the dominant race, and, whether emancipated or not, yet remained subject to their authority, and had no rights or privileges but such as those who held the power and the Government might choose to grant them.
>
> (*Dred Scott v. Sandford* 1856, 404–405)

African slaves and their descendants were, therefore, not recognized as citizens until ratification of the Fourteenth Amendment on July 28, 1868. The amendment granted citizenship to "all persons born or naturalized in the United States," including former slaves who had just been freed after the Civil War. Known as one of the "Reconstruction Amendments," the Fourteenth Amendments forbids any state to deny any person "life, liberty or property, without due process of law" or to "deny to any person within its jurisdiction the equal protection of the laws."

In 1886, the Supreme Court further challenged the racial binary by extending the protection of the Fourteenth Amendment to Chinese immigrants. In *Yick Wo v. Hopkins*, a case involving the regulation of laundry facilities in San Francisco, the Court held that an ordinance prohibiting the operation of wooden laundry facilities discriminated against Chinese laundry owners. The issue was whether an ordinance that is facially neutral yet permits the board to discriminate on the basis of race violates the equal protection clause.

The city of San Francisco ordinance required laundromats in wooden buildings to have a permit and also established a board to decide who would be issued a permit. The data showed that no Chinese applicant was ever granted a permit to operate a laundry in a wooden building, despite the fact that nearly 90 percent of the city's laundries were operated by Chinese persons. Plaintiffs were held in custody by the sheriff of the city and county of San Francisco, ordered to pay a $10 fine, and in default of payment, imprisoned in the local jail at a rate of one day for each dollar of the fine (*Yick Wo v. Hopkins* 1886, 357).

The Court held that, although the ordinance did not discriminate on its face, its administration was arbitrary and racially unequal. The Court concluded:

> The fact of this discrimination is admitted. No reason for it is shown, and the conclusion cannot be resisted that no reason for it exists except hostility to the race and nationality to which the petitioners belong, and which, in the eye of the law, is not justified. The discrimination is, therefore, illegal, and the public administration which enforces it is a denial of the equal protection of the laws and a violation of the Fourteenth Amendment of the Constitution. The imprisonment of the petitioners is, therefore, illegal, and they must be discharged.
>
> (*Yick Wo v. Hopkins* 1886, 374)

In *Yick Wo*, the Supreme Court also took an important step in holding that the Fourteenth Amendment to the Constitution is not solely confined to the protection of citizens, noting "Nor shall any State deprive any person of life, liberty, or property without due process of law; nor deny to any person within its jurisdiction the equal protection of the laws." In addition, the provisions

> are universal in their application to all persons within the territorial jurisdiction, without regard to any differences of race, of color, or of nationality, and the equal protection of the laws is a pledge of the protection of equal laws.
>
> (*Yick Wo v. Hopkins* 1886, 369)

Notwithstanding ratification of the Fourteenth Amendment which ensured full rights for former slaves and its universal application in *Yick*

Wo, Mexicans were not afforded its protection until 1954. The question before the Court in *Hernandez* was whether the equal protection clause of the Fourteenth Amendment was violated when a state tries a person of a particular race or ancestry before a jury in which all persons of that race or ancestry have been excluded from serving. *Hernandez v. Texas* held that the exclusion of Mexicans from juries denied them equal protection of the law guaranteed by the Fourteenth Amendment. Incredibly, between 1788 and 1954, Mexicans were not considered "persons" and did not exist under the law.

Jury Exclusion and the Fourteenth Amendment

De Jure *Jury Exclusion:* Strauder v. West Virginia

The United States Supreme Court first addressed the issue of racial discrimination in jury selection in *Strauder v. West Virginia* in 1880. Under a West Virginia statute no colored man was eligible to serve on grand or petit juries. The statute, enacted on March 12, 1873 (Acts of 1878: 102), stated: "All white male persons who are twenty-one years of age and who are citizens of this State shall be liable to serve as jurors, except as herein provided."[5]

The plaintiff, a colored man, was indicted for murder in the Circuit Court of Ohio County, West Virginia (*Strauder v. West Virginia,* 100 U.S. 304) on October 20, 1874. Upon trial, he was convicted and sentenced. The case was appealed to the state Supreme Court, which affirmed the judgment of the Circuit Court. The plaintiff appealed to the U.S. Supreme Court, claiming he was denied rights entitled under the Constitution and the laws of the United States (*Strauder v. West Virginia* 1880, 100 US. 304).

Strauder set the standard for discrimination in jury selection, which continues today. The question before the Court was not whether a colored man, when an indictment has been preferred against him, has a right to a grand or a petit jury composed in whole or in part of persons of his own race or color. Instead it asks whether or not, in the composition or selection of jurors by whom he is to be indicted or tried, all persons of his race or color may be excluded by law solely because of their race or color, so that by no possibility can any colored man sit upon the jury.

The Supreme Court overturned Strauder's conviction, holding that the purpose of the framers of the Fourteenth Amendment was that

> no State shall deprive any person of life, liberty, or property without due process of law, or deny to any person within its jurisdiction the equal protection of the laws. What is this but declaring that the law in the States shall be the same for the black as for the white; that all persons, whether colored or white, shall stand equal before the laws of the

States, and, in regard to the colored race, for whose protection the amendment was primarily designed, that no discrimination shall be made against them by law because of their color? The words of the amendment, it is true, are prohibitory, but they contain a necessary implication of a positive immunity, or right, most valuable to the colored race.

(*Strauder v. West Virginia* 1880, 307–308)

De Facto *Jury Exclusion:* Hernandez v. Texas

The Court noted in *Hernandez v. Texas* that exclusion of otherwise eligible persons from jury service solely because of their ancestry or national origin is prohibited by the Fourteenth Amendment, although the Texas statute did not discriminate on this basis (*Hernandez v. Texas,* 1954, 479). In rejecting his appeal, the Texas Supreme Court initially held that Mexicans are White people, and are entitled at the hands of the state to all the rights, privileges, and immunities guaranteed under the Fourteenth Amendment. So long as they are so treated, the guarantee of equal protection has been accorded to them. The grand jury that indicted appellant and the petit jury that tried him being composed of members of his race. [*Hernandez v. Texas,* 1952, 246 (Texas Decision)]

Because Mexicans were defined as legally White, it could not be said in the absence of proof of actual discrimination, that Hernandez was discriminated against and therefore denied equal protection of the law. According to the Texas Supreme Court, he had been tried by his peers. To insist that members of various nationalities that compose the White race should be proportionately represented on grand and petit juries "would destroy our jury system" (*Hernandez v. Texas* 1952).

The petitioner, therefore, had a duel burden when the case came before the U.S. Supreme Court. His initial burden was proving group discrimination by showing that persons of Mexican descent constituted a separate class in Jackson County, which was distinct from Whites (*Hernandez v. Texas* 1954, 479). One method was to show community attitudes. Testimony from responsible persons and community members showed that residents readily distinguished between Whites and Mexicans, and that the participation of Mexicans in business and community groups was slight (*Hernandez v. Texas* 1954, 479). Until recently, Mexican children were also required to attend segregated schools for the first four grades (*Hernandez v. Texas* 1954, 479). At least one restaurant displayed a sign announcing "No Mexicans Served." Ironically, on the courthouse grounds at the time of the hearing, there were two men's bathrooms; one unmarked and the other marked "Colored Men" and "Hombres Aquí" (*Hernandez v. Texas* 1954, 479–480).

Having demonstrated the existence of a separate class, Hernandez had the additional burden of proving discrimination (*Hernandez v. Texas* 1954, 480).

He relied on the "rule of exclusion" first established in *Norris v. Alabama* (1935, 587), and used in other cases, which was that Negroes constituted a substantial segment of the population, that there were Negroes who were qualified to serve, and that none had been called for jury service over a substantial period of time. This was held to constitute *prima facie* evidence of discrimination. Hernandez demonstrated that 14 percent of the population of Jackson County were persons with Mexican or Latino surnames and that 11 percent of the males over 21 had such names (*Hernandez v. Texas*, 1954, 480). The County Tax Assessor also testified that 6 or 7 percent of the persons on the tax rolls of the County were of Mexican descent (*Hernandez v. Texas* 1954, 480–481). The parties stipulated that there were eligible persons of Mexican or Latin American descent in Jackson County to serve as jury commissioners and grand or petit jurors, yet "for the last twenty-five years, there is no record of any person with a Mexican or Latin American name having served on a jury commission, grand jury or petit jury in Jackson County" (*Hernandez v. Texas* 1954, 481).

Once a *prima facie* case was established, the burden shifted to the defense to offer a non-discriminatory explanation for the exclusion. The State offered the testimony of five jury commissioners who stated that they had not discriminated against Mexicans or Latinos in selecting jurors, but the testimony was not sufficient to rebut the strong *prima facie* presumption established in *Norris v. Alabama,* "That showing as to the long-continued exclusion of negroes from jury service, and as to the many negroes qualified for that service, could not be met by mere generalities" (*Hernandez v. Texas* 1954, 481).

Hernandez established that Mexicans were a class, separate, and apart from Blacks or Whites. Just as Blacks were defined as non-persons and not one of the people in *Dred Scott,* prior to *Hernandez,* Mexicans were rendered legally invisible as "White" and therefore incapable of being victims of racial discrimination given they had been tried and convicted by members of their own race.

Discrimination in Peremptory Challenges: Batson v. Kentucky

While *Strauder, Norris,* and *Hernandez* dealt with discrimination in the composition of the *venire,* or panel of prospective jurors, it is also important to discuss discrimination of potential jurors during the *voir dire* examination. The term *voir dire* comes from the French, meaning "to speak the truth." It refers to the preliminary examination of prospective jurors to determine their qualifications and fitness to serve, based on questions asked by the judge and the attorneys. It is used to assess whether a prospective juror is biased or acquainted with any of the parties, counsel, or witnesses.

There are two basic types of jury challenges during *voir dire:* for cause and peremptory. For cause, challenges are unlimited. They occur when a determination is made by the court that a challenged juror should be excluded because the person is presumed to be biased and disqualified because they cannot be fair, impartial, and/or objective. The bias may be overt or implied. The "cause" for exclusion may be that the person has a close relationship with one of the parties or the attorneys as, for example, when a prospective juror is a friend or relative of the judge or one of the attorneys.

Several years ago I was excluded from the jury pool, after I made it to the final 18 empaneled jurors when the judge asked if any of the prospective jurors was acquainted with one or more of the attorneys. I raised my hand and told the court that the defense lawyer had been my undergraduate student and that I had been one of his law school references. When the judge asked whether I could be fair and impartial in the upcoming trial I admitted that I could not and I was dismissed for cause.[6] A person may be similarly excluded because they have a spouse or close relative who works for the police department or the District Attorney; in a DUI trial, because they have had a close friend or relative that was killed or seriously injured by a drunk driver; or in a domestic violence case because the prospective juror or a close friend and/or family member has been a victim of domestic abuse. The defense or the government can make a motion to exclude someone for cause, but the judge makes the ultimate determination.

Peremptory challenges, on the other hand, do not require "cause" and can be made by either party without providing a reason or justification for excluding the prospective juror. Unlike cause challenges, the number of peremptories is limited by statute in the jurisdiction. Because a party need not articulate a justification for excluding a juror, it is obvious that peremptory challenges can be abused and used to exclude prospective jurors because of their race, national origin, and/or gender.

In *Batson v. Kentucky* (1986), the Supreme Court reaffirmed the principle first established in *Strauder* that a State denies a defendant equal protection when it puts him on trial before a jury from which members of his race have been purposefully excluded (*Batson v. Kentucky* 1986, 84–89). While a defendant does not have a right to a jury trial made up in whole or in part of members of his own race, the equal protection clause guarantees that the state will not exclude members of his race from the jury *venire* because of their race. In addition, selection procedures based on race undermine the public's confidence in the fairness of the judicial system.

Batson, a Black man, was indicted in Kentucky on charges of second-degree burglary and receipt of stolen goods. On the first day of trial, the judge excluded certain jurors for cause during the *voir dire*. The prosecution then used peremptory challenges to exclude all Black persons on the *venire*. After an all-White jury was selected, the defense made a motion to discharge the jury. It argued that exclusion of Black jurors from the venire violated Batson's rights under the Sixth and Fourteenth

Amendments to a jury selected from a cross-section of the community, and under the Fourteenth Amendment to the equal protection of the law. The judge denied the motion and the jury convicted him on both counts. In affirming the conviction, the Kentucky Supreme Court held that a defendant alleging lack of a fair cross-section must demonstrate systematic exclusion of a group of jurors from the *venire*.

The Supreme Court reversed, holding that the same principles used to determine discrimination in the selection of the *venire*, also apply in the State's use of peremptory challenges to strike individual jurors from the petit jury. While the prosecution is entitled to use peremptory challenges for whatever reason, as long as it is related to their perception of the outcome of the case, the equal protection clause forbids the exclusion of persons simply because of their race (*Batson v. Kentucky* 1986, 88–89).

The Supreme Court went on to reject the portion of *Swain v. Alabama*, which held that a Black defendant could make out a *prima facie* case of purposeful discrimination only by proving that the peremptory challenge system as a whole was discriminatory. The Court held, in other words, that a defendant may make a *prima facie* cased based simply on the facts concerning the selection of the jury in their case (*Batson v. Kentucky* 1986, 89–96). The Court concluded that

> In deciding whether the defendant has made the requisite showing, the trial court should consider all relevant circumstances. For example, a "pattern" of strikes against black jurors included in the particular venire might give rise to an inference of discrimination. Similarly, the prosecutor's questions and statements during voir dire examination and in exercising his challenges may support or refute an inference of discriminatory purpose. These examples are merely illustrative …
> (*Batson v. Kentucky* 1986, 96–97)[7]

Once a defendant makes a *prima facie* case, the burden shifts to the State to provide a non-discriminatory explanation for excluding the Black juror. While this requirement may in some cases limit the character of the peremptory challenge, the Court stressed that the prosecutor's explanation need not rise to the level necessary in justifying a challenger for cause. However,

> the prosecutor may not rebut the defendant's prima facie case of discrimination by stating merely that he challenged jurors of the defendant's race on the assumption – or his intuitive judgment – that they would be partial to the defendant because of their shared race.
> (*Batson v. Kentucky* 1986, 96–97)

In a line of cases going back to *Strauder* (1879), and including *Norris* (1935), and *Hernandez* (1954), the Supreme Court has consistently held that the use of race to exclude people from jury service is unconstitutional and a viola-tion of the Fourteenth Amendment equal protection clause. In *Batson* (1986), the Court held that the same equal protection principles applied to determine whether there is discrimination in selecting the *venire* also apply to the State's use of peremptory challenges to strike individual jurors from the petit jury.

While discrimination in jury selection based on race, national origin, and gender is unconstitutional, it is not clear whether language discrimination is also a violation of equal protection. This important issue was addressed in a second and more recent, Hernandez case, *Hernandez v. New York.*

Is Use of Peremptories to Exclude Bilingual Jurors Prohibited Under the Fourteenth Amendment?

Hernandez v. New York

Dionisio Hernandez was accused of firing several shots at his estranged wife, Charlene Calloway and her mother Ada Saline on a Brooklyn street, where Calloway suffered three shotgun wounds. The petitioner allegedly missed Saline and hit two men in a nearby restaurant. Although the victims sur-vived the incident, Hernandez was convicted on two counts of attempted murder and criminal possession of a weapon. He appealed his conviction to the United States Supreme Court and asked the court to review the New York state courts' rejection of his claim that the prosecution had used per-emptory challenges in his trial to exclude Latinos because of their ethnicity (*Hernandez v. New York* 1991, 355). He argued that per the Court's ruling in *Batson* (1986), the use of peremptory challenges to exclude people because of their ethnicity violated the equal protection clause (*Hernandez v. New York* 1991, 355).

The trial was held in the New York Supreme Court, Kings County. In the appeal, the U.S. Supreme Court focused only on the jury selection process and the proper application of *Batson*. After 63 prospective jurors were questioned and nine empaneled, the defense objected, claiming the prosecutor used four peremptory challenges to exclude potential Latino jurors (*Hernandez v. New York* 1991, 355–356). Two of the excluded Latino *venire* persons had brothers convicted of crimes, and the brother of one potential juror was being prosecuted by the same District Attorney for a parole violation (*Hernandez v. New York* 1991, 356). Yet, these jurors were not excused for cause. Because petitioner did not press his *Batson* claim relative to these jurors, the court focused on the other two excluded jurors (*Hernandez v. New York* 1991, 356).

Once Hernandez's raised his *Batson* objection, the prosecution volun-teered reasons for excluding the jurors before the court had an opportu-nity to rule on whether the defense attorney had made a *prima facie* case.

The prosecutor justified the exclusion, claiming not knowing whether or not they were Hispanics but because of language. He felt uncertain that "they would be able to listen and follow the interpreter" (*Hernandez v. New York* 1991, 356). The prosecutor explained:

> We talked to them for a long time; the Court talked to them, I talked to them. I believe that in their heart they will try to follow it, but I felt there was a great deal of uncertainty as to whether they could accept the interpreter as the final arbiter of what was said by each of the witnesses, especially where there were going to be Spanish-speaking witnesses, and I didn't feel, when I asked them whether or not they could accept the interpreter's translation of it, I didn't feel that they could. They each looked away from me and said with some hesitancy that they would try, not that they could, but that they would try to follow the interpreter, and I feel that, in a case where the interpreter would be for the main witnesses, they would have an undue impact upon the jury.
>
> (*Hernandez v. New York* 1991, 356–357)

After the defense counsel renewed the objection, the prosecutor responded by noting that the case involved four complainants who were all Hispanic, that all of his witnesses were Hispanic, and that he had absolutely no reason to exclude them (*Hernandez v. New York* 1991, 357).

The Court followed the three-step process used to evaluate claims of violations of equal protection in the use of peremptory challenges under *Batson* (1986, 96–98). First, the moving party must make a *prima facie* case that the prosecutor used race as a basis for exercising peremptory challenges (*Batson v. Kentucky 1986*, 96–97). Once the *prima facie* basis is made, the prosecution then has the burden of providing a race-neutral explanation for striking the jurors (*Hernandez* 1991, 358–359). Finally, the court makes the final determination as to whether the moving party has carried his burden of proving intentional discrimination.

It should be noted that the Court took a significant departure from the previous standard for establishing equal protection violations by insisting that the petitioner had the burden of proving that the discrimination is intentional. This was not the standard employed in previous cases, including *Strauder, Yick Wo, Norris, Hernandez v. Texas*, or even *Batson*. The Court relied instead on recent cases involving discrimination in employment, noting that a court addressing the issue of discrimination in the use of peremptory challenges must adhere to the fundamental principle that "official action will not be held unconstitutional solely because it results in a racially disproportionate impact ... Proof of racially discriminatory intent or purpose is required to show a violation of the Equal Protection Clause" (*Arlington Heights v. Metropolitan Housing Development Corp.*, 429 U.S. 252,

429 U.S. 264–265 (1977); see also *Washington v. Davis*, 426 U.S. 229, 426 U.S. 239 (1976)).

The Court added that,

> 'Discriminatory purpose' … implies more than intent as volition or intent as awareness of consequences. It implies that the decision-maker … selected … a particular course of action at least in part 'because of,' not merely 'in spite of,' its adverse effects upon an identifiable group.[8]

In addition, a neutral explanation within the context of this analysis means an explanation based on something other than the race or ethnicity of the juror (*Hernandez v. New York* 1991, 360). At this point in the analysis, the ultimate issue is the face validity of the prosecutor's explanation, and "[u]nless a discriminatory intent is inherent in the prosecutor's explanation, the reason offered will be deemed race-neutral" (*Hernandez v. New York* 1991, 360).

Hernandez maintained that Spanish language ability was closely related to ethnicity and that as a result, the exclusion of Latino potential jurors because they speak Spanish violates the equal protection clause (*Hernandez v. New York* 1991, 360). The petitioner also pointed to the close relationship between Spanish-speaking ability and ethnicity in New York City. The Court noted that it did not have to address this argument here because the prosecutor did not rely on Spanish language ability alone as a reason for excluding the jurors. He also used potential juror's response and demeanor during the *voir dire,* which made him doubt their ability to defer to the official translation (*Hernandez v. New York* 1991, 360). The prosecutor, therefore, offered a race-neutral basis for their exclusion, not based on his intent to exclude bilingual or Latino jurors or on stereotypical beliefs about Latinos or bilingual persons (*Hernandez v. New York* 1991, 361).

In upholding Hernandez's conviction, the Supreme Court concluded that it found no clear error in the state trial court's ruling that the prosecutor did not discriminate on the basis of the ethnicity of the prospective Latino jurors (*Hernandez v. New York* 1991, 369). But the Court stressed that the decision does not imply that exclusion of bilinguals from jury service is wise, or even necessarily constitutional in all cases.

"In the Land of the Blind, the One-Eyed Person is King": Implications of Hernandez v. New York

The decision in *Hernandez v. New York* has important and negative implications for Latinas/os. First, as noted by the Court, it is a harsh paradox that one may become proficient enough in English to be eligible to participate in a trial, only to be disqualified because they know a second language (1991, 371). Second, the case is significant because it deals with discrimination against bilingual persons and not monolingual limited English speakers. My father, for example, could not be on a jury because he didn't speak English and now, potentially, I may not be able to serve on one either because I do. A third, related, point is that while Latinos are often subjected to differential and unequal treatment because of some real or perceived deficiency, in this instance they are being excluded from jury service because they are overqualified and know too much.

The saying in Spanish, "*En la Tierra del Ciego, el Tuerto es Rey*" ("In the Land of the Blind, the One-Eyed Person is King"), is applicable to the exclusion of bilingual jurors because, ironically, they actually are the only ones who understand the Spanish language testimony being presented to the court. They hear and are able to understand both the original witness testimony in Spanish, and then the interpreter's English translation of the testimony. As members of the jury, they could provide an important check or corrective function against potential translation errors in a trial.

The prosecutor's concern in *Hernandez* was that, if bilingual jurors disagreed with the translated testimony, they might not be able to "disregard what they heard and accept the official translation." The truth, however, is that once one hears testimony, it is impossible to block out and/or disregard what you just heard. It will be recalled that the excluded jurors said that they would "try" to disregard the actual testimony and that the prosecutor "believed that in their heart they will try to follow it, but I felt here was a great deal of uncertainty as to whether they could accept the interpreter as the final arbiter of what was said by each of the witnesses" (*Hernandez v. New York* 1991, 356).

An additional problem with the decision is that because bilingual jurors are being evaluated through monolingual lenses, they are being asked to control something that is difficult, if not impossible, to control. One of the reasons that the Fourteenth Amendment prohibits the government from denying persons the equal protection of the law because of their race, gender, religion, national origin, or ethnicity is precisely because these are immutable or relatively immutable characteristics that the person either cannot control, or like religion or sexual orientation, are so fundamental to their identity or sense of self that they should not have to change or alter them.

In evaluating such classifications, courts generally use strict scrutiny, meaning that regulations based on immutable or relatively immutable characteristics such as race, national origin, or gender are presumptively unconstitutional. In order for the government to pass the rigorous strict scrutiny standard, it must carry the heavy burden of demonstrating that: (1) In regulating a protected category it is seeking to attain a compelling state interest such as an imminent danger or national security, and (2) The means used to attain such an interest are necessary. In other words, if one can articulate a less restrictive alternative, the state action is presumptively unconstitutional.[9]

Finally, there is a body of literature on bilingual speakers supported by the experience of bilinguals which suggests that they are not generally consciously aware of the language they are speaking at a given moment, particularly when interacting with other bilinguals (Albert and Obler 1978, 95). When bilinguals converse with one another, they code switch between one language and another without being fully conscious or aware of the language they are speaking. As an attorney who often represents Spanish-speaking clients and interacts with them in Spanish outside of court, I find it difficult during trial to ask them questions in English and then wait for the translation by the interpreter. I also often found myself unconsciously beginning a sentence in Spanish before the interpreter has an opportunity to translate the response. Although bilinguals may try to control the language they are speaking, they may not be able to consciously do so. In short, monolingual judges and courts err in viewing language like a faucet, which can be readily turned on or off, because bilingualism is much more complex and not readily controllable at a conscious level.

Bilingual Classifications Should be Subjected to Strict Scrutiny Because Bilingualism is a Fixed, Relatively Immutable Characteristic

The argument in *Hernandez v. New York* (1991) that the jurors were not excluded because they were Latino or bilingual is unpersuasive because there is, as the Petitioner maintained, a very close relationship between bilingualism and Latino ethnicity. In fact, about 97 percent of all bilingual Spanish speakers in the United States are Latinos and most Latinos claim some knowledge of Spanish.[10] In addition, regardless of language competency, the fear that Latinos will not abide by the official translation can be used as a pretext for excluding them from juries, just as having a wooden laundry facility became a proxy for Chinese heritage in *Yick Wo*. Given the double standard of Justice, or injustice, that has prevailed in the United States historically, it is especially important that Latinos not be excluded from juries where there will be Spanish language testimony. Significantly, the prosecutor in *Hernandez* did not question non-Latinos about their knowledge of Spanish or whether they would have difficulty abiding by the official translation. The prosecutor also made assumptions about the language competency of the two excluded jurors without first assessing it.

Hernandez set a dangerous precedent because the decisions will likely lead to the wholesale exclusion of Latinos from juries and, by extension, their participation in the judicial process. The holding in *Hernandez v. New York* was extended by the Third Circuit Court of Appeals, for example, which held that the "Equal Protection Clause does not prohibit a trial attorney from peremptorily challenging jurors because of their ability to understand a foreign language, the translation of which will be disputed at trial" (*Pemberthy v. Beyer* 1994). In *Pemberthy v. Beyer*, the prosecutor used five peremptory challenges to strike Latinos who spoke Spanish because the translation of wiretap tapes would be contested at trial. The defendants moved to suppress all of the wiretap evidence, "arguing, among other things, that the interceptions had not been properly minimized due to the monitors' deficient knowledge of Spanish."

The prosecutor in *Hernandez* maintained that the jurors were not excluded because they were Latino or because they spoke Spanish but because of their hesitancy in answering whether they would abide by the official translation as the ultimate arbiter of what was said. However, based on research on bilingualism and the lived experience of bilinguals, I argue that they were excluded because they were Latinos, bilingual, and, therefore, unable to ignore or disregard the testimony they heard. In short, the bilingual jurors in *Hernandez v. New York* answered the prosecutor's questions precisely the way that any honest reasonable bilingual person would have answered when they said that they would try to disregard what they heard and abide by the official translation. I further argue that bilingualism is a discrete and immutable characteristic over which bilingual persons have little if any control, and the exclusion of bilinguals from juries should be subjected to strict scrutiny. In addition to research suggesting that language processing occurs rather automatically among bilinguals, there are postmortem studies of polyglot brains providing evidence that knowledge of more than one language has anatomical consequences (Albert and Obler 1978, 95).

The Court in *Hernandez v. New York* was careful to note that it was not suggesting that all Latino bilingual jurors be excluded from juries or that their exclusion is always necessarily constitutional. Bilinguals are different from other protected classes for whom language is not a primary basis of difference, identity, and discrimination. As with race and national origin, bilingual children learn the language or languages spoken in the home and have little choice in acquisition of language. I argue that if equality is to be attained, law and equal protection analysis must recognize bilingualism as a relatively immutable characteristic that cannot be turned on and off like a faucet and take into account the anatomical difference in the bilingual brain. Otherwise, the *Hernandez v. New York* analysis of equal treatment is bound to perpetuate inequality and serve as a pretext for excluding Latinas and Latinos from juries.

Exclusion from Grand Juries: The East LA Thirteen and Common-Sense Racism

In *Hernandez v. Texas,* the state of Texas stipulated that over the previous 25 years no person with a Mexican or Latin American surname had ever served on a jury commission, grand jury, or petit jury in Jackson County.

While grand and petit (trial) juries are both made up of ordinary citizens subpoenaed for jury service, they serve very different functions. Grand juries are especially important because they determine whether felony charges should be brought against a person, while trial juries render a verdict on the charges. Grand juries are also standing entities usually consisting of 23 people, and jurors may have jury duty for months at a time but individual jurors will have to work only a few days out of the month (FindLaw 2017). Because grand juries work closely with prosecutors and rules of evidence are relaxed, defense attorneys often remark that "one could indict a ham sandwich" before a grand jury.

In March 1968, thousands of high school students in East Los Angeles participated in a massive walkout demanding that school curriculum be radically altered to reflect the history, heritage, and culture of Chicanas/os. Thirteen organizers of the protest were arrested and faced 45-year prison sentences after being charged with 16 counts of conspiracy, a felony (Stavans 1996).

Oscar "Zeta" Acosta, a brash, inexperienced Chicano lawyer and creative writer agreed to take the case, representing all of the defendants.[11] Acosta had served as a legal aid lawyer in Oakland for a year but this was his first criminal case. The 13 defendants were indicted by the Los Angeles grand jury and charged with what was essentially a concocted charge of conspiracy to disrupt the schools (Acosta 1973). Acosta moved to quash the indictment before the California Court of Appeal arguing that the method of selecting grand jurors in Los Angeles discriminated against Mexicans, led to their under-representation, and denied them the equal protection of the law (Stavans, 1996: 285).

Although the 1968 East LA Thirteen case occurred almost a century after *Strauder v. West Virginia* (1880) and 14 years after *Hernandez v. Texas* (1954), the motion to quash was denied and the judgment was upheld by the Court of Appeals. Approximately one million Mexicans resided in Los Angeles at the time and constituted the largest minority in the country's most populous county (ibid.). However, in a span of ten years 178 Superior Court Judges, who nominated grand jurors in Los Angeles County, nominated 1,501 people; only 20 (1 percent) of the nominees were Spanish surnamed (ibid.). Grand jurors were selected from a random list of nominees and 96.1 percent of the judges had never nominated a Spanish surnamed person (ibid.). As a result, only four of the 210 (1.9 percent) grand jurors had a Spanish-surname and one of these individuals was black (ibid.).

Despite his lack of experience, Acosta boldly subpoenaed 30 Superior Court judges. From their testimony one is able construct a demographic profile of the 1959–1968 grand jurors:

He is wealthy, of independent financial means. He is comparatively advanced in years. He is, or was, a business owner, executive, or professional – or married to one. He is a close personal friend, occasionally once removed, of a Superior Court Judge. He is of the White race ... In a word, as characterized by an Appellate Judge: WASP.

(ibid,: 285)

All but 2 of the 30 subpoenaed judges reported that they did not nominate any Mexicans for the grand jury, because they did not know any who were qualified and they did not feel personally obligated to take affirmative steps to find people who were qualified among the several minorities in the area (ibid.). "The trial court denied the motion to quash because since in its opinion there was no showing of intentional discrimination, since in each of the last ten years at least one Mexican was nominated" (ibid., 285). This ruling was contrary to the conclusion in *Hernandez v. Texas* (1954, 482) where the Court noted that

> it taxes our credulity to say that mere chance resulted in their being no members of this class among the over six thousand jurors called in the past 25 years. The result bespeaks discrimination, whether or not it was a conscious decision on the part of any individual jury commissioner.

Ian Haney López (2004, 109) notes that in analyzing the testimony presented in the East Los Angeles Thirteen case, it is clear that "most judges engaged in widespread discrimination without forming intent to do so." In fact, like the prosecutor in *New York v. Hernandez*, all of the judges vehemently denied being prejudiced or that they intended to discriminate against Mexicans or other racial minorities in making their nominations for the grand jury (ibid.).

Haney López dismisses the notion that the judges were lying or simply trying to cover up their racism and suggests that they probably genuinely believed that they were not racist or biased in making their nominations. In order to explain the judges' behavior and the contradiction between their professed lack of intent to discriminate and the exclusion of Mexicans from grand juries, Haney López proposes a "common-sense" theory of discrimination, which posits that much of our racial beliefs and behavior are neither overt nor intentional. In other words, the type of racism the judges exhibited is not the old-fashioned overt racism, but one that is subtle, covert, and unknowing. While some judges may have harbored racial animus against Mexicans, "the era and general social context of the cases, though, make it unlikely that the majority of the judges intentionally embraced and acted on racial hatred" (ibid., 110).

Recognizing that it would be difficult to prove intentional discrimination, Acosta told the court: "I am not suggesting that the Judges wake up every morning and say, 'I'm not going to look for any Mexicans today. I'm not going to submit any Mexican names today'" (ibid., 110). While Acosta insisted that the judges did in fact discriminate, as in *Hernandez v. Texas,* he focused not on the intent of the judges but on the results of a discriminatory system, reporting that "We are talking about facts; we are talking about the results of a system" (ibid., 110). Clearly, one can see the power of common-sense racism in jury nominations by analyzing the extent to which the judges tended to completely disregard the criteria given to them for the selection of grand jurors.

The California Code of Civil Procedure listed five prerequisites for grand jurors but only two focused on the personal capacity of prospective jurors. They were simply expected to possess: "sufficient knowledge of the English language" and to be "of ordinary intelligence" (ibid., 113). Given these nominal requirements, almost any citizen would qualify to serve on a grand jury.

Several U.S. Supreme Court decisions also governed nomination prac-tices, as they held that officials selecting grand juries "*must not* simply draw on their acquaintances," cautioning that "Where jury commissioners limit those from whom grand juries are selected to their own personal acquaintances, discrimination can arise from commissioners who know no negroes as well as from commissioners who know but who eliminate them" (ibid., 114). In another case, the Supreme Court ruled:

> The statements of the jury commissioners that they chose only whom they knew, and that they knew no eligible Negroes in an area where Negroes made up so large a proportion of the popula-tion, prove the intentional exclusion that is discrimination in viola-tion of constitutional rights.
>
> (ibid., 114)

Finally, Superior Court judges received a yearly directive from the presiding judge with instructions that the Grand Jury should be representative of a cross-section of the population and that judges should make nominations from the various geographical areas in the city (ibid., 114).

Although it is difficult to understand how the judges could have inter-preted the relevant Supreme Court decisions and the cross-sectional mandate issued by the presiding judge as legitimating the selection of their friends as grand jurors, this is precisely how the judges interpreted these directives. Judge William Levit, for instance, responded to Acosta's admonishment that the grand jury should be representative of a cross-section of the community:

> I have no quarrel with that. I would assume that with a hundred and thirty-four Judges, selected as they are and each one given the right to nominate up to two people, that this would be what I would consider a cross-section of the community, broadly defined,
>
> (ibid., 117)

But for these judges nominating their friends was part of a powerful script, or common sense, which became not only a routine practice but assumed a normative and self-righteous character (ibid., 119).

One judge, for example, said, "It wouldn't make any difference who came before me if they are *qualified* as a nominee, but I don't want to nominate people I don't know" (ibid., 123). Another judge said, "I think it is the duty of each judge to pick a nominee who he feels is *qualified* for the position, regardless of what race, nationality, or religion he may be" (ibid., 123–124). The common-sense script carried a strong, unstated implication, not only that grand jurors should be qualified but that "qualified persons were White, and non-Whites were unqualified," as illustrated by the testimony of Judge Richard Fildew. When Acosta asked Judge Fildew whether he believed that the grand jury should be represented by the various racial and ethnic groups, he responded: "If the people are qualified, definitely; if they are not qualified, no" (ibid.:125).

What is perhaps most revealing about the judges' emphasis on qualifications is that the criteria for serving on a grand jury are minimal and entail simply "sufficient knowledge of the English language" and be of "ordinary intelligence." Essentially, an indirect, disturbing, and unstated assumption of the testimony of the judges was that Mexicans were inferior, not qualified, and too stupid to serve on grand juries.

Conclusion

One of the cornerstones of the U.S. justice system is the right to a trial by a jury of one's peers. The Sixth Amendment provides that one has a right to a speedy and public trial by an impartial jury and the Fourteenth Amendment that no state shall "deny to any person within its jurisdiction the equal protection of the law."

In *Strauder v. West Virginia* (1880), the Supreme Court invalidated the conviction of a Black man who was convicted by an all-White jury because of a specific statute that limited jury service to "All White male persons who are twenty-one years of age and who are citizens of this State." Strauder unsuccessfully sought to have his case moved to federal court, and the Supreme Court held that removal should have been granted and that the statute was a violation of the Fourteenth Amendment and thus unconstitutional.

In 1935, the Supreme Court similarly overturned the conviction of Clarence Norris, one of nine young Negro boys indicted for rape after he was sentenced to death in Jackson County, Alabama. Although there were Negroes who were qualified for service, for a generation or longer, no Negro had been called to serve on any jury in the county (Norris v. Alabama 1935, 596). According to the practice the jury commission had—the names of eligible Negroes would normally appear on the preliminary list of eligible male citizens but no names of any Negroes were placed on a jury roll. The Supreme Court held that the exclusion of all Negroes from a grand jury by which a Negro is indicted, or from the petit jury by which he is tried for the offense, resulting from systematic and arbitrary exclusion of the African race from the jury lists solely because of their race or color, is a denial of the equal protection of the laws guaranteed by the Fourteenth Amendment (*Norris v. Alabama* 1935, 589).

Hernandez v. Texas (1954) similarly overturned the murder conviction of a young Mexican farm worker by an all-White jury, thereby challenging the racial binary and recognizing Mexicans as a distinct and cognizable entity, separate and apart from Blacks and Whites. Previously Mexicans were viewed as "legally White" but not accepted or treated equally with Whites. Thus, just as Blacks were rendered as not being persons protected by the Constitution of the United States in *Dred Scott*, prior to 1954, Mexicans did not exist as a legally cognizable category. Although the Texas statute did not exclude Mexicans from jury service, the Court uncovered a widespread *de facto* pattern of discrimination in injury selection against Mexicans in Jackson County, where in the previous 25 years no person with a Mexican or Latino surname had served on as a jury commissioner, grand jury, or petit jury.

Hernandez was important in challenging the racial binary in that it established Mexicans as a class apart, separate and distinct from Blacks or Whites. They are what Justice Stone termed a discrete and insular minority in Footnote 4 of *Carolene Products* (1938). Stone noted that while courts are generally deferential to legislative bodies when it comes to regulation of economic activities, greater judicial scrutiny may be warranted when legislations seeks to regulate fundamental rights protected by the Constitution. He also suggested in the famous Footnote 4 that strict scrutiny should be used in evaluating statutes directed at particular religious groups or racial minorities, suggesting that

> prejudice against discrete and insular minorities may be a special condition, which tends seriously to curtail the operation of those political processes ordinarily to be relied upon to protect minorities, and which may call for a correspondingly more searching judicial inquiry.
> (*Carolene Products* 1938)

In *Swain v. Alabama* (1965), however, the Supreme Court held that it was not a violation of equal protection for a prosecutor to use peremptory challenges to strike all Blacks from a jury pool and that "[To] subject the prosecutor's challenge in any particular case to the demands [of equal protection] would entail a radical change in the nature and operation of the challenge" given that the "essential nature of the peremptory challenge is that it [is] exercised without a reason stated, without inquiry and without being subject to the court's control."

Batson v. Kentucky (1986) overturned *Swain*, holding that the equal protection clause forbids the prosecutor from challenging potential jurors solely because of their race or on the assumption that Black jurors as a group will be unable to be impartial in considering the State's case against a Black defendant (*Batson v. Kentucky*, 1986, 86). *Batson* further held that a defendant can make a *prima facie* case of purposeful racial discrimination by relying solely on the facts concerning jury selection in his particular case.

Despite these U.S. Supreme Court precedents, Mexicans and other Latino groups continue to be discriminated against and are grossly underrepresented in both grand and petit juries (Forde-Mazrui 1999). Arguably, most of this discrimination is not de jure; formally and legally mandated and purposeful, but covert, indirect discrimination, or what has been termed common-sense racism.

Hernandez v. New York turned *Hernandez v. Texas* on its head by upholding the exclusion of bilingual jurors during peremptory challenges. As long as the prosecution could articulate a racially neutral reason such as that a prospective juror might not be able to disregard what they heard and accept the interpreter's official translation as the ultimate arbiter of the witness' testimony, bilingual persons could continue to be excluded. Given that much discrimination is common sense, it also set an onerous burden on the plaintiff to show that the discrimination was intentional or had a discriminatory purpose (*Hernandez v. New York* 1991, 360).

This is a dangerous precedent that opens the door to the use of language ability as a proxy for race and potentially to the wholesale exclusion of Mexicans and other Latino groups from grand and petit juries. It also places the burden on the defendant who must now demonstrate that the discrimination was intentional and motivated by racial animus. Ironically, as the Supreme Court acknowledged, "It is a harsh paradox that one may become proficient enough in English to participate in trial, only to encounter disqualification because he knows a second language as well" (*Hernandez v. New York* 1991, 371).[12]

Notes

1 The extent to which Pete worked as a cotton picker is unclear, as one newspaper account claimed he was working as service station attendant at the time of the shooting (García 2009, 17).
2 Pete got into a heated argument and ballroom fight with Espinosa, after Espinosa had insulted him. Hernandez left the bar and returned with a gun, shooting and killing Espinosa.
3 Hernandez was subsequently re-tried and convicted.
4 While the Supreme Court's official recording of the case name spells the respondent's name as "Sandford," his name was actually "Sanford" (Oyez, 1 September 2017).
5 Women of all races were also excluded from jury service but this issue was not addressed by the Court. Notes deleted.

6 I also handled a case as an attorney where the prosecutor was a disgruntled White, former student of mine who was overly zealous in prosecuting my client. I argued, unsuccessfully that he should have been recused from the case.
7 Citations omitted.
8 Citations omitted.
9 In *Korematsu v. United States* 1944,, the Supreme Court upheld the internment of persons of Japanese ancestry during World War II, including U.S. citizens and children because it was deemed necessary to attain the compelling state interest of national security. In retrospect, it is clear that the action was overbroad and not narrowly tailored to attain the national security interest. Also, the fact that person of German or Italian origin were not treated similarly suggests that racial animus against the Japanese motivated the action.
10 Amici Curiae Brief in Support of Petitioner on behalf of the Mexican American Legal Defense and Education Fund (MALDEF) and the Commonwealth of Puerto Rican Community Affairs in the United States. *Hernandez v. New York*, 1990, at 3.
11 Given possible conflicts of interest in one lawyer representing multiple defendants, courts generally insist that each party have independent counsel.
12 Citations omitted.

References

Acosta, Oscar Zeta. 1973. *The Revolt of the Cockroach People*. New York: Vintage Books.
Albert, Martin L. and Loraine K. Obler. 1978. *The Bilingual Brain: Neuropsychological and Neurolinguistic Aspects of Bilingualism*. New York: Academic Press.
FindLaw. 2017. Available at: http://criminal.findlaw.com/criminal-law-basics/differ ence-between-grand-jury-and-trial-jury.html/ (accessed October 4, 2017).
Forde-Mazrui, Kim. 1999. "Jural Districting: Selecting Impartial Juries Through Community Representation." *Vanderbilt Law Review*, 52: 351.
García, Ignacio. 2009. *White But Not Equal*. Tucson. AZ: The University of Arizona Press.
Haney López, Ian F. 2004. *Racism on Trial: The Chicano Fight for Justice*. New York: Belknap Press.
Olivas, Michael A. (Ed.). 2006. *"Colored Men and Hombres Aquí": Hernandez v. Texas and the Emergence of Mexican-American Lawyering*. Houston, TX: Arte Público Press.
Oyez. 2017. "Dred Scott v. Sandford." 1 September 2017. Retrieved from www. oyez.org/cases/1850-1900/60us393
Perea, Juan Francisco. 2006. "Mi Profundo Azul: Why Latinos Have a Right to Sing the Blues." In Michael A. Olivas (Ed.), *"Colored Men and Hombres Aquí"*: *Hernandez v. Texas and the Emergence of Mexican-American Lawyering*. Houston, TX: Arte Público Press, pp. 91–110.
Stavans, Ilan (Ed.). 1996. *Oscar "Zeta" Acosta: The Uncollected Works*. Houston, TX: Arte Publico Press.

Cases Cited

Arlington Heights v. Metropolitan Housing Development Corp. 429 U. S. 252 (1977).
Batson v. Kentucky 476 U.S. 79 (1986).

Carolene Products (1938).

Hernandez v. New York 500 U.S. 352 (1991).

Hernandez v. State of Texas 160 Tex. Crim. 72, 251 S.W.2D 531 (1952) (State decision)

Hernandez v. Texas 347 U.S. 475 (1954).

Korematsu v. United States 323 U.S. 214 (1944).

Norris v. Alabama 294 U.S. 587 (1935).

Pemberthy v. Beyer (1994).

Scott v. Sandford 60 U.S. 393 (1856).

Strauder v. West Virginia 100 U.S. 303 (1880).

Swain v. Alabama 380 U.S. 202 (1965).

Washington v. Davis 426 U. S. 229 (1976).

Yick Wo v. Hopkins 118 U.S. 356 (1886).

Chapter 10

Whiteness, Mexican Appearance and the Fourth Amendment

Alfredo Mirandé

> In the 1930s, some years after my mother's family became part of the great river of Black migration that flowed north, my Mississippi-born grandmother was confronted with the harsh matter of economic survival for herself and her two daughters … [S]he took one long hard look at her choices and presented herself for employment at a major retail store in Chicago's central business district … in so doing she was presenting herself as a white woman. In the parlance of racist America, she was "passing." Her fair skin, straight hair, and aquiline features had not spared her from the life of sharecropping into which she had been born in … but in the burgeoning landscape of urban America, anonymity was possible for a Black person with "white" features. She was transgressing boundaries, crossing borders, spinning on margins, traveling between dualities of Manichean space, rigidly bifurcated into light/dark, good/bad, white/Black. [S]he could thus enter the white world, albeit on a false passport, not merely passing, but trespassing.
>
> (Harris 1993, 1710–1711)

Cheryl Harris' moving description of how her grandmother passed as a White person is a powerful illustration of how "Race Matters" in American society and how it is socially constructed. Historically, Whiteness was property that conferred certain legal rights, privileges, and benefits on persons accorded this status. The status of becoming White, therefore, became a valued asset that Whites sought to protect and attain.

Whites have come to expect and rely on these benefits, and over time these expectations have been affirmed, legitimated, and protected by the law. Even though the law is neither uniform nor explicit in all instances, in protecting settled expectations based on White privilege, American law has recognized a property interest in Whiteness (ibid., 1713).

Gaining "legal" immigration status in the United States also confers rights and privileges on persons. DACA (Deferred Action for Childhood Arrivals) recipients, for example, were granted temporary legal status in the United States, only to have it stripped away by a Presidential Executive Order (Department of Homeland Security 2017; Molina 2017). Like Harris' grandmother, thousands of immigrants who cross the US/Mexico border yearly with fake documents are similarly traversing the White world, "on a false passport, not merely passing, but trespassing."

This chapter[1] focuses on the racialization of immigration status and how the social construction of Whiteness is part and parcel of the designation of persons as being labeled as "illegal," "unauthorized," or "undocumented." Terms such as "illegal" and "undocumented" have become virtually synonymous with Mexican, and race and immigration status are often conflated. There are a large number of White European undocumented persons, for example, who can more readily pass themselves off as documented because of White privilege. While these immigrants may initially be forced to work in low status, poorly paying jobs because of their undocumented status and lack of papers, they are accorded certain privileges by virtue of their race and real or perceived Whiteness.

I focus here not only on the social construction of Whiteness and White privilege but also on how Whiteness affects immigration and citizen status via the selective enforcement of the Fourth Amendment prohibition against unreasonable searches and seizures by Immigration and Customs Enforcement (ICE) and the Border Patrol, as well as the legal doctrine surrounding the constitutionality of border stops. Specifically, I interrogate how socially constructed racial categories, such as being perceived as "Mexican-looking" are embedded in border enforcement and immigration stops. The Supreme Court has ruled, for example, that so-called "Mexican appearance" is so closely linked to immigration status that it can be used as a legitimate factor in making an immigration stop. In short, I look at how the racialization of "Mexican-looking" persons now serves as a proxy for immigration status.

I begin with a brief overview of the concept of "Whiteness as Property" before turning to a discussion of the historical origins of the Fourth Amendment prohibition against unreasonable government searches and seizures, and the various exceptions to that doctrine. I conclude by analyzing a line of cases that shows how courts have gradually eroded Fourth Amendment protections for Mexicans and Latinos/a in an immigration context by carving out what I call the border or Mexican exception to the Fourth Amendment.

Whiteness as Property

Cheryl Harris demonstrates how in American society, Whiteness has historically functioned as property with all of the rights and privileges accorded other types of property. Arguing that racial identity and property are inextricably linked, Harris maintains that Whiteness was initially constructed as a form of racial identity but evolved into a form of property, which was acknowledged and protected in American law (Harris 1993, 1709). Because of her fair skin, straight her, and white features, her maternal grandmother, Alma, as noted, was able to "pass" and gain employment in a major department store in downtown Chicago, a fancy establishment that did not hire Blacks and catered to an exclusively White clientele (ibid, 1710). While this decision would have been unremarkable for a White woman in similar circumstances, for Harris' grandmother, it proved to be "an act of both great daring and self-denial" (ibid., 1710). Harris poignantly remarks that by passing, she "walked into forbidden worlds impaled on the weapon of her own pale skin, she was a sentinel at impromptu planning sessions of her own destruction" (ibid., 1709).

Although passing was difficult and painful, Whiteness conferred legal rights and privileges to people. Whiteness not only determined White identity and whether one assumed the status of slave but "conferred tangible and economically valuable benefits, and it was jealously guarded as a valued possession, allowed only to those who met a strict standard of proof" (ibid., 1726).

Harris describes the evolution of Whiteness as property. Through the institutionalization of slavery, the privilege of Whites to subordinate Blacks was linked through a legal regime that attempted to convert Blacks into objects of property. Just as the concept of Manifest Destiny nullified Native American claims to land ownership, slavery linked the privilege of Whites to the subordination of Blacks through a legal regime that attempted the conversion of Blacks into objects of property. The settlement and seizure of Native American land similarly supported White privilege through a system of property rights in land in which the "race" of the Native Americans rendered their first possession rights invisible and justified conquest (ibid., 1721). For a discussion of the Indigenous as Alien, see Volpp (2015).

The liberal, modern conception of property is counter to the classic view espoused by early theorists such as John Locke and Jeremy Bentham. According to the classic view, property rights were generally determined by one or two basic principles—the rights of possession and labor. The right of first possession was obviously not respected for Native Americans and Mexicans in the American Southwest. Whites disregarded the right of first possession and displaced Native Americans from their native lands. The US-Mexican War and the Treaty of Guadalupe Hidalgo, which ended the hostilities between the two nations, similarly led to the acquisition of more than one-half of Mexico's territory (see Chapter 1). Article IX of the Treaty stipulated that after one year, those who did not choose to remain Mexican citizens would be considered "to have elected" to become US citizens (Griswold del Castillo 1990, 66). Mexicans who did not elect to remain Mexican citizens were nonetheless entitled

> to the enjoyment of all the rights of citizens of the United States according to the principles of the Constitution; and in the meantime shall be maintained and protected in the free enjoyment of their liberty and property, and secured in the free exercise of their religion without restriction.
>
> (Bevans 1972)

The labor principle was similarly not observed for Blacks as African slaves provided the labor for maintaining the plantation economy in the South. The Mexican and Asian colonial labor force also provided labor for the expansion of agriculture, mines, and railroads in the Southwestern and Western United States. Blauner notes, for example, that

> In a historical sense, people of color provided much of the hard labor (and the technical skills) that built up the agriculture base and the mineral-transport-communication infrastructure necessary for industrialization and modernization, whereas the Europeans worked primarily within the industrialized, modern sectors ... The placement of nonwhite groups, however, imposed barrier upon barrier on such mobility, freezing them for long periods of time in the least favorable segments of the economy.
>
> (1972, 62)

Fourth Amendment: Origins and Historical Overview

This chapter examines whether Latinos in the United States have a Fourth Amendment right to be protected against unreasonable searches and seizures relative to their real or perceived immigration status. I conclude that in the context of immigration searches and seizures, Fourth Amendment protections for Mexican-looking persons have been consistently eviscerated by judicial rulings. As with slavery for Blacks and displacement of Indians from their native land, federal courts have substantially eroded the rights of Mexican and "Mexican-looking" persons, creating a tacit, unstated "Mexican Exception" to the Fourth Amendment.

While the Fifth and Sixth Amendments provide protections to an individual or to an accused person, the language of the Fourth Amendment clearly ascribes the right to "the people" rather than individuals against excessive government intrusion. The Fourth Amendment ostensibly provides the people protection against unreasonable searches and seizures, stating that

> The right of the people to be secure in their persons, houses, papers, and effects, against unreasonable searches and seizure, shall not be violated, and no Warrants shall issue, but upon probable cause, supported by Oath or affirmation, and particularly describing the place to be searched, and the persons or things to be seized.
>
> (US Constitution, Amendment IV)

"The people" are protected against unreasonable government searches and seizures not only of their property, including their houses, papers, and effects, but also of their person. While the Amendment does not provide direct prohibition of warrantless searches, such searches are suspect and presumptively unreasonable (Amar 1994, 759). A guiding principle of the Amendment is that "searches conducted outside the judicial process, without prior approval by judge or magistrate are *per se* unreasonable under the Fourth Amendment—subject only to a few specifically established and well-delineated exceptions."

The Fourth Amendment was adopted by the framers of the United States Constitution as a way to protect American colonists from wholesale violations of the right to privacy carried out by the British government. So-called Writs of Assistance were mechanisms used to conduct searches of homes of private citizens, primarily as a way of discovering violations of strict British customs laws that sought to limit criticisms of the King. Such abuses resulted in increased sensitivity by the Founders to limit the power of the government to engage in unwarranted searches and seizures and to stifle political dissent against the British government and the King.

The origins of the Fourth Amendment can be traced directly to seventeenth- and eighteenth-century English common law and more precisely to public response to three high profile cases in the 1760s: two in England and one in the American colonies. *Wilkes v. Wood*, 19 Howell's State Trials 1153 (C.P. 1763) and *Entick v. Carrington*, 19 Howell's State Trials 1029 (C. P. 1765), dealt with pamphleteers charged with seditious libel for criticizing ministers of the King and, indirectly, the King himself. Wilkes, a Member of Parliament, had published an anonymous critique of King George III in a 1763 pamphlet. Lord Halifax, a Crown Officer had issued a sweeping warrant in response (Amar 1994, 772). In these cases, the King's agents had issued a warrant authorizing the search and raiding of the pamphleteers' homes and seizure of their books, papers, and belongings. Wilkes and Entick each sued for damages, claiming that the warrants were void and that the searches were therefore illegal.

The third case dealt with so-called Writs of Assistance issued by British customs inspectors which permitted them to search any place in the Colonies where they felt smuggled goods might be found. The Writs also empowered the inspectors to force private citizens to assist them in carrying out the searches. First introduced in Massachusetts in 1751, the Writs sought to bring order via strict enforcement of the Acts of Trade, which regulated commerce throughout the British Empire. Many merchants, however, were able to develop creative ways of evading the Acts of Trade and were skillful in smuggling contraband items. The Writs of Assistance served as general warrants, which authorized government officials to inspect not only shops and warehouses but private residences as well.

James Otis, Advocate General of Massachusetts when the Writs were issued, promptly resigned his post when asked to represent several Boston merchants who sued in the Massachusetts Superior Court. Otis, in turn, sued on behalf of the merchants in 1761, drawing great attention by arguing that the Writs violated the natural rights of the colonists and were, therefore, unconstitutional and invalid. Although the merchants lost, Otis delivered a powerful five-hour speech and his argument and eloquent defense of the individual's right to privacy further intensified opposition to British rule. The Writs of Assistance drew public attention once again with the enforcement of the Townshend Duties in 1767. However, courts continued to uphold the constitutionality of the orders during the 1770s, and as time passed and public passions intensified, British officials became increasingly reluctant to enforce them.

There is general consensus that the Fourth Amendment was designed to affirm the results of *Wilkes* and *Entick* and to overturn the Writs of Assistance cases. The Amendment essentially incorporates three principles. The first principle is that the government should not be permitted to search, absent some compelling justification and substantial reason to believe that the place or person being searched contains evidence that is being sought. Second, searches, especially of private homes, should be limited and should not go beyond their justification. Finally, the government should be prohibited from issuing blanket warrants. In fact, under English common law it was a trespass to invade someone's home without some kind of authorization, but the warrants in *Wilkes* and *Entick* and the Writs of Assistance appeared to have been designed to evade the common law.

In *Wilkes v. Wood* (C.P. 1763), a civil action of trespass, the defendant, Wood had been served the Writ of Assistance in entering Wilkes' home. He first pleaded not guilty and then gave a special justification (Kurland and Lerner 2000). The Lord Chief Justice Camden summoned the evidence of the whole, stating that it was an action of trespass and then went through the particulars as to the justification, the King's Speech, libel No. 45. Camden noted that if the jury found that every step was properly taken as represented in the justification, they must find for the defendant. On the other hand, if they found that Wood was a party in the affair, they must find a verdict for the plaintiff, with damages.

After presenting the evidence, the Lord Chief Justice also noted that if the jury found that Wilkes was the author and publisher of No. 45, it would be filed, stand upon record in the Court of Common Pleas, and would be offered as proof in the criminal case. The jury deliberated for half an hour and found for the plaintiff on both issues, with a £1,000 in damages.

Entick v. Carrington (C.P. 1765) was also an action in trespass brought by Entick against Carrington. Entick declared that on November 11, 1762, defendants with force and arms broke and entered his dwelling house and continued there for hours without his consent and against his peaceable possession thereof. He further alleged that the defendants broke open the doors to the rooms, the locks, and iron bars. Once inside, they broke open boxes, chests, drawers, and other items, and they broke the door locks, searching and examining all the rooms and all the boxes in his dwelling house, whereby his secret affairs were wrongfully discovered and made public. Both Wilkes and Entick brought actions in trespass against the defendants and both won verdicts, with powerful opinions issued by Lord Camden who presided in both cases.

The history of the Fourth Amendment is that it was clearly drafted to address the issues raised by Wilkes and Entick and the Writs of Assistance (Amar 1994; 2000). The opening clause declares that people have a right to be "secure in their persons, houses, papers, and effects, against unreasonable searches and seizures," focusing precisely on infringements viewed as especially intrusive in *Wilkes* and *Entick*. In fact, per the last clause of the Fourth Amendment, "no Warrants shall issue, but upon probable cause, supported by Oath or affirmation, and particularly describing the place to be searched, and the persons or things to be seized."

Although modern courts have focused on the exclusionary rule, or suppression of illegally seized items, as the primary remedy for Fourth Amendment violations, *Wilkes* and *Entick* were clearly not cases subject to the exclusionary rule (Amar 2000). England has never had an exclusionary rule and American courts did not implement the exclusionary rule for the first one hundred years after independence. Indeed, during colonial times the federal government authorized outrageous and incredibly intrusive searches. Nevertheless, as in *Wilkes* and *Entick*, citizens could bring suit against the officers for civil trespass and seek compensatory and punitive damages (Amar 1994). In fact, none of the three cases, which gave impetus to the Fourth Amendment, were traditional criminal law enforcement cases such as murder, rape, or burglary but cases involving violations of the rights of political dissidents, who were strongly opposed to the laws they were accused of disobeying. None involved searches by people whom we would consider enforcement officers because police forces as we know them did not exist either in England or in the United States until the nineteenth century (Russell et al. 2005).

In practice and over time, however, the exclusionary rule has not been carefully observed, as the Supreme Court has carved out a number of exceptions to the per se rule. So many exceptions have been made that some observers have wondered whether the exceptions may have swallowed up the rule. Justice Scalia has identified at least twenty exceptions, such as automobile searches incident to arrest, and plain view (*California v. Acevedo* 1967, 582 (Scalia, J., concurring)). In a concurring opinion in *California v. Acevedo,* Justice Scalia remarked that by the 1960s, the warrant requirement "had become so riddled with exceptions that it was basically unrecognizable" (*California v. Acevedo* 1967, 581–582).

Since 1967, in *Terry v. Ohio*, the Supreme Court has continued to carve out a number of exceptions to the warrant requirement. Terry, for example, established a "search and frisk" exception. The Court wrote that a proper balance needs to be struck between the Fourth Amendment right of the individual and society's right to protect law enforcement officers. It concluded that

> there must be a narrowly drawn authority to permit a reasonable search for weapons for the protection of the police officer, where he has reason to believe that he is dealing with an armed and dangerous individual, regardless of whether there is probable cause to arrest the individual for a crime.
>
> (*Terry v. Ohio* 1968, 27)

Although the officer need not be absolutely certain that the individual is armed, the question is whether a reasonably prudent person in similar circumstances would believe that the officer's safety or the safety of others was in peril.

> And in determining whether the officer acted reasonably in such circumstances, due weight must be given not to his inchoate and unparticularized suspicion or "hunch," but to the specific reasonable inferences which he is entitled to draw from the facts in light of his experience.
>
> (*Terry v. Ohio* 1968, 27)

The primary deterrent for law enforcement has been the Exclusionary Rule, a legal doctrine which basically holds that evidence resulting from an illegal search and the fruit of that search are inadmissible in a criminal trial.

Does the Exclusionary Rule Apply in Civil Deportation Hearings?

Lopez-Mendoza

Adan Lopez-Mendoza, a citizen of Mexico, was arrested by Immigration and Naturalization Service (INS) agents at the transmission repair shop where he worked in San Mateo, California (*Lopez-Mendoza* 1984, 1037). Working on a tip, the agents went to the shop just before 8:00 a.m. but failed to obtain a warrant to search the premises or arrest any of the employees. Although the proprietor of the shop refused to allow the agents to interview employees during working hours, as one agent spoke with the proprietor, another entered the shop through a back entrance and engaged Lopez-Mendoza (*Lopez-Mendoza* 1984, 1037). The respondent gave his name, indicated he was from Mexico and did not have any close relatives in this country. He was placed under arrest and underwent further questioning at the INS offices, where he subsequently admitted to being born in Mexico and entering the country "without inspection." The agents prepared a "Record of Deportable Alien" (Form I-213) and an affidavit which he signed, admitting illegal entry into the country (*Lopez-Mendoza* 1984, 1035).

While the Supreme Court has held on numerous occasions that the Exclusionary Rule applies in a criminal proceeding, the issue before the Supreme Court in *Lopez-Mendoza* was whether the Rule also applies in a civil deportation hearing. At a hearing before an immigration judge, his attorney made a motion to terminate the proceedings because the respondent had been arrested illegally but the judge ruled that the legality of the arrest was not relevant in a deportation hearing. The Form I-213 and the affidavit were admitted into evidence without objection from Lopez-Mendoza, and the judge found that Lopez-Mendoza was deportable (*Lopez-Mendoza* 1984, 1036).

An appeal was dismissed by the Bureau of Internal Affairs (BIA), noting that "[t]he mere fact of an illegal arrest has no bearing on a subsequent deportation proceeding" (*Lopez-Mendoza* 1984, 1036), and that Lopez-Mendoza had not objected either to the admission of the Form I-213 or his signed affidavit (*Lopez-Mendoza* 1984, 1036). The Ninth Circuit Court of Appeals, however, vacated the order of deportation and remanded the case to determine whether or not the respondent's Fourth Amendment rights were violated during his arrest.

A majority opinion, written by Supreme Court Justice O'Connor, reversed the Ninth Circuit and held that "credible evidence gathered in connection with peaceful arrests by INS officers does not have to be suppressed in an INS deportation hearing" (*Lopez-Mendoza* 1984, 1038). In other words, the sole authority of the judge in a deportation hearing is to adjudicate deportation, not to assess guilt or to punish respondents, as is the case in a criminal trial (*Lopez Mendoza* 1984, 1038). Because of the civil nature of a deportation hearing, various protections of a criminal proceeding such as the Exclusionary Rule do not apply. For example, a respondent must be given a reasonable opportunity to attend but the hearing can be held in his or her absence (*Lopez-Mendoza* 1984, 1039). Similarly, the standard for deportability required by the BIA is "clear, unequivocal and convincing evidence," not proof beyond a reasonable doubt, as is required in a criminal trial (*Lopez-Mendoza* 1984, 1039). The absence of Miranda warnings also do not render an otherwise voluntary statement inadmissible in a deportation hearing (*Lopez-Mendoza* 1984,1039).

The Court held that the body or identity of respondent in a criminal or civil case, is never itself suppressible because it was the fruit of an unlawful arrest (*Lopez-Mendoza* 1984, 1039). Accordingly, "On this basis alone, the Court of Appeals' decision as to respondent Lopez-Mendoza must be reversed" (*Lopez-Mendoza* 1984, 468). The Court noted, in fact, that at the deportation hearing Lopez-Mendoza objected to being summoned to a deportation hearing following an unlawful arrest, not to the evidence offered against him relative to his deportability (*Lopez-Mendoza* 1984, 1040).

After balancing the social costs of applying the Exclusionary Rule in a civil deportation hearing against the benefits of applying the rule, the Court concluded that the societal costs would outweigh any benefits. The deterrent benefits of applying the rule, in other words, would not justify the costs that would result from its application in allowing large number of unauthorized immigrants to remain in the United States. Even if the Exclusionary Rule were applied, deportation would still be possible because evidence obtained directly from the arrest could be used to justify the deportation, since the only thing that the Government must establish to establish deportability is identity and alienage status (*Lopez-Mendoza* 1984, 1043). Once this burden is met, the burden shifts to the respondent to prove the time, location, and mode of entry into the United States (*Lopez-Mendoza* 1984, 1043).

The second factor identified by the Court in justifying its ruling is a practical one. During a typical year, an INS agent arrests approximately 500 unauthorized immigrants. Because 97.5 percent of these persons agree to voluntary departure without a formal hearing, the deterrent effect of applying the Exclusionary Rule would be minimal, according to the Court (*Lopez-Mendoza* 1984, 1044). Moreover, there is very little deterrent effect because among those who request a formal hearing, few challenge the circumstances of their arrest (*Lopez-Mendoza* 1984, 1044). The third and most important factor noted by the Court is that the INS has its own comprehensive scheme for deterring Fourth Amendment violations, and it has implemented rules restricting stop, interrogation, and arrest practices (*Lopez-Mendoza* 1984, 1044).

The Court acknowledged the respondent's contention that retention of the Exclusionary Rule was important to protect the Fourth Amendment rights of ethnic Americans, especially the Hispanic-Americans who are lawfully in this country, "but application of the exclusionary rule to civil deportation proceedings can be justified only if the rule is likely to add significant protection to these Fourth Amendment rights" (*Lopez-Mendoza* 1984, 1045–1046).

One cost to application of the exclusionary rule, according to Justice O'Connor, would be allowing the Court to "close its eyes" to ongoing violations of the law:

> Presumably no one would argue that the exclusionary rule should be invoked to prevent an agency from ordering corrective action at a leaking hazardous waste dump if the evidence underlying the order had been improperly obtained, or to compel police to return contraband explosives or drugs to their owner if the contraband had been unlawfully seized.
>
> (*Lopez-Mendoza* 1984, 1066)

The Supreme Court's ruling in *Lopez-Mendoza* is objectionable on several grounds. First, Justice O'Connor likens Mexicans to "hazardous waste" and justifies Fourth Amendment violations based on practical, policy grounds rather than on constitutional considerations or criteria. I argue that perhaps more persons would challenge their arrests if courts enforced the prohibition against unreasonable searchers and seizures. Finally, her paraphrasing of Justice Cardozo's famous quote that "The constable's blunder may allow the criminal to go free ... but he should not go free within our borders" (*Lopez-Mendoza* 1984, 1047) is also cruelly ironic and contradictory. The reference to not letting the "criminal go free" within our border also belies her contention that deportation hearings are civil proceedings, not criminal, where the Exclusionary Rule does not apply.

Are INS Factory Raids Seizures?

INS v. Delgado

In *INS v. Delgado,* the Supreme Court overturned a Ninth Circuit Court of Appeals decision that "factory surveys" entailed the seizure of an entire workforce without INS agents having reasonable suspicion that the employees questioned were in the country illegally (*INS v. Delgado* 1984). In overturning the case, the Supreme Court held that the factory raids did not constitute an impermissible detention or seizure.

The agents had obtained two warrants in which the INS demonstrated probable cause that the Davis Pleating Plant in Southern California employed a large number of "illegal aliens." During the raid, armed agents guarded the building exits as others moved through the factory questioning employees. The agents used walkie-talkies, showed their badges, and were armed.

The respondents in *Delgado* were four employees questioned in one of the three "surveys" who were legal residents of the United States. They maintained that the factory raids "violated their Fourth Amendment right to be free from unreasonable searches [and] seizures and the equal protection component of the Due Process Clause of the Fifth Amendment" (*INS v. Delgado* 1984, 213).

Relying on *Terry v. Ohio*, the Court stated that "not all personal intercourse between policemen and citizens involves 'seizures' of persons. Only when the officer, by means of physical force or show of authority, has restrained the liberty of a citizen may we conclude that a 'seizure' has occurred" (*INS v. Delgado* 1984, 215). The standard that has evolved over time is that an initially consensual encounter becomes a seizure or detention, only "if, in view of all of the circumstances surrounding the incident, a reasonable person would have believed that he was not free to leave" (*INS v. Delgado* 1984, 215). The Supreme Court held that the INS factory raids did not constitute impermissible seizures.

The *Delgado* Court stated that the fact that most people will respond positively to such a request does not negate its consensual nature, "unless the circumstances of the encounter are so intimidating as to demonstrate that a reasonable person would have believed he was not free to leave if he had not responded ... ." Writing for the *Delgado* majority, Chief Justice Rehnquist observed that the way the respondents were questioned could hardly have resulted in their having a reasonable fear that they were not free to continue working or to move about the work site. The Court, therefore, held that these were classic consensual stops that are not constitutionally prohibited.

From the record, according to the Court, it is clear the agents simply questioned employees and proceeded to arrest only those that they had probable cause to believe were unlawfully in this country because they ran, hid, or sought to avoid detection (*INS v. Delgado* 1984, 211). Because mere questioning did not constitute a "seizure" inside the factory, neither was it one when it occurred at the exits (*INS v. Delgado* 1984, 217–219). "Since there was no seizure of the workforces by virtue of the method of conducting the factory surveys, the issue of individual questioning could be presented only if one of the named respondents had in fact been seized or detained," but their deposition testimony showed that none was (*INS v. Delgado* 1984, 211).

While the Court ruled these were classic consensual encounters rather than seizures, it failed to consider how the race or national origin status of a respondent might impact how they view factory raids. The concept of the "reasonable person" is one the courts have traditionally used to establish an objective standard for how a fictive person would or should have acted under similar circumstances and conditions. For example, a reasonable motorist should not drive a motor vehicle while intoxicated.

While a reasonable, educated White man like Justice Rehnquist might have known that they were free to leave even though there were armed guards at the doors, it is not clear that a reasonable Mexican or reasonable immigrant would have felt that he or she was free to leave. Perhaps there is a need for the court to establish a reasonable Mexican, or reasonable non-White person, standard.

Are Mexican Nationals Protected by the Fourth Amendment?

Verdugo-Urquidez

The basic issue addressed by the Supreme Court in the case of *Verdugo-Urquidez* is whether a Mexican national accused of a crime and tried in the United States has the same Fourth Amendment protection as a resident of the United States. Rene Martín Verdugo-Urquidez, a Mexican citizen and resident was believed by the United States Drug Enforcement Agency (DEA) to be a leader of a large, violent organization involved in smuggling narcotics into the United States (*United States v. Verdugo-Urquidez* 1990, 262). Based on a complaint charging Verdugo-Urquidez with a number of narcotics-related offenses, the United States Government obtained a warrant for his arrest in July. The following January, after discussions with United States marshals, Mexican police arrested the respondent in Mexico and took him to the US Border Patrol station in Calexico, California. He was then apprehended by US Marshals who transported him to a correctional facility in San Diego, where he remained awaiting trial (*United States v. Verdugo-Urquidez* 1990, 262).

Subsequent to the arrest, a DEA agent assigned to the Calexico Border office decided to organize searches of two of Verdugo-Urquidez's residences in Mexicali and San Felipe. The DEA agent believed the searches would turn up evidence of various alleged drug trafficking activities (*Verdugo-Urquidez* 1990, 262). Subsequently, DEA agents, working in concert with Mexican police, carried out two warrantless searches of respondent's properties, seizing various documents, including a tally sheet, which allegedly indicated the quantities of marijuana smuggled into the United States (*Verdugo-Urquidez* 1990, 262–263).

Verdugo-Urquidez was subsequently tried in Federal Court on various drug trafficking charges. The US District Court granted a motion to exclude evidence seized in the searches (*Verdugo-Urquidez* 1990, 263), finding that the searches were protected by the Fourth Amendment and governed by the Exclusionary Rule, and that DEA agents had failed to justify the warrantless searches (*Verdugo-Urquidez* 1990, 263). The Court of Appeals for the Ninth Circuit affirmed the lower court decision (*Verdugo-Urquidez* 1988, 1214) citing parallel cases where the Supreme Court had held that American citizens tried by military authorities in a foreign county were entitled to the protection of the Fifth and Sixth Amendments (*Verdugo Urquidez* 1990, 263).

Citing the case of *INS v. Lopez-Mendoza* (1984, 1032), in which a majority indicated that illegal aliens (undocumented persons) in the United States had Fourth Amendment rights, the Ninth Circuit Court of Appeal wrote:

> [i]t would be odd indeed to acknowledge that Verdugo-Urquidez is entitled to due process under the Fifth Amendment, and to a fair trial under the Sixth Amendment, ... and deny him the protection from unreasonable searches and seizures afforded under the Fourth Amendment.
>
> (*Verdugo-Urquidez* 1988, 1224)

The Ninth Circuit decided that the searches were unconstitutional because the DEA agents failed to obtain a search warrant. While recognizing that "an American search warrant would be of no legal validity in Mexico," the Court of Appeals noted that it would have "substantial constitutional value in this country" because it would show that a magistrate had determined that there was probable cause to search the residence and would have limited the scope of the search (*Verdugo-Urquidez* 1988, 1229–1230).

In the majority opinion, Chief Justice Rehnquist reasoned that unlike the Fifth and Sixth Amendments, which are personal rights, the reach of the Fourth Amendment extends only to "the people" and that the term "the people" appears as a term of art that "refers to a class of persons who are part of a national community or who have otherwise developed sufficient connection with this country to be considered part of that community" (*Verdugo-Urquidez*, 1990, 265). The Fourth Amendment, therefore, did not protect Verdugo-Urquidez because he was insufficiently connected to the United States to be considered one of the people. The Court added that the Fourth Amendment was never "intended to restrain the actions of the federal government against aliens outside of the United States territory" or on foreign soil or international waters (*Verdugo-Urquidez* 1990, 266). Although Verdugo-Urquidez was lawfully present in the United States and brought across the border against his will to face criminal charges, the Court determined that he was insufficiently connected to the United States to be one of the people.

Contrary to the Court's ruling, I contend that unless we are willing to accept a dual system of justice in which most criminal defendants are protected by the Constitution and Mexicans are not, Verdugo-Urquidez became one of "the people" the minute he became a suspected drug dealer and most certainly once a warrant was issued for his arrest in the United States.

Are Fixed Checkpoints and Secondary Inspections Constitutional?

Martinez-Fuerte

The Border Patrol conducts three types of stops in seeking to apprehend undocumented immigrants along inland roadways: (1) permanent checkpoints are operated at certain key, heavily trafficked intersections; (2) temporary checkpoints established from time to time at various locations; and (3) roving patrols like the one that stopped and search automobiles within a reasonable distance from any external boundary of the United Sates (*Almeida-Sanchez* 1973, 268).

In the case of *United States v. Martinez-Fuerte*, the Supreme Court upheld the constitutionality of Border Patrol stops at permanent checkpoints operated away from the international border (*United States v. Martinez-Fuerte*

1976, 543). Routine car stops at permanent checkpoints on major highways away from the Mexican border to briefly question its occupants were not a violation of the Fourth Amendment. Such stops and questioning, moreover, may be made even in the absence of particularized suspicion that the vehicle contains persons who are in the country illegally (*Martinez-Fuerte* 1976, 556–564).

Martinez-Fuerte approached the San Clemente checkpoint driving a car which contained two female passengers, illegal Mexican aliens, who had entered through the San Isidro border crossing with false documents. They then met Martinez-Fuerte and were transported northward by the respondent. At the checkpoint, the vehicle was directed to a secondary checkpoint. Martinez-Fuerte presented documents which showed him to be a lawful resident alien but the two passengers were found to be in the country illegally. The respondent was charged with two counts of illegally transporting aliens (428 U.S. 548) in violation of 8 U.S.C. 1324 (a) (2). Prior to his trial, Martinez-Fuerte's motion to suppress the evidence because it was in violation of the Fourth Amendment was denied, and he was subsequently convicted on both counts.

The case actually involved three separate cases which were consolidated by the Ninth Circuit. The Court of Appeals reversed the convictions, holding that these stops violated the Fourth Amendment. The Ninth Circuit held that a stop for inquiry is constitutional only if the Border Patrol reasonably suspects the presence of illegal aliens on the basis of articulable facts, reversing Martinez-Fuertes' conviction, and affirming the orders to suppress the illegally obtained evidence in the other cases (514 F.2d. 308 (1975)).

The Supreme Court reversed, holding that requiring such stops be made based on reasonable suspicion would be impractical because of the heavy flow of traffic and they do not serve as a deterrent to well-organized smuggling operations, which are known to use these highways (*Martinez-Fuerte* 1976, 556–565). Using a balancing test once again, the Court reasoned that while the societal need to make routine checkpoints is great, the resulting intrusion on Fourth Amendment interests is limited. Interference with legitimate traffic is minimal, given that such fixed checkpoints entail less discretionary activity than the roving patrol stops (*Martinez-Fuerte* 1976, 557–560). The Court also affirmed that it was constitutional to selectively refer motorists to the secondary inspection area on the basis of criteria that would not sustain a roving patrol (*Martinez-Fuerte* 1976, 543).

> Thus, even if it be assumed that such referrals are made largely on the basis of apparent Mexican ancestry, we perceive no constitutional violation. [Citation omitted]. As the intrusion here is sufficiently minimal that no particularized reason need exist to justify it, we think it follows

that the Border Patrol officers must have wide discretion in selecting the motorists to be diverted for the brief questioning involved.

(*Martinez-Fuerte* 1976, 563–564)

In his dissenting opinion, Justice Brennan noted that this decision continues the "evisceration of Fourth Amendment protections," and "virtually empties the Amendment of its reasonableness requirement" (*Martinez-Fuerte* 1976, 567–568). Since the focus is almost exclusively on Mexicans in the country illegally, checkpoint officials unguided by any objective standards will be free to stop all motorists without explanation or justification and will undoubtedly target Mexican-looking motorists (*Martinez-Fuerte* 1976, 572).

Roving Patrols and Racial Profiling of Mexicans

Almeida-Sanchez

In *Almeida-Sanchez v. United States* (413 U.S. 266 (1973)), the Petitioner, a Mexican citizen holding a valid permit to work in the United States, challenged the constitutionality of a Border Patrol search of his automobile some 25 air miles north of the Mexican border. The evidence obtained in the search, made without either probable cause or consent, was used to convict him in federal court (413 U.S. 266) of knowingly receiving, concealing, and facilitating the transportation of a large quantity of marijuana in violation of 21 U.S.C. § 176a (1964 ed.). His only contention on appeal was that the search of his car that resulted in the discovery of the marijuana was unconstitutional and a violation of the Fourth Amendment, and that per the rule articulated in *Weeks v. United States*, 232 U.S. 383, the marijuana should not have been admissible as evidence against him. In *Weeks*, the United States Supreme Court unanimously held that the warrantless search of a private residence is a violation of the Fourth Amendment.

The government sought to justify the search based on § 287 (a)(3) of the Immigration and Nationality Act, which permits warrantless searches of automobiles and other modes of transportation, "within a reasonable distance from any external boundary of the United Sates," as authorized by regulations to be promulgated by the Attorney General. The Attorney General, in turn, defines "reasonable distance" as being "within 100 air miles from any external boundary of the United States." The Court of Appeals upheld the search based on the Act and the regulation.

The US Supreme Court overturned the conviction, holding that the warrantless search of Almeida-Sanchez's automobile made without probable cause or the consent of the petitioner violated the Fourth Amendment protection against unreasonable searchers and seizures (413 U.S. 269–275). It held that the search could not be justified either on the basis of any special rules applicable to automobile searchers, as probable cause was absent. Nor could it be justified by analogy with administrative inspections, as the officers lacked a warrant or reason to believe that the petitioner had crossed the border or committed an offense, and because there was no consent by petitioner (413 U.S. 269–272).

The underlying facts of the case are simple and undisputed. Almeida-Sanchez was stopped by the United States Border Patrol on California State Highway 78 and his car was carefully searched. Highway 78 runs essentially east to west and runs partly through an undeveloped area. At the point where petitioner was stopped, the highway winds north and east. Significantly, the road never reaches the Mexican border and it lies north of U.S. 80, a major east-west Interstate that connects the Southwest and the West Coast (413 U.S. 267–268). Almeida-Sanchez was approximately 26 air miles from the border when he was stopped.

The Government maintained that all of these stops and searches were constitutional without a warrant or probable cause, with the only asserted justification being § 287 (a)(3) of the Immigration and Nationality Act, 66, Stat. 233, U.S.C. § 1357(a)(3), which provides for warrantless searches of automobiles and other conveyances "within a reasonable distance of any external boundary of the United Sates, as authorized by regulations established by the Attorney General" (413 U. S. 268). The Attorney General defined "reasonable distance" as being "within 100 air miles of the external boundary of the United States" (413 U.S. 268). The Court of Appeals for the Ninth Circuit acknowledged that the search of the petitioner's automobile was not a border search but upheld it, based on the Immigration and Nationality Act and the accompanying regulations promulgated by the Attorney General (413 U.S. 268–269).

The Court acknowledged that certain searches, such as those conducted at fixed checkpoints near the border or the search of the passengers or cargo of an airplane, might be functional equivalents of border searches, but the search of the petitioner's automobile by a roving patrol more than 20 miles from the border absent probable cause or consent, "violated the petitioner's Fourth Amendment right to be free of "'unreasonable searches and seizures'" (413 U. S. 273). The Court recalled the words of Justice Jackson after returning from the Nuremberg Trials:

> These [Fourth Amendment rights], I protest, are not mere second-class rights, but belong in the catalog of indispensable freedoms. Among deprivations of rights, none is so effective in cowing a population, crushing the spirit of the individual and putting terror in every heart. Uncontrolled search and seizure is one of the first and most effective weapons in the arsenal of every arbitrary government.
>
> (413 U.S. 274)

Brignoni-Ponce

While *Almeida-Sanchez* was an important victory for Mexicans and Latinos, *United States v. Brignoni-Ponce* (1975) is perhaps the most significant negative Fourth Amendment Supreme Court decision in that it constitutionally legitimated racial profiling and the use of race as a factor in making immigration stops. The holding in the case is double-edged. On the one hand, the Court held that a roving patrol is not justified in making an immigration stop *solely* because the occupants of a vehicle appear to be Mexican-looking but, on the other hand, Mexican appearance was sufficiently related to immigration status to make it a valid and legitimate factor in making such a stop.

As previously noted (*Martinez-Fuerte* 1976), the Border Patrol operates a fixed checkpoint on Interstate Highway 5, south of San Clemente. On the night of March 11, 1973, the checkpoint was closed because of inclement weather, and two officers were observing northbound traffic from a car parked on the side of the road (*Brignoni-Ponce* 1975, 874–875). Because of the lack of lighting, the Border Patrol officers were using the patrol car's headlights to observe passing cars. They stopped Brignoni-Ponce's car and questioned him and his two passengers about their citizenship status and discovered that the two passengers were in the country illegally (*Brignoni-Ponce* 1975, 875). Later, the officers admitted that the only reason they had for stopping the vehicle was that the occupants "appeared to be of Mexican descent" (*Brignoni-Ponce* 1975, 875). All three were then arrested and "respondent was charged with two counts of knowingly transporting illegal immigrants, a violation of § 274(a)(2) of the Immigration and Nationality Act, 66 Stat. 228, 8 U.S.C. § 1324(a)(2)."

During the trial, Brignoni-Ponce's motion to suppress the testimony relative to the two passengers because it was the fruit of an illegal seizure, was denied. The two passengers testified and the respondent was convicted on both counts of smuggling people into the United States (*Brignoni-Ponce* 1975, 875).

The Supreme Court held that the Border Patrol agents failed to furnish reasonable grounds to believe that the three occupants of the car were illegal aliens. Even if they had reason to believe that the occupants were of Mexican descent, this factor alone would not justify the stop, or the belief that the car was carrying illegal aliens (*Brignoni-Ponce* 1975, 886).

> Large numbers of native born and naturalized citizens have the physical characteristics identified with Mexican ancestry, and, even in the border area, a relatively small proportion of them are aliens. [Footnote omitted]. The likelihood that any given person of Mexican ancestry is an alien is high enough to make Mexican appearance a relevant factor, but, standing alone, it does not justify stopping all Mexican-Americans to ask if they are aliens.
>
> (*Brignoni-Ponce* 1975, 886–887)

Conclusion

Although the Fourth Amendment to the US Constitution ostensibly protects the people against unreasonable searches and seizures of their property, persons, and effects, a number of exceptions have been carved out of the reasonableness requirement of the Amendment. In this chapter, I argued that in an immigration context, there is an unstated Mexican or Latino exception to the Amendment, which has led to an evisceration of Fourth Amendment protections for Mexicans and "Mexican-looking" people.

As in the infamous *Dred Scott* case, the Supreme Court held in *Verdugo-Urquidez* that the Fourth Amendment protection does not apply to Mexican residents who are charged with crimes in the United States because they are insufficiently connected to the United States to be one of the people. *Martinez-Fuerte* upheld routine border checkpoints absent reasonable suspicion because they were deemed minimal intrusions on the Fourth Amendment even though it recognized that it would primarily target Mexicans for arbitrary secondary inspections. Finally, *Brignoni-Ponce* further legitimated the racialization of border stops by holding that Mexican appearance was a legitimate factor that could be taken into account in making an immigration stop, although it could not be the only factor.

Just as slavery linked White privilege to the subordination of Blacks by making them the object of property, justified the settling on and seizing of Native American lands, and abrogating Mexican land titles guaranteed by the Treaty of Guadalupe Hidalgo, the courts today have systematically eviscerated the Fourth Amendment rights not only of Mexican citizens but of all Brown persons residing in the United States, regardless of their place of birth, citizenship, or immigration status. In addition, because Fourth Amendment violations entail not only the seizure of property but of their person, these are also due process violations. As Justice Brennan admonished in his eloquent *Martinez-Fuerte* dissent:

> Every American citizen of Mexican ancestry, and every Mexican alien lawfully in this country, must know after today's decision that he travels the fixed checkpoint highways at the risk of being subjected not only to a stop, but also to detention and interrogation, both prolonged and to an extent far more than for non-Mexican appearing motorists. To be singled out for referral and to be detained and interrogated must be upsetting to any motorist. One wonders what actual experience supports my Brethren's conclusion that referrals "should not be frightening or offensive because of their public and relatively routine nature."
>
> (*Martinez-Fuerte* 1976, 572)

Note

1 This chapter is a revision and expanded version of an earlier, shorter draft essay which was published in a special dossier issue of *Aztlán: A Journal of Chicano Studies* 43(2) Fall (2018). The chapter expands on the concept of Whiteness as property to show how courts today have systematically eviscerated the Fourth Amendment rights not only of Mexican citizens but of all Brown persons residing in the United States,

References

Amar, Akhil Reed. 1994. "Fourth Amendment First Principles." *Harvard Law Review*, 107(4): 757–819.

Amar, Akhil Reed. 2000. "Introduction." In Philip B. Kurland and Ralph Lerner (Eds.), *The Founders' Constitution*, vol. V, *Amendment IV*. Chicago: University of Chicago Press.

Barrera, Mario. 1979. *Race and Class in the Southwest: A Theory of Racial Inequality.* Notre Dame, IN: University of Notre Dame Press.

Bevans, Charles (Ed.). 1972. *Treaties and Other International Agreements of the United States of America, 1776–1949*, vol. 9. Washington, DC: Department of State, pp. 791–806.

Blauner, Robert. 1972. *Racial Oppression in America.* New York: Harper & Row.

Department of Homeland Security. 2017. "Consideration of Deferred Action for Childhood Arrivals (DACA)." Retrieved from www.uscis.gov

Griswold del Castillo, Richard. 1990. *The Treaty of Guadalupe Hidalgo: A Legacy of Conflict.* Norman, OK: University of Oklahoma Press.

Harris, Cheryl I. 1993. "Whiteness as Property." *Harvard Law Review*, 106(8): 1707–1791.

Kurland, Philip B. and Ralph Lerner (Eds.). 2000. *The Founder's Constitution*, vol. V, *Amendment IV*. Chicago: University of Chicago Press.

Molina, Alejandra. 2017. "Data: Discontinuing DACA Would Cost State $12 Billion." *The Press Enterprise*, October 20, 1.

Russell, Gregory D., Rebecca Paynich, James A. Conser, and Terry E. Gingerich. 2005. *Law Enforcement in the United States.* Boston: Jones and Bartlett.

Volpp, Leti. 2015. "The Indigenous as Alien." *UC Irvine Law Review*, 5(2): 289–326.

Cases Cited

Almeida-Sanchez v. United States (413 U.S. 266 1973).

California v. Acevedo 500 U.S. 565 (1991).

Entick v. Carrington 19 Howards State Trials (C.P. 1765).

INS v. Delgado 466 U.S. 210 (1984).

INS v. Lopez-Mendoza 468 U.S. 1032 (1984).

Katz v. United States 389 U.S. 347 (1967).

Martinez-Fuerte 514 F.2d 308 (1975).

Terry v. Ohio 392 U.S. 1 (1968).

United States v. Brignoni-Ponce 422 U.S. 873 (1975).

United States v. Martinez-Fuerte 428 U.S. 543 (1976).

United States v. Verdugo-Urquidez 856 F.2d 1214 (1988).
United States v. Verdugo-Urquidez 494 U.S. 259 (1990).
Weeks v. United States 232 U.S. 383 (1914).
Wilkes v. Wood 19 Howell's State Trials 1153 (C.P. 1763).

Index